First World War
and Army of Occupation
War Diary
France, Belgium and Germany

2 DIVISION
6 Infantry Brigade
Essex Regiment
13th Battalion
16 November 1915 - 31 January 1918

WO95/1358/1

The Naval & Military Press Ltd
www.nmarchive.com
Published in association with The National Archives

Published by

The Naval & Military Press Ltd

Unit 10 Ridgewood Industrial Park,
Uckfield, East Sussex,
TN22 5QE England
Tel: +44 (0) 1825 749494

www.naval-military-press.com

www.nmarchive.com

This diary has been reprinted in facsimile from the original. Any imperfections are inevitably reproduced and the quality may fall short of modern type and cartographic standards.

© **Crown Copyright**
Images reproduced by permission of The National Archives, London, England, 2015.

Contents

Document type	Place/Title	Date From	Date To
Heading	WO95/1358/1		
Heading	33rd Division 100th Infy Bde 2 Div 6 B D E 13th Bn Essex Regt. 1915 Nov & Dec		
Heading	100th Infantry Brigade 33rd Division, 13th Battn. The Essex Regiment. November 1915 (16.11.15-25.11.15)		
Heading	War Diary of 13th (S) Battn The Essex Regt From November 16th 1915 To December 31st 1915		
War Diary	Terham Down Camp Andauer	16/11/1915	17/11/1915
War Diary	Terham Down Camp	17/11/1915	17/11/1915
War Diary	Terham Down Camp Andauer	17/11/1915	17/11/1915
War Diary	Baulogne France	19/11/1915	25/11/1915
Heading	6th Infantry Brigade. 2nd Division War Diary 13th Battn. The Essex Regiment. December 1915		
War Diary	Le Pieriere France	02/12/1915	02/12/1915
War Diary	Bethune France	03/12/1915	03/12/1915
War Diary	Essars	04/12/1915	09/12/1915
War Diary	Annezin	10/12/1915	10/12/1915
War Diary	Le Preol	10/12/1915	22/12/1915
War Diary	Bethune	24/12/1915	24/12/1915
Heading	2nd Division 6th Infy Bde 13th Battalion Essex Regiment Jan-Dec 1916		
Heading	6th Brigade. 2nd Division. 13th Battalion The Essex Regiment January 1916		
Heading	War Diary of 13th (S) Battn. The Essex Regiment. From 11th To January 31st 16		
War Diary	Manqueville	11/01/1916	16/01/1916
War Diary	Les Choquaux	17/01/1916	18/01/1916
War Diary	B 3	19/01/1916	26/01/1916
War Diary	Gorre	27/01/1916	27/01/1916
War Diary	B 2	28/01/1916	30/01/1916
War Diary	Gorre	31/01/1916	31/01/1916
Heading	6th Brigade. 2nd Division. 13th Battalion The Essex Regiment February 1916		
Heading	War Diary of 13th (S) Battn Essex Regt From 1st-29th February 1916		
War Diary	B2	02/02/1916	03/02/1916
War Diary	Les Chocquaux	05/02/1916	05/02/1916
War Diary	Village Line C.2	11/02/1916	15/02/1916
War Diary	Sub Section C2	16/02/1916	19/02/1916
War Diary	Les Choquaux	20/02/1916	22/02/1916
War Diary	Les Harisoirs	25/02/1916	25/02/1916
War Diary	Pt Sains	26/02/1916	26/02/1916
War Diary	Bully Grenay	27/02/1916	28/02/1916
Heading	6th Brigade. 2nd Division.13th Battalion The Essex Regiment March 1916		
Heading	War Diary of 13th Essex Regiment From March 1st 1916 To March 31st 1916		
War Diary	Calonne L Sect.	05/03/1916	06/03/1916
War Diary	Horthern Sub. Section	13/03/1916	13/03/1916
War Diary	Bully Grenay	17/03/1916	17/03/1916

War Diary	Coupigny	18/03/1916	18/03/1916
War Diary	Bruay	20/03/1916	28/03/1916
Heading	6th Brigade & 2nd Division. 13th Battalion The Essex Regiment April 1916		
Heading	War Diary of 13th (S) Bn Essex Regt From 1/4/16 Until 30/4/16 Inclusive		
War Diary	Bruay	02/04/1916	02/04/1916
War Diary	Coupigny	09/04/1916	12/04/1916
War Diary	Bruay	13/04/1916	13/04/1916
War Diary	Delettes	14/04/1916	17/04/1916
War Diary	Bruay	18/04/1916	18/04/1916
War Diary	Coupigny	18/04/1916	18/04/1916
War Diary	Northern Sub Section	19/04/1916	22/04/1916
War Diary	Support Area	23/04/1916	26/04/1916
War Diary	Aorthern Subsection	27/04/1916	30/04/1916
Heading	6th Brigade. 2nd Division. 13th Battalion The Essex Regiment May 1916		
Heading	War Diary of 13th (S) Battn. The Essex Regt From May 1st 1916 To May 31st 1916 Vol 6		
War Diary	Bully Grenay	04/05/1916	06/05/1916
War Diary	Aorthern Subsection	07/05/1916	08/05/1916
War Diary	Support Area	09/05/1916	12/05/1916
War Diary	Northern Sub Section	13/05/1916	15/05/1916
War Diary	Bully Grenay	16/05/1916	18/05/1916
War Diary	Compigny	19/05/1916	19/05/1916
War Diary	Fresnicourt	21/05/1916	21/05/1916
War Diary	Divion	21/05/1916	22/05/1916
War Diary	Maisnil Bouche	23/05/1916	25/05/1916
War Diary	Vimy Ridge	26/05/1916	30/05/1916
War Diary	Support Area	31/05/1916	31/05/1916
War Diary	Vimy Ridge	31/05/1916	31/05/1916
Heading	6th Brigade. 2nd Division. 13th Battalion The Essex Regiment June 1916		
Heading	War Diary of 13th (S) Bn The Essex Regt From June 1st To June 30th 1916 Vol 7		
War Diary	Souchez	01/06/1916	12/06/1916
War Diary	Estree Cauchie	18/06/1916	22/06/1916
War Diary	Southen Sub Section	22/06/1916	30/06/1916
Heading	6th Inf Bde. 2nd Div. War Diary 13th Battn. The Essex Regiment. July 1916		
Heading	War Diary of 13th (S) Bn. The Essex Regt From July 1st 1916 To July 31st 1916		
War Diary	Southen Sub Section Berthonval	01/07/1916	03/07/1916
War Diary	Camblain L'abbe	05/07/1916	05/07/1916
War Diary	Estree Cauchie	10/07/1916	15/07/1916
War Diary	Northern Subsection Carency	16/07/1916	17/07/1916
War Diary	Gouy Servins	18/07/1916	18/07/1916
War Diary	Beugin	20/07/1916	20/07/1916
War Diary	Welcome Wood	23/07/1916	23/07/1916
War Diary	Bois de Tailes	25/07/1916	28/07/1916
War Diary	Breslau Support	28/07/1916	28/07/1916
War Diary	Delville Wood	29/07/1916	31/07/1916
Heading	6th Infantry Brigade, 2nd Division 13th Battalion The Essex Regiment August 1916 Report On Operations 8/9th August 1916		

Heading	War Diary of 13th (S) Bn.The Essex Regt. From 1st August 1916 31st August 1916 Vol 9		
War Diary	Breslau Support Trenches	01/08/1916	05/08/1916
War Diary	Waterlot Farm Section	06/08/1916	06/08/1916
War Diary	Trenches Mine Alley	07/08/1916	09/08/1916
War Diary	Trones Wood	09/08/1916	10/08/1916
War Diary	Happy Valley	12/08/1916	12/08/1916
War Diary	Meaulte	13/08/1916	13/08/1916
War Diary	Bois Du Warnimount	19/08/1916	19/08/1916
War Diary	Right Subsection	22/08/1916	22/08/1916
War Diary	Courcelles	24/08/1916	27/08/1916
War Diary	Left Subsection	28/08/1916	28/08/1916
War Diary	Courcelles	29/08/1916	31/08/1916
Miscellaneous	6th. Infantry Brigade.	10/08/1916	10/08/1916
Miscellaneous Diagram etc	Star S42/195		
Heading	6th Brigade. 2nd Division 13th Battalion The Essex Regiment September 1916		
Heading	War Diary of 13th (S) Bn The Essex Regt From September 1st-30th 1916 Vol 10		
War Diary	Courcelles	01/09/1916	01/09/1916
War Diary	Left Sub Section	03/09/1916	05/09/1916
War Diary	Courcelles	06/09/1916	09/09/1916
War Diary	Left Sub Section	10/09/1916	13/09/1916
War Diary	Courcelles	14/09/1916	17/09/1916
War Diary	Left Sub Section	18/09/1916	19/09/1916
War Diary	Bois Du Warnimount	20/09/1916	30/09/1916
Heading	6th Brigade. 2nd Division. 13th Battalion The Essex Regiment October 1916		
Heading	War Diary of 13th (S) Bn The Essex Regt From 1.10.16 To 31.10.1916 Vol XI		
War Diary	Bois Du Warnimount	01/10/1916	01/10/1916
War Diary	Right Sub Section Sailly Au Bois Section	02/10/1916	03/10/1916
War Diary	Bertrancourt	04/10/1916	07/10/1916
War Diary	Puchevillers	08/10/1916	18/10/1916
War Diary	Bertrancourt	19/10/1916	21/10/1916
War Diary	Mailly Wood East	22/10/1916	26/10/1916
War Diary	Brigade Front	27/10/1916	28/10/1916
War Diary	Bertrancourt	29/10/1916	31/10/1916
Heading	6th Brigade. 2nd Division 13th Battalion The Essex Regiment November 1916		
Heading	War Diary of 13th (S) Bn The Essex Regt From November 1st-30th 1916 Vol 12		
War Diary	Bertrancourt	01/11/1916	07/11/1916
War Diary	Mailly Maillet	08/11/1916	11/11/1916
War Diary	Brigade Front Regan Sector	12/11/1916	12/11/1916
War Diary	Regan Sector	12/11/1916	16/11/1916
War Diary	Vauchelles Les Authie	19/11/1916	19/11/1916
War Diary	Doullens	21/11/1916	21/11/1916
War Diary	Bernaville	23/11/1916	23/11/1916
War Diary	Coulonvillers	24/11/1916	24/11/1916
War Diary	Marcheville	25/11/1916	25/11/1916
War Diary	Le Titre	27/11/1916	27/11/1916
War Diary	Capennes	28/11/1916	30/11/1916
Heading	6th Brigade. 2nd Division. 13th Battalion The Essex Regiment December 1916		

Heading	War Diary of 13th (S) Battn The Essex Regt December 1st To 31st 1916 Vol 13		
War Diary	Gapennes	01/12/1916	31/12/1916
Heading	2nd Division 6th Infantry Bde, 13th Essex Regt January To 30th June, 1917		
Heading	6th Brigade. 2nd Division. 13th Battalion The Essex Regiment January 1917		
Heading	War Diary of 13th (S) Battn. The Essex Regt January 1st To January 31st 1917 Vol 14		
War Diary	Gapennes	01/01/1917	09/01/1917
War Diary	Boisbergues	10/01/1917	11/01/1917
War Diary	Rancheval	12/01/1917	12/01/1917
War Diary	Bouzincourt	13/01/1917	20/01/1917
War Diary	Wolfe Huts Ovillers	21/01/1917	24/01/1917
War Diary	Right Subsector	25/01/1917	28/01/1917
War Diary	Bouzincourt	30/01/1917	31/01/1917
Heading	6th Brigade. 2nd Division. 13th Battalion The Essex Regiment February 1917		
Heading	War Diary of 13th (S) Battn The Essex Regt February 1st To 28th 1917 Vol 15		
War Diary	Bouzincourt	01/02/1917	05/02/1917
War Diary	Ovillers Huts	06/02/1917	15/02/1917
War Diary	Wolfe Huts	16/02/1917	18/02/1917
War Diary	Left Subsector	19/02/1917	23/02/1917
War Diary	Albert	23/02/1917	28/02/1917
Heading	6th Brigade. 2nd Division. 13th Battalion The Essex Regiment March 1917		
Heading	War Diary of 13th (S) Bn Essex Regt March 1st 1917 To March 31st 1917 Vol 16		
War Diary	Albert	01/03/1917	03/03/1917
War Diary	Ovillers Huts	03/03/1917	10/03/1917
War Diary	Ovillers Huts To Line	11/03/1917	11/03/1917
War Diary	Loupart Sector	12/03/1917	14/03/1917
War Diary	Dyke Valley Camp	15/03/1917	18/03/1917
War Diary	Loupart Wood	18/03/1917	19/03/1917
War Diary	Loupart Wood to Sapighies to Courcelette	19/03/1917	19/03/1917
War Diary	Courcelette Camp	20/03/1917	21/03/1917
War Diary	Ovillers Huts	21/03/1917	21/03/1917
War Diary	Ovillers Huts To Warloy	22/03/1917	22/03/1917
War Diary	Warloy	23/03/1917	25/03/1917
War Diary	Warloy To Beauval	26/03/1917	26/03/1917
War Diary	Beauval To Haute Visee	27/03/1917	27/03/1917
War Diary	Haute Visse To Sibiville	28/03/1917	28/03/1917
War Diary	Sibiville	29/03/1917	29/03/1917
War Diary	Sibiville to Comteville & Huclier	30/03/1917	30/03/1917
War Diary	Conteville & Huclier	30/03/1917	31/03/1917
Miscellaneous	A Form. Messages And Signals.		
Miscellaneous	O C A Coy		
Miscellaneous	O C B Coy		
Miscellaneous	O C D Coy		
Miscellaneous	6th Brigade		
Miscellaneous	A Form. Messages And Signals.		
Heading	6th Brigade 2nd Division. 13th Battalion The Essex Regiment April 1917		
Heading	War Diary of 13th (S) Bn. Essex Regt. April 1st 1917 To April 30th 1917 Vol 17		

War Diary	Comteville & Huclier	01/04/1917	06/04/1917
War Diary	Conteville To Ourtin	07/04/1917	07/04/1917
War Diary	Ourtim	08/04/1917	10/04/1917
War Diary	Ourtim To "X" Huts	11/04/1917	11/04/1917
War Diary	Ecoivres "X" Huts To Roclincourt (Oppy Sector)	12/04/1917	12/04/1917
War Diary	Roclincourt	13/04/1917	18/04/1917
War Diary	Roclincourt To Line	18/04/1917	18/04/1917
War Diary	Line	19/04/1917	22/04/1917
War Diary	Line To Roclincourt	23/04/1917	23/04/1917
War Diary	Roclincourt	24/04/1917	25/04/1917
War Diary	Roclincourt To Marcevil	26/04/1917	26/04/1917
War Diary	Maroeuil to Roclincourt And Line	27/04/1917	27/04/1917
War Diary	Roclincourt And Line	27/04/1917	27/04/1917
War Diary	Line	27/04/1917	28/04/1917
War Diary	Line To Roclincourt	28/04/1917	28/04/1917
War Diary	Roclincourt To Ecurie	29/04/1917	29/04/1917
War Diary	Ecurie	29/04/1917	29/04/1917
War Diary	Ecurie To Maroeuil	30/04/1917	30/04/1917
Diagram etc			
Diagram etc	Scale 1/10,000		
Operation(al) Order(s)	Operation Orders No. 100 By Lieut Col C. Martim Cmdg 13th Bn. Essex Rgt.	27/04/1917	27/04/1917
Miscellaneous	Narrative of Operations on 28th April, 1917	01/05/1917	01/05/1917
Heading	6th Brigade 2nd Division.13th Battalion The Essex Regiment May 1917		
Heading	War Diary of 13th Bn. Essex. Rgt. From May 1st 1917-May 31st 1917 Vol 18		
War Diary	Ecurie To Maroeuil	01/05/1917	01/05/1917
War Diary	Maroeuil	02/05/1917	03/05/1917
War Diary	Maroeuil To Roclincourt	04/05/1917	04/05/1917
War Diary	Roclincourt	05/05/1917	17/05/1917
War Diary	Roclincourt To Camblain-Chatelaine	18/05/1917	18/05/1917
War Diary	Camblain Chatelaine	18/05/1917	24/05/1917
War Diary	Camblain-Chatelaine To Roclincourt	25/05/1917	25/05/1917
War Diary	Roclincourt	26/05/1917	31/05/1917
Operation(al) Order(s)	13th Bn. Essex Regt Operation Order No. 101	05/05/1917	05/05/1917
Operation(al) Order(s)	13th Bn. Essex Regt. Order No 103		
Operation(al) Order(s)	13th Bn. The Essex Regt Operation Orders No. 102	17/05/1917	17/05/1917
Miscellaneous	Notes	16/05/1917	16/05/1917
Miscellaneous	13th Bn. The Essex Regt Programme		
Heading	6th Brigade. 2nd Division. 13th Battalion The Essex Regiment June 1917		
Heading	War Diary of 13th Bn Essex Regt From June 1st 1917-June 30th 1917 Vol 19		
War Diary	Ecurie	01/06/1917	03/06/1917
War Diary	Ecurie To Line	03/06/1917	03/06/1917
War Diary	Line	04/06/1917	08/06/1917
War Diary	Line To Support Line	09/06/1917	09/06/1917
War Diary	Support Line Roclincourt	10/06/1917	13/06/1917
War Diary	Support Line to Roclincourt	14/06/1917	14/06/1917
War Diary	Roclincourt	15/06/1917	18/06/1917
War Diary	Mont St Eloy To Return	19/06/1917	19/06/1917
War Diary	Bethune to Gorre	20/06/1917	20/06/1917
War Diary	Gorre	20/06/1917	25/06/1917
War Diary	Gorre to Line	26/06/1917	26/06/1917
War Diary	Line	27/06/1917	30/06/1917

Operation(al) Order(s)	13th Essex Regt. Order No. 105	02/06/1917	02/06/1917
Operation(al) Order(s)	13th Bn. Essex Regt Order No. 106	08/06/1917	08/06/1917
Operation(al) Order(s)	13th Bn. Essex Regt Order No. 107	10/06/1917	10/06/1917
Operation(al) Order(s)	13th Bn. Essex Regt Order No. 108	10/06/1917	10/06/1917
Operation(al) Order(s)	13th Bn. Essex Regt Order No. 109	13/06/1917	13/06/1917
Operation(al) Order(s)	13th Bn. Essex Regt Order No. 110	26/06/1917	26/06/1917
Operation(al) Order(s)	13th Bn. Essex Regt Order No. 111	20/06/1917	20/06/1917
Heading	2nd Division 6th Infantry Bde.13th Essex Regt July To 31st December 1917		
Heading	6th Brigade. 2nd Division. 13th Battalion The Essex Regiment July 1917		
Heading	War Diary of 13th (Service) Bn. Essex Regt. From July 1st To July 31st 1917 Vol 20		
War Diary	Givenchy Sector Festubert	01/07/1917	02/07/1917
War Diary	Support Area Windy Corner	03/07/1917	08/07/1917
War Diary	Left Subsector	09/07/1917	14/07/1917
War Diary	Gorre	15/07/1917	19/07/1917
War Diary	Left Subsector	20/07/1917	24/07/1917
War Diary	Support Area	25/07/1917	25/07/1917
War Diary	Windy Corner	25/07/1917	29/07/1917
War Diary	Left Subsector	29/07/1917	31/07/1917
Heading	6th Brigade 2nd Division. 13th Battalion The Essex Regiment August 1917		
Heading	War Diary of 13th (S) Bn. The Essex Regt From August 1st-31st 1917 Vol 21		
War Diary	Left Subsector Givenchy Sector	01/08/1917	03/08/1917
War Diary	Gorre	04/08/1917	09/08/1917
War Diary	Gorre & Left Subsector	09/08/1917	10/08/1917
War Diary	Left Subsector Givenchy Sector	10/08/1917	13/08/1917
War Diary	Left Subsector	13/08/1917	15/08/1917
War Diary	Windy Corner	15/08/1917	20/08/1917
War Diary	Left Subsector	21/08/1917	21/08/1917
War Diary	Left Subsector Givenchy Sector	21/08/1917	26/08/1917
War Diary	Left Subsector	26/08/1917	27/08/1917
War Diary	Gorre	28/08/1917	31/08/1917
Heading	6th Brigade. 2nd Division. 13th Battalion The Essex Regiment September 1917		
Heading	War Diary of 13th (S) Bn. The Essex Regt From September 1st-30th 1917 Vol 22		
War Diary	Gorre	01/09/1917	02/09/1917
War Diary	Left Subsector Givenchy Sector	02/09/1917	02/09/1917
War Diary	Gorre and Left Subsector	02/09/1917	02/09/1917
War Diary	Left Subsector Givenchy Sector	03/09/1917	07/09/1917
War Diary	Left Subsector & Bethune	07/09/1917	07/09/1917
War Diary	Bethune	08/09/1917	17/09/1917
War Diary	Bethune & Windy Corner	18/09/1917	18/09/1917
War Diary	Windy Corner	19/09/1917	23/09/1917
War Diary	Windy Corner & Left. Subsector Givenchy Sector	24/09/1917	24/09/1917
War Diary	Left Subsector Givenchy Sector	25/09/1917	30/09/1917
Heading	6th Brigade. 2nd Division. 13th Battalion The Essex Regiment October 1917		
Heading	War Diary of 13th (Service) Battn Essex Regiment October 1st To 31st 1917 Vol 23		
War Diary	Gorre	01/10/1917	05/10/1917
War Diary	Bethune	06/10/1917	06/10/1917
War Diary	Bethune & Lozinghem	07/10/1917	07/10/1917

War Diary	Lozinghem	08/10/1917	31/10/1917
Heading	6th Brigade. 2nd Division. 13th Battalion The Essex Regiment November 1917		
Heading	War Diary of 13th (S) Battn Essex Regiment November 1st To 30th 1917 Vol 24		
War Diary	Lozinghem	01/11/1917	04/11/1917
War Diary	Lozinghem & Steenbecque	05/11/1917	05/11/1917
War Diary	Steenbecque & Eeche Area	06/11/1917	06/11/1917
War Diary	Eeche Area & Houtkerque	07/11/1917	07/11/1917
War Diary	Houtkerque area	08/11/1917	22/11/1917
War Diary	Houtkerque area And Proven	23/11/1917	23/11/1917
War Diary	Proven And Rocquigny	24/11/1917	25/11/1917
War Diary	Rocquigny And Doignies	25/11/1917	25/11/1917
War Diary	Doignies	26/11/1917	26/11/1917
War Diary	Trenches	27/11/1917	30/11/1917
Miscellaneous	6th Infantry Brigade.	07/12/1917	07/12/1917
Miscellaneous	Notes on Recent Operations I beg to forward following with reference to the operations described above	07/12/1917	07/12/1917
Miscellaneous	13th (S) Bn. Essex Regiment Ref 6th Bn G S 916/36	07/12/1917	07/12/1917
Miscellaneous	6th Infantry Bde		
Miscellaneous	A Form. Messages And Signals.		
Diagram etc	Rough Sketch Shewing disposition of Troops under Cond. of o/c Left Support Bn. at 7 Pm 12/13.12.17		
Operation(al) Order(s)	13th Essex Regt. Order No. 144	19/12/1917	19/12/1917
Miscellaneous	Defence Scheme		
Miscellaneous	Addendum To Defence Scheme		
Heading	6th Brigade 2nd Division. 13th Battalion The Essex Regiment December 1917		
Heading	War Diary of 13th (S) Bn Essex Regt From Dec 1st-31st 1917 Vol 25		
War Diary	Moeuvres Sector	01/12/1917	03/12/1917
War Diary	K 3.a	04/12/1917	04/12/1917
War Diary	Le Bucquiere	05/12/1917	08/12/1917
War Diary	Support Area	09/12/1917	14/12/1917
War Diary	Le Bucquiere	15/12/1917	20/12/1917
War Diary	Support Area	21/12/1917	23/12/1917
War Diary	Front Line	24/12/1917	26/12/1917
War Diary	Hermies	27/12/1917	29/12/1917
War Diary	Support Area	30/12/1917	31/12/1917
Operation(al) Order(s)	Short Narrative of the Recent Operations From November 30th, 1917 To Night Of 4th/5th December 1917		
Heading	6th Brigade. 2nd Division Battalion Disbanded 10.2.18 1/13th Battalion The Essex Regiment January 1918		
Heading	War Diary of 13th (S) Bn. Essex Regt January 1918 Vol 26		
War Diary		01/01/1918	04/01/1918
War Diary	Rocquigny	05/01/1918	23/01/1918
War Diary	Rocquigny & Metz	24/01/1918	24/01/1918
War Diary	Metz	25/01/1918	28/01/1918
War Diary	Metz-Right Sub Sector Left Brigade Sector	28/01/1918	28/01/1918
War Diary	Right Sub Sector	29/01/1918	31/01/1918
Operation(al) Order(s)	13th Bn The Essex Regt Relief Order No. 5	02/02/1918	02/02/1918
Heading	2nd Division 6th Infy Bde 1-13th Battalion The Essex Regiment Jan 1918 (Disbanded 10th Feb)		
Diagram etc	Standard Hutting.		

WO 95/1358/1

33RD DIVISION
100TH INFY BDE

2 DIV

6 BDE

13TH BN ESSEX REGT.

~~NOV 1915 ONLY~~

1915 NOV & DEC

100th Infantry Brigade.

33rd Division.

(Battn. disembarked at
Boulogne from England
17.11.15)

13th BATTN. THE ESSEX REGIMENT.

N O V E M B E R

1 9 1 5

(16.11.15-25.11.15)

Army Form C. 2118.

WAR DIARY
or
INTELLIGENCE SUMMARY.
(Erase heading not required.)

Instructions regarding War Diaries and Intelligence Summaries are contained in F. S. Regs., Part II. and the Staff Manual respectively. Title pages will be prepared in manuscript.

Hour, Date, Place	Summary of Events and Information	Remarks and references to Appendices
	CONFIDENTIAL. WAR DIARY. of 13th (S) Battn THE ESSEX. REGT 16th From November 11th 1915 To December 31st 1915.	

Army Form C. 2118.

WAR DIARY
or
INTELLIGENCE SUMMARY.

(Erase heading not required.)

Instructions regarding War Diaries and Intelligence Summaries are contained in F. S. Regs., Part II. and the Staff Manual respectively. Title pages will be prepared in manuscript.

Place	Date	Hour	Summary of Events and Information	Remarks and references to Appendices
Perham Down Camp Andover	Nov 19th 1915.	2 pm	The Transport and Advance Party, with Capt. S. E. Collier in command, and Lieut T.S. Biddulph-Pinchard, Lieut G. Simpson, and 2nd Lieut G. A. T. Ross, and 134 N.C. Officers and Men, left Camp and proceeded to Ludgershall Station where they entrained for Southampton, and from thence by boat to France.	27T

Army Form C. 2118.

WAR DIARY
or
INTELLIGENCE SUMMARY.
(Erase heading not required.)

Place	Date	Hour	Summary of Events and Information	Remarks and references to Appendices
Parham Down Camp Andover	Nov 14th 1915	6 am	**Parades** Headquarters (less Second in Command – Major A. L. Brown and Batman – Pte T. Garwood) and A + B Coys under the following Officers:- Lieut Col. T. R. Papillon. — Commanding Officer. Capt. J. J. Trimble. — Adjutant Lieut L. E. Holthouse. — O.C. Signalling Section Capt A. J. Hayward — O.C. Machine Gun Section Lieut A. M. Holthouse R.A.M.C — O.C Stretcher Bearer Hon Lieut. Quartermaster T. E. Brunt + Medical Officer Rev. T. L. B. Westerdale (Chaplain.) **A Coy** Capt R. A. Swann Lieut A. E. Bunting 2/Lieut T. T. Toleman 2/Lieut A. W. Lee. **B Coy** Major W. H. Winthrop Lieut E. J. Lawson 2/Lieut R. J. Norman 2/Lieut T. R. Keile	JF

Army Form C. 2118.

WAR DIARY
or
INTELLIGENCE SUMMARY.
(Erase heading not required.)

Instructions regarding War Diaries and Intelligence Summaries are contained in F. S. Regs., Part II. and the Staff Manual respectively. Title pages will be prepared in manuscript.

Place	Date	Hour	Summary of Events and Information	Remarks and references to Appendices
Perham Downs Camp	Nov 14th 1915	6.10 a.m	Parade. Major A. L. Brown, (Second in command) and 13 other and C & D Companies under the following officers:— Capt Patterson Capt & O Stafford Lieut. F Young. Lieut. W. W. Buckley Lieut. B. F Tyne Lieut. F. E. Howell Lieut. d'Fountain W. Hestele. Capt F. G. R. Page Capt H. H. Shannon	77

WAR DIARY
INTELLIGENCE SUMMARY
(Erase heading not required.)

Army Form C. 2118.

Place	Date	Hour	Summary of Events and Information	Remarks and references to Appendices
Pecham Down Camp Andover	Nov 14th 1915	4 am	The Battalion paraded 26 officers & 869 Other ranks which proceeded to Hurstpierpoint Station where they entrained for Folkestone Harbour Station, arriving at 12 noon. The Battalion then embarked on the Princess Victoria for Boulogne, which port was reached at 6pm. After disembarking, the Battalion proceeded by road to Ostrohove Large Rest camp where it rested, under canvas, until 6 am Sunday Nov 19th.	391
Boulogne France	Nov 19th 1915	6 am	The Battalion paraded at 6 am and marched off at 6:45 a.m. under Lieut Col. F.R. Papillon, to Pont de Briques Station, where the Transport, and the Advance Party under Capt. S.E. Collier joined the Battalion.	391

			Appx
Boulogne France	Nov 19th 1915	9.50 a.m	The Battalion proceeded to TWEENNES.C STATION (nr ST OMER) arriving at this Station at 3.45 pm after detraining, the Battalion proceeded to the village of BOESEGHEM, where billets had been prepared	397
Boeseghem France	Nov 25th	9 a.m	The Battalion marched to the Village of LE PIERIERE a distance of about 4 Miles. Billets had been prepared here (Time of arrival 12 Noon)	397

6th Infantry Brigade.

2nd Division.

(Battn. transferred from
100th Bde. 33rd Div.
22.12.15)

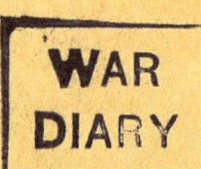

13th BATTN. THE ESSEX REGIMENT.

D E C E M B E R

1 9 1 5

13th Battn. The Essex Regiment.

December 1915

$(2.12.15 - 22.12.15)$

Pont Remy, France 2nd Dec 1915	9 am	The Battalion marched to the town of BETHUNE a distance of about 10 Miles, arriving at 1.30pm The Battalion billeted at a Tannery factory	39.1
Bethune, France 3rd Dec 1915	10 am	The Battalion marched to the village of ESSARS a distance of 2 Miles arriving at 11 am	39.1

WAR DIARY or INTELLIGENCE SUMMARY.

Army Form C. 2118.

Place	Date	Hour	Summary of Events and Information	Remarks and references to Appendices
Essars	4/10/15		Battalion transferred to the 5th Infantry Brigade, Second Division for instructions	Appx.1
Essars	9/10/15	9 am	Battalion marched to ANNEZIN arriving at 11 a.m.	Appx.II
Annezin	10/10/15	10 am	Battalion marched to LE PREOL arriving at 11 a.m. "B" Company under Major M. Winthrop, and "C" Company under Capt J. N. Patterson proceeded to the trenches.	Appx.II
Le Preol	10/10/15	1 pm	"A" Company under Capt R. A. Surman, and "D" Company under Capt H. H. Shannon relieved "B" & "C" Coys in the trenches	Appx.II
R.O.	11/10/15		No 11555 Pte T. V. Price "B" Coy was killed whilst in the trenches. This was the first casualty in the Regiment.	Appx.I

WAR DIARY
or
INTELLIGENCE SUMMARY.
(Erase heading not required.)

Instructions regarding War Diaries and Intelligence Summaries are contained in F.S. Regs., Part II. and the Staff Manual respectively. Title pages will be prepared in manuscript.

Hour, Date, Place	Summary of Events and Information	Remarks
Tue 23rd 1915	Battalion transferred to :- 1st Army, 1st Corps, 1st Division & 6th Infantry Brigade.	

Army Form C. 2118

WAR DIARY
or
INTELLIGENCE SUMMARY.
(Erase heading not required.)

Instructions regarding War Diaries and Intelligence Summaries are contained in F.S. Regs., Part II. and the Staff Manual respectively. Title pages will be prepared in manuscript.

Hour, Date, Place	Summary of Events and Information	Remarks and references to Appendices
Le Preol. 23/12/15. 10 a.m.	The Battalion marched to the town of BETHUNE arriving at 12 Noon	39.T.
Bethune. 24/12/15. 8 a.m.	The Battalion marched to the village of MANQUEVILLE a distance of about 10 Miles, arriving at 1 p.m. for a period of rest and training	

D.J. Trumble
Capt & Adj.
13th Essex Regt.

2ND DIVISION
6TH INFY BDE

13TH BATTALION
ESSEX REGIMENT
JAN - DEC 1916

6th Brigade.

2nd Division.

13th BATTALION

THE ESSEX REGIMENT

JANUARY 1916.

Army Form C. 2118.

WAR DIARY
or
INTELLIGENCE SUMMARY.
(Erase heading not required.)

CONFIDENTIAL

WAR DIARY

of

13th (S) BATTN. THE ESSEX
REGIMENT.

FROM DECEMBER 2nd/15 11th Jan TO JANUARY 31st/16

1916
Marquville
Sept 11th 16 26 | Regimental canteen opened under
Lieut. W. Roang.

Army Form C. 2118.

WAR DIARY
or
INTELLIGENCE SUMMARY.
(Erase heading not required.)

Instructions regarding War Diaries and Intelligence Summaries are contained in F.S. Regs., Part II. and the Staff Manual respectively. Title pages will be prepared in manuscript.

Hour, Date, Place	Summary of Events and Information	Remarks and references to Appendices
Mazinguarde Jan 19th 8-15 am	Battalion marched to BERGUETTE STATION and entrained for BETHUNE STATION, and from thence marched to the village of LES CHOQUAUX arriving at 12 noon	
Les Choquaux Jan 19th 12-30pm	Battalion marched to the village of LE QUESNOY arriving at 2-30pm HQ's B+C Coys occupied the Reserve trenches at B3 with No's 1+2 Coys Huts under the Command of Lieut Col. P.R. Papillon. Heavy shelling at 4am + 3 am for Reserve Trenches at Sub Section B3	
B3 Jan 19th 20th	Heavy Shelling at 11 am 11.40 am & 1am 4am	

WAR DIARY
or
INTELLIGENCE SUMMARY.
(Erase heading not required.)

Army Form C. 2118.

Hour, Date, Place	Summary of Events and Information	Remarks and references to Appendices
B3. Jan 30th 1916	Heavy Shelling at 10 am + 4 pm (4 Casualties (Wounded) No 14244 L/Cpl A. Trench " 14554 Pte J.T. Newling " 18661 " W. Allister " 14414 " S. Ward Bn. 3rd Infantry Battalion relieved South Staffs Regt in front line trenches at 2nd line Trenches at WINDY CORNER and billets at 5.30 pm. B3 heavily shelled at intervals. 4 Casualties (1 Killed 6 Wounded) No 14980. Pte. W.J. King (Killed) " 12889 " W. Shannan } " 14949 " E.W. Mills } Wounded " 14747 " H. Holden } " 14545 " A. Timslow } " 14505 " G. Greenwood } " 14660 " H.E. Heighway }	

Army Form C. 2118.

WAR DIARY
or
INTELLIGENCE SUMMARY.
(Erase heading not required.)

Hour, Date, Place	Summary of Events and Information	Remarks and references to Appendices
B3. Jan 31st 1916 22nd day 6pm	Headquarters Area heavily shelled. Mine blown up by Enemy (No Casualties) No 1361 Pte. A. Wade wounded (Self Inflicted)	
3pm	Battalion relieved by the O's, Herts. & No's 1st Regt Herts & "A" + "C" Coys. Essex, under the Command of Lieut Col Croft with Major A.b. Brown (Essex) 2nd in Command.	
	Relieved Battalion took over billets vacated by 1st Kings Regt at GORRE.	
6.15 pm 9.15 pm	Repeated bombardment by the enemy, all ranks ordered to "Stand to Arms" throughout the night of 31st/1st.	

Army Form C. 2118.

WAR DIARY
or
INTELLIGENCE SUMMARY.
(Erase heading not required.)

Instructions regarding War Diaries and Intelligence Summaries are contained in F.S. Regs., Part II. and the Staff Manual respectively. Title pages will be prepared in manuscript.

Hour, Date, Place	Summary of Events and Information	Remarks and references to Appendices
Jan 27th 16 Gorre. 4:30pm	H.Q's "B" + "C" Coys (Essex) + No's 1+2 Coys (Hants) occupy the trenches at Sub Sections B2, vacated by the 1st King's Regt.	
B2 Jan 28th 10.5am	Rifle Bombardment by the Enemy's Artillery which lasted for 4½ hours viz:- 10.5am — 5.30pm. Slight damage done to buildings in the vicinity of WINDY CORNER, including the Dressing Stations at B2. (No Casualties.) Our Artillery replied effectively. Battalion relieved by 1st King's Regt and occupied billets at GORRE. Casualties (Wounded) No 14948 Pte Coleman 14352 Pte R Buck " 14229 " W Smith 14919 " E.W. Kunkel " 18203 " J. Harlow 18533 " A. Hyatt " 14386 " R. Cook 4596 " St. Smith No 18139 Pte E.T. Rower accidentally shot by Comrade	
B2. Jan 30th.		Jan 29th Nothing of Importance to report.

(73989) W4141—463. 400,000. 9/14. H.&J.Ltd. Forms/C. 2118/10.

Army Form C. 2118.

WAR DIARY
or
INTELLIGENCE SUMMARY.
(Erase heading not required.)

Instructions regarding War Diaries and Intelligence Summaries are contained in F.S. Regs., Part II. and the Staff Manual respectively. Title pages will be prepared in manuscript.

Hour, Date, Place	Summary of Events and Information	Remarks and references to Appendices
Gorre. Jan 31st	Battalion in Billets at GORRE and LE QUESNOY. Nothing of importance occurred.	

6th Brigade.
2nd Division.

13th BATTALION

THE ESSEX REGIMENT

FEBRUARY 1916.

Army Form C. 2118.

WAR DIARY
or
INTELLIGENCE SUMMARY.
(Erase heading not required.)

CONFIDENTIAL

WAR DIARY

of

13th (S) BATTN ESSEX REGT

From 1st – 29th FEBRUARY 1916

Army Form C. 2118.

WAR DIARY
or
INTELLIGENCE SUMMARY.
(Erase heading not required.)

Instructions regarding War Diaries and Intelligence Summaries are contained in F. S. Regs., Part II. and the Staff Manual respectively. Title pages will be prepared in manuscript.

Place	Date	Hour	Summary of Events and Information	Remarks and references to Appendices
B3	2/3/16	5pm	H.Q's, B + T Coys + No's 1 + 3 Coys 1st Herts Regt relieved 1st King's Regt at B3. 14th Middlesex Regt took over billets vacated at GORRE	S.W.O.R.
	3/3/16	6pm	Battalion relieved by 22nd Royal Fusiliers + moves to billets at LES CHOCQUAUX arriving about 10.30pm. A halt was made en route for tea about 8.30pm which was much appreciated. Lieut.Colonel C.R. Papillon proceeded to England on leave. Major A.H. Brown (Second in Command) took over the Command of the Battalion.	S.W.O.R.
Les Chocquaux	5/3/16		Battalion under the Command of Major A.H. Brown relieved 1st Oxford + Bucks Light Infantry at VILLAGE LINE - FESTUBERT - C3 - at 4pm. 14th Royal Fusiliers took over billets vacated at LES CHOCQUAUX.	S.W.O.R.
Village Line C3	11/3/16	4pm		S.W.O.R.

Army Form C. 2118.

WAR DIARY
or
INTELLIGENCE SUMMARY.
(Erase heading not required.)

Instructions regarding War Diaries and Intelligence Summaries are contained in F. S. Regs., Part II. and the Staff Manual respectively. Title pages will be prepared in manuscript.

Place	Date	Hour	Summary of Events and Information	Remarks and references to Appendices
Village Line C3	12/3/16		VILLAGE LINE Shelled between 11.15 a.m. & 1.15 p.m. also RUE DU CAILLOUX.	A/228
Do	13/3/16		Heavy Shelling at intervals.	A/228
Do	15/3/16	5.30 p.m.	Battalion relieved by the 3rd South Staffs Battalion	A/228
Do	Do	Do	VILLAGE LINE. Battalion relieved 1st Herts Regt in Sub Station C3. "A" + "B" Coys occupied Right + Left front trenches, "C" Coy 1st Support, Headquarters and "D" Coy the Reserve line.	
Sub Station C3	16/3/16		Nothing of importance to report. Lieut Colonel F.R. Papillon returned from leave and resumed command of the Battalion.	A/228
	19/3/16	7.30 p.m.	"C" Coy relieved by E Coy with the exception of No 11 Platoon	A/228
			"B" Coy relieved by F Coy	

Continued

2353   W: W2544/1454   700,000   5/15   D. D. & L.   A.D.S.S./Forms/C. 2118.

WAR DIARY
or
INTELLIGENCE SUMMARY.
(Erase heading not required.)

Army Form C. 2118.

Place	Date	Hour	Summary of Events and Information	Remarks and references to Appendices
Sub Section C3	18/3/16	4.30pm	Casualties (Wounded) No 14534 L/Sergt M.G. Burden B Co. (Slightly) " 10468 Pte " Cowell Co " 14501 " A. Fowler Co Accidentally shot by comrade. Capt. Adjutant & J. Trundle proceeded to England on leave & Lieut T.A. Fountaine took over the duties of Adjutant	JMcK
	19/3/16		Casualties Killed No 18463 Pte H. Bagley " 11112 " R. Brown Casualties Wounded No 18345 Pte L. Farmer " 13396 " J.E. Gardner " 21308 " A. Berkles " 11114 L/Cpl H. T. Cook	JMcK

Army Form C. 2118.

WAR DIARY
or
INTELLIGENCE SUMMARY.
(Erase heading not required.)

Place	Date	Hour	Summary of Events and Information	Remarks and references to Appendices
Sub Section C.	19/9/16	6.15 pm	Battalions relieved by 11th South Wales Borderers and moved into billets at LES CHOQUAUX arriving at 11 pm. Sapping Platoon relieved at LE TOURET by the 10th South Wales Borderers + marched independently to billets at LES CHOQUAUX. En route a halt was made by Battalions about 10 pm when that sapfs was served out and much enjoyed. There was a bright moon out some excitement was caused during this halt by the appearance of what seemed to be a Zeppelin, which met with fire from our Aerial Guns. Bombs were dropped in the neighbourhood of LES CHOQUAUX.	AJK

Army Form C. 2118.

WAR DIARY
or
INTELLIGENCE SUMMARY.
(Erase heading not required.)

Instructions regarding War Diaries and Intelligence Summaries are contained in F. S. Regs., Part II. and the Staff Manual respectively. Title pages will be prepared in manuscript.

Place	Date	Hour	Summary of Events and Information	Remarks and references to Appendices
Les Eloquent	20/9/16	9.30 am	Battalions moved into Billets at LES HARISOIRES and MONT BERMENCHON, a distance of about 8 miles, arriving at 1pm. Heavy bombardment of Enemy's positions by our Artillery lasting from 6pm to 1am until 6pm did not. Lieut E. & C. Moon transferred from B. Coy, and appointed to the Command of A. Coy vice Capt H. A. Shannon (Sick) in England.	A.M.2K.
	21/9/16		A demonstration Parade at GONNEHEM. Every available man paraded.	A.M.2K.
	24/9/16			A.M.2K.
Les Harisoires	25/9/16	9.30 am	Battalions marched to ST SAINS to billets vacated by the French, a distance of about 13 miles, arriving at 3 pm. The road en route was	A.M.2K.

2353 Wt. W2511/1454 700,000 5/15 D. D. & L. A.D.S.S./Forms/C. 2118.

WAR DIARY
or
INTELLIGENCE SUMMARY.
(Erase heading not required.)

Army Form C. 2118.

Place	Date	Hour	Summary of Events and Information	Remarks and references to Appendices
Pt. Sains	26/2/16	5.30pm	frozen and heavy snow fell at intervals. Battalion marched to billets at BULLY GRENAY a distance of about 3 Miles, arriving at 6.30 pm	3HQR
Bully Grenay	27/2/16		Shelling at Intervals 2 Men wounded by shell fire Pte W. E. Loughlin 'B' Co. No 14586 S C. No. 14519	
			2 Lt S. P. Fountain (Acting Adjutant) admitted to Hospital and Lieut S. H. T. Ross took over the duties of Acting Adjutant	3HQR
	28/2/16		Shelling at Intervals	3HQR
	29/2/16		Shelling at Intervals Capt. St. G. Collier appointed to the Command of 'A' Co	3HQR

6th Brigade.

2nd Division.

13th BATTALION

THE ESSEX REGIMENT

MARCH 1916.

WAR DIARY
or
INTELLIGENCE SUMMARY.
(Erase heading not required.)

Army Form C. 2118.

2nd Army

13 Essex
Vol 4.
2nd Div

CONFIDENTIAL

WAR DIARY of

13th ESSEX REGIMENT

FROM MARCH 1st 1916 TO MARCH 31st 1916

WAR DIARY
or
INTELLIGENCE SUMMARY.

(Erase heading not required.)

Army Form C. 2118.

Instructions regarding War Diaries and Intelligence Summaries are contained in F.S. Regs., Part II. and the Staff Manual respectively. Title pages will be prepared in manuscript.

Place	Hour, Date	Summary of Events and Information	Remarks and references to Appendices
Calonne Tr. Sect.	5/3/16 6pm	Battalion relieved by 14th Middlesex Regt. and took over the Support Area vacated by 1st King's Regt.	Map 36.b & 36.c. 1/40000 J.T.
	6/3/16	The undermentioned men died during the night of 5th & 6th in their billet, from C.O. poisoning. (Carbon monoxide).	Trench Map 1/10000 J.T.

		14942 Loffhofl E
		 14948 Pte. rfk.
		 14995 Ryan 80 } "C"
		 18535 Byrnes 96 Coy
		 18029 Barber a.
		 18098 Carter t.a.
		 18028 Busby A.J.
		  Parker
		  Chaplin	

		No. 18013 Pte. C.A. Payne died from the effects of C.O. poisoning on 7/3/16 during evacuation.	
Support Area	9/3/16 5pm	Battalion relieved 14th Middlesex Regt. in Trenches in Northern Sub. Section. 14th Middlesex took over Support Area.	J.T.

Army Form C. 2118.

WAR DIARY
or
INTELLIGENCE SUMMARY.
(Erase heading not required.)

Instructions regarding War Diaries and Intelligence Summaries are contained in F.S. Regs., Part II. and the Staff Manual respectively. Title pages will be prepared in manuscript.

Place	Hour, Date		Summary of Events and Information	Remarks and references to Appendices
Northern Sub. Section	12/3/16	5pm	Battalion relieved by 14th Middlesex Regt. & took over billets vacated by 1st Kings Regiment at BULLY-GRENAY. Billet Area shelled at intervals.	T.J.T
Bully Grenay	14/3/16	5.30pm	Battalion relieved by 11th Bn. Northumberland Fusiliers & marched to COUPIGNY & took over billets vacated by 13th Durham Light Infantry.	36b. 1/40000 T.J.T
Coupigny	15/3/16	12.35pm	Battalion marched to the town of BRUAY arriving about 3-30pm. Leave for Battalion commenced.	T.J.T
Bruay	20/3/16		Lieut. Col. P.R. Papillon took over the Command of the 6th Infantry Bde during the absence on leave of Brig. Gen. A.C. Daly.	T.J.T
	25/3/16		Major W.A. Witheth took over the Command of the Battalion.	T.J.T

T.J. Rumpler
Capt. & Adjt.
13th Essex Regt.

(73989) W4141—463. 400,000. 9/14. H.&J.Ltd. Forms/C. 2118/10.

6th Brigade.

&2nd Division.

13th BATTALION

THE ESSEX REGIMENT

APRIL 1916.

13 Essex

Army Form C. 2118.

WAR DIARY
or
INTELLIGENCE SUMMARY.
(Erase heading not required.)

Confidential

War Diary
of
13th (S) Bn Essex Regt

from 1/4/16 until 30/4/16 inclusive

Army Form C. 2118.

WAR DIARY
or
INTELLIGENCE SUMMARY.
(Erase heading not required.)

Instructions regarding War Diaries and Intelligence Summaries are contained in F. S. Regs., Part II. and the Staff Manual respectively. Title pages will be prepared in manuscript.

Place	Date	Hour	Summary of Events and Information	Remarks and references to Appendices
Bruay	3/4/16	9.15am	Battalion marched to Bruay Station and entrained to BABLIN and from thence marched to COUPIGNY and took over billets vacated by the 2nd R.I. arriving about 12 Noon.	36.L 1/40000 Starting Point BRUAY J.26 d.c.4
Coupigny	9/4/16		Lieut Col P.R. Papillon resumed the command of the Battalion	
"	11/4/16		2nd Lieuts. Pts. J. Stradfords was at the West Riding Casualty Clearing Station	
"	11/4/16		Capt. & Adjt. J. J. Trimble granted Special leave to England. 2/Lt. W.T. Mortimore took over the duties of Acting Adjutant	
"	14/4/16	11.0am	Battalion marched to HERSIN Station + entrained for BRUAY and took over billets vacated by the 2nd Royal Fusiliers, arriving at 3.30 pm	Starting Point Q11 a.6.3

Army Form C. 2118.

WAR DIARY
or
INTELLIGENCE SUMMARY.
(Erase heading not required.)

Instructions regarding War Diaries and Intelligence Summaries are contained in F. S. Regs., Part II. and the Staff Manual respectively. Title pages will be prepared in manuscript.

Place	Date	Hour	Summary of Events and Information	Remarks and references to Appendices
Burny	13/4/16	10.30 am	Battalion marched to CALONNE RICOUART Station, a distance of about 4 Miles and entrained for AIRE Station and thence marched to DFLETTES (in First Army Training Area) a distance of about 10 Miles - arriving about 4 pm.	I 10 & S.

WAR DIARY
or
INTELLIGENCE SUMMARY.
(Erase heading not required.)

Army Form C. 2118.

Place	Date	Hour	Summary of Events and Information	Remarks and references to Appendices
Roellette	14/4/16 15/4/16 16/4/16		Battalion + Brigade Training at GREUPPE & RUPIGNY	
Do	17/4/16	8.15am	Battalion marched to AIRE Stn arriving about 12 Noon & entrained for CALONNE RICOUART STATION & thence marched into Billets previously occupied by the Battalion on the night of the 12/13th Apl at BRUAY	
Bruay	18/4/16	9.45 am 10.30am	Battalion marched to BRUAY Stn and entrained at for HERSIN Station and from thence marched to Huts in COUPIGNY arriving about 12 Noon.	36b + 36e 1/40000
Coupigny	18/4/16	5.30pm	Battalion relieved 13th & whom light Infantry in Northern Sub Section at 6pm. Heavy Shelling at intervals. No Casualties.	
Northern Sub Section	19/4/16 20/4/16 21/4/16 22/4/16	4pm	Heavy Shelling at intervals. Battalion relieved by 14th M Lucas Regt and took over billets in the Support Area CITÉ CALONNE vacated by the 1st Kings Regt	

Army Form C. 2118.

WAR DIARY
or
INTELLIGENCE SUMMARY.
(Erase heading not required.)

Instructions regarding War Diaries and Intelligence Summaries are contained in F.S. Regs., Part II. and the Staff Manual respectively. Title pages will be prepared in manuscript.

Place	Date	Hour	Summary of Events and Information	Remarks and references to Appendices
Support trenches	23/4/16 24/4/16 25/4/16 26/4/16 27/4/16		Nothing to report with the exception of heavy Artillery fire at intervals. Capt. Adjt. to of Trensules returned from leave (Adjutant)	
To KOY	28/4/16	1.15pm	Battalion relieved 14th Middlesex Regt in trenches # in Northern Subsection	
Northern Subsection	29/4/16 30/4/16		Heavy Bombardment heard on our right. Casualties 2nd Lieut A.O.Olleitt Killed by Sniper. 4/19458 Pte Cooper Killed by Sniper. 4/11391 Pte A.M.Bollenger 14509 Pte A. Wilkenson (Accidentally) Wounded Sergt R Barker	
KOY	30/4/16		Heavy Artillery duel on our Right	

WAR DIARY
or
INTELLIGENCE SUMMARY.
(Erase heading not required.)

Army Form C. 2118.

Place	Date	Hour	Summary of Events and Information	Remarks and references to Appendices
Northern Sub Section B [?]	29/4/16	4.55 am	at 5AM Gas alarm. Gas came over our lines and every man was ordered to Stand to Arms + put on Gas Helmet. The Gas passed over about 6.10 am. No Casualties Gas Shell burst on "B" Coys lines. No Casualties	
Do	Do	4 pm		
Do	30/4/16	4 pm	Battalion relieved by 14th Middlesex Regt and took over billets vacated by 1st Kings Regt at BULLY - GRENAY.	

D. Trimble
LtCol 18th KLR

6th Brigade.

2nd Division.

13th BATTALION

THE ESSEX REGIMENT

M A Y 1916.

Army Form C. 2118.

WAR DIARY
or
INTELLIGENCE SUMMARY.
(Erase heading not required.)

13 Essex

Vol II

CONFIDENTIAL

WAR DIARY

of

13th (S) BATTN THE ESSEX REGT

FROM MAY 1st 1916 TO MAY 31st 1916

WAR DIARY
or
INTELLIGENCE SUMMARY.
(Erase heading not required.)

Army Form C. 2118.

Instructions regarding War Diaries and Intelligence Summaries are contained in F.S. Regs., Part II. and the Staff Manual respectively. Title pages will be prepared in manuscript.

Hour, Date, Place	Summary of Events and Information	Remarks and references to Appendices
5pm. 4/5/16 Bully Grenay	Battalion relieved 14th Middlesex Regt in trenches at NORTHERN Subsectors CALONNE. Heavy Shelling during relief. Casualties <u>Killed</u> No 21414 Pte G. H. Totter. <u>Wounded</u> No 14182 Pte J. Skevitt 18055 " W. J. Bowen. 21831 " W. O'Brunne. 14851 " J. Tinnen (duty)	36c + 36c. Map Trench Map 1/10000
5/5/16 6/5/16	Heavy Shelling at intervals. on both sides by Rifle Grenades &c. Casualties. <u>Killed</u> No 14530 L/cpl J. M. Barford 14633 Pte S. Woodward <u>Wounded</u> No 14544 Pte A. E. Canter (duty) 14645 " A. Preston	

Army Form C. 2118.

WAR DIARY
or
INTELLIGENCE SUMMARY.
(Erase heading not required.)

Instructions regarding War Diaries and Intelligence Summaries are contained in F.S. Regs., Part II. and the Staff Manual respectively. Title pages will be prepared in manuscript.

Hour, Date, Place	Summary of Events and Information	Remarks and references to Appendices
7/5/16 Northern Subsection	Heavy Shelling at intervals. Trench Mortar + Grenade activity on both sides. Quiet on Casualties Wounded No. 18844 Pte R.B. Ferguson & No. 18154 Pte Hawkins } 1st/4th	29 T.
8/5/16	Battalion relieved by 14th Middlesex Regt + took over the Support area CITE CALONNÉ vacated by the 1st KINGS Regt	29 T
Support Area 9/5/16	No 1134H Pte W CLARK slightly wounded.	29 T
10/5/16	No 1464& Pte J.B. Moon do	29 T
2.30p 10/5/16	Battalion relieved by Middlesex Regt in Trenches at NORTHERN Subsection Casualties Nil P.T.O.	29 T

Army Form C. 2118.

WAR DIARY
or
INTELLIGENCE SUMMARY.
(Erase heading not required.)

Instructions regarding War Diaries and Intelligence Summaries are contained in F.S. Regs., Part II. and the Staff Manual respectively. Title pages will be prepared in manuscript.

Hour, Date, Place	Summary of Events and Information	Remarks and references to Appendices
Northern Sub Section 13/5/16	Shelling & hostile grenade & trench Mortar activity. Casualties. Wounded	29T
14/5/16	2nd Lieut A.W. KAYE Heavy Shelling on both sides at intervals. Casualties. Wounded No. 18653 Pte G. GIBBS " 18081 " P.G. WINDLEY " 21660 " A.E. SEEKER	29T
15/5/16	Heavy shelling at intervals. Casualties Killed No. 18052 L/Cpl J.W. DUTTON Battalion relieved by 14th Middlesex Regt and took over billets vacated by the 1st KINGS Regt in BULLY GRENAY	29T

(73989) W4141—463. 400,000. 9/14. H.&J.Ltd. Forms/C. 2118/10.

Army Form C. 2118.

WAR DIARY
or
INTELLIGENCE SUMMARY.
(Erase heading not required.)

Instructions regarding War Diaries and Intelligence Summaries are contained in F. S. Regs., Part II. and the Staff Manual respectively. Title pages will be prepared in manuscript.

Place	Date	Hour	Summary of Events and Information	Remarks and references to Appendices
Bully Grenay	13/5/16		Transport lines at FOSSE 10 shelled Casualties Wounded No 18496 Pte W. THORNE. Working parties found by Battalion and the following casualties occurred. Killed No 3146 Pte J. L. LYGOE Wounded No 14998 Pte E. GIBBONS	39.T
"	14/5/16		Lieut Col. P. R. PAPILLON proceeds to England on leave of absence and Major W. H. WINTHROP takes over the Command of the Battalion, with Capt J. J. PATERSON as 2nd in Command	39.T
"	15/5/16	4pm	Battalion relieved by 1st CAMERON Highlanders and marched to COUPIGNY and took over billets vacated by the 2nd H. L. I. Arrived at 6pm	39.T

Army Form C. 2118.

WAR DIARY
or
INTELLIGENCE SUMMARY.
(Erase heading not required.)

Instructions regarding War Diaries and Intelligence Summaries are contained in F.S. Regs., Part II. and the Staff Manual respectively. Title pages will be prepared in manuscript.

Hour, Date, Place	Summary of Events and Information	Remarks and references to Appendices
9 am 19/5/16 Cauchy	Battalion marched to the village of FRESNICOURT, a distance of about 4 Miles arriving at 10.30 am where billets were taken over from the 23rd LONDON Regt.	36c + 36b 1/40000 O i/c 2nd T
Fresnicourt 9 am 20/5/16	Battalion marched to DIVION, a distance of about 6½ Miles, arriving at 11.45 am and took over billets vacated by the 23rd ROYAL FUSILIERS	2nd T
DIVION. 21/5/16 11 am 22/5/16 1 am 8.40 8 am	Battalion under orders to move to CARENCY VALLEY at one hours notice. Battalion under orders to be prepared to move by Motor lorries at 8 am. Battalion less Transport Section proceeded to MAISNIL BOUCHÉ by Motor lorries arriving about 11 am. Battalion	2nd T

Army Form C. 2118.

WAR DIARY
or
INTELLIGENCE SUMMARY.
(Erase heading not required.)

Instructions regarding War Diaries and Intelligence Summaries are contained in F.S. Regs., Part II. and the Staff Manual respectively. Title pages will be prepared in manuscript.

Hour, Date, Place	Summary of Events and Information	Remarks and references to Appendices
Mairie Bouches 23/5/16.	under orders to move off at an hours Notice. Heavy bombardment heard on our front. Large numbers of troops observed being conveyed to the surrounding villages by Motor lorries and a number of batteries of Artillery passed through going toward CARENCY.	29.T
25/5/16 2½pm	Battalion relieved the 19th Dist. 33rd Bde LONDON Regt at VIMY RIDGE. Relief en route North of CARENCY owing to road being heavily shelled by enemy. Heavy rain was falling which continued for some hours. Relief Complete by 3 am 24/5/16.	29.T
Vimy Ridge 24/5/16	Heavy shelling on our front by Minnenwerfers Our Artillery replied effectively as	29.C

(73989) W4141—463. 400,000. 9/14. H.&J.Ltd. Forms/C. 2118/10.

Army Form C. 2118.

WAR DIARY
or
INTELLIGENCE SUMMARY.
(Erase heading not required.)

Instructions regarding War Diaries and Intelligence Summaries are contained in F. S. Regs., Part II. and the Staff Manual respectively. Title pages will be prepared in manuscript.

Place	Date	Hour	Summary of Events and Information	Remarks and references to Appendices
Vimy Ridge	26/5/16		The Minnenwerfers were quiet again for a considerable time. Casualties 2nd Lieut W. F MARTINSON Wounded No 14659 L/Cpl G.W. KEET " 14418 Pte W. BAKER " 18331 " A.C. GILES } Remained at duty Gas alert on	28 T
do	27/5/16		Heavy Shelling on both sides. Gas alert on Casualties Killed No 14435 Pte A.S. MOTTON " 14181 " A.W. PERCIVAL Wounded No 18594 A/Cpl F.T. GEVAUX " 18348 Pte F. BRANTON (Remained at duty) " 18333 " W. WAVING " 18355 " G.W. CARTER (Since died 29/5/16)	29 T

WAR DIARY
or
INTELLIGENCE SUMMARY.

Army Form C. 2118.

Place	Date	Hour	Summary of Events and Information	Remarks and references to Appendices
Vimy Ridge	29/5/16		Continuous shelling on both sides during day & night. Casualties 2nd Lieut. H.E.G. WEST Wounded. No. 18499 Pte H.G. WESTON "	App. T
Do	30/5/16		Continuous shelling on both sides	App. T
Do	30/5/16		Lieut Colonel T.R. TAPILLON returned from leave and resumed the Command of the Battalion.	App. T
Do	30/5/16		Battalion relieved by 19th Middlesex Regt. H.Q's remained in previous quarters and were designated H.Q's of SUPPORT Battalion & dispositions of Battalion "B" Coy at CARENCY, also 3 platoons of "A" Coy. "C" Coy at ZOUAVE VALLEY, South of UHLAN VALLEY. "D" Coy at ZOUAVE VALLEY, NORTH of UHLAN VALLEY. 1 Platoon of "A" Coy at BATOLLE LINE NORTH of CABARET ROAD. SAPPING Platoon with "C" Coy & LEWIS GUN SECTION at CARENCY.	App. T

Army Form C. 2118.

WAR DIARY
or
INTELLIGENCE SUMMARY.
(Erase heading not required.)

Place	Date	Hour	Summary of Events and Information	Remarks and references to Appendices
Subsect Sec Vimy Ridge	31/5/16		Heavy Shelling at intervals. Battalion engaged on Working parties. Casualties Killed No 18881 L/Cpl H THOMAS. Wounded No 14465 Pte J W TULLY 14909 " A A SPURLING " 14580 " T J LLEWELLYN	26/T
		8pm	Battalion ordered to Stand to Arms. Major W H WINTHROP proceeds on leave to ENGLAND	80/T

6th Brigade.

2nd Division.

13th BATTALION

THE ESSEX REGIMENT

J U N E 1916.

Army Form C. 2118.

WAR DIARY
or
INTELLIGENCE SUMMARY.
(Erase heading not required.)

13 Essex

CONFIDENTIAL

WAR DIARY

of

13th (S) Bn THE ESSEX REGT

FROM JUNE 1st to JUNE 30th 1916

WAR DIARY
or
INTELLIGENCE SUMMARY.
(Erase heading not required.)

Army Form C. 2118.

Place	Date	Hour	Summary of Events and Information	Remarks and references to Appendices
Souchez	1/6/16		CARENCY Battalion occupied Support Area & 3 Mines were exploded by us. The 19th Middlesex Regt succeeded in holding craters. Violent artillery duel lasting from 4.30 pm until 10 pm. Enemy kept up a heavy Artillery barrage on Support Area & on ZOUAVE VALLEY & Support to the 1st Kings Regt who raided the German trenches for which they received valuable assistance from Lieut. Col. & officers of the Supporting Platoon. The Commanding Officer & Lieut. Col. & officers of the Supporting Platoon also came under very heavy shell fire. The trenches in front of Battalion H.Q. were severely damaged. 'C' Coy acted as carrying party in the consolidation of the new Craters. Killed W 10831 Pte T. Quinton Wounded W 3104 L/Cpl T. C. Roy Pte J. H. Farrell 18440 Pte M. Beam 18483 L/Cpl R. Knight 18494 Pte S. D. Turner 18801 #A. Burnett 18050 #14459 Pte A. Lewis W18350 Pte A. Paine 18408 Cpl A. Robinson 14474 #A. G. Stone 18408 L/Sgt M. Coughlan M.T. Emery 18421 Pte B. Townley #Pte W. S. Pearsall 18381 #L/Cpl A. Fleming Pte W. Smith 18050 #Pte A. Hemming Pte E. W. Crisp 14669 #Since of No 18558 Pte	Q.

WAR DIARY
or
INTELLIGENCE SUMMARY.
(Erase heading not required.)

Army Form C. 2118.

Place	Date	Hour	Summary of Events and Information	Remarks and references to Appendices
Sunday	2/6/16		Heavy Shelling at intervals also Machinegun Casualties Killed	Ol.
			No 18484 Pte J Newman	
			Wounded	
			No 11404 Pte J Williamson (6/1 TMB)	
	3/6/16 8 pm		No 14498 Sgt J Cotton No 14512 Life H Clark No 14545 Life H C Archer 18533 Pte S Quest No 21626 Pte F. C. Baker No 14493 Pte A E Buckley 14440 J McCain 11689 W L Cooper 12851 Life F G Mulvey Battalion relieved the 1/4th Middlesex Regt in NORTHERN Suburbs of CAMBRAI as follows:—	
			a Coy .... Right B " .... Right centre C " .... Left centre D " .... Left Heavy shelling on both sides. Wounded No 14426 Pte J H Scott. Slightly Wounded Remained at duty	
			Heavy Shelling at intervals Casualties	
	4/6/16		Wounded No 18919 Pte C Cross 18182 E Langley No 21439 Pte J J Turner. 21164 L H Waite	Ol.

WAR DIARY
or
INTELLIGENCE SUMMARY.
(Erase heading not required.)

Army Form C. 2118.

Place	Date	Hour	Summary of Events and Information	Remarks and references to Appendices
Bouchez	6/6/16	10pm	Battalion relieved by 14th Middlesex Regt & took over billets vacated by the 1st Kings Regt at VILLERS AU BOIS S.O.R. Wounded.	1130 Pte J.E. Mark 1435 - Pte Ewing 1930 - Pte Ridley 1930 - 3 Pte Shaw
	10/6/16	6.45 pm	Battalion relieved by 1st K.R.R. Corps & marched to ESTREE CAUCHIE and took over billets vacated by the 2nd Royal Fusiliers.	
	15/6/16		Capt. & Adjt. J. Trumble admitted to Hospital & Lieut. L.G. B. Lyne took over the duties of Acting Adjutant.	3 O.R. 11.0000 Trench Mortar
Estree Cauchie	18/6/16	6pm	Battalion relieved the 2nd H.L.I. in the SOUTHERN Sub section BERTHONVAL	
	20/6/16		A Party of 60 Other Ranks (riding horses) under Capt A.G. HAYWARD. Lieut F.R KEEBLE & Lieut W.W BUSBY proceeded to the CHATEAU DE LA HAIE for training. No 1936 Pte B.Bell Wounded.	
	2/6/16		Heavy shelling of Interned on both sides. Artillery engaged in Wire Cutting No 14145 L/Cpl E Graham & No 2161 Pte E.J Godfrey Wounded	

Army Form C. 2118.

WAR DIARY
or
INTELLIGENCE SUMMARY.
(Erase heading not required.)

Instructions regarding War Diaries and Intelligence Summaries are contained in F. S. Regs., Part II. and the Staff Manual respectively. Title pages will be prepared in manuscript.

Place	Date	Hour	Summary of Events and Information	Remarks and references to Appendices
Southern Sub Sector	22/6/16	10.45pm	Battalion relieved by 1st. Kings Regt - took over the Subsect area as follows:- Battn HQs CABARET ROUGE. "A" Coy ALHAMBRA - COLISEUM. "B" " CABARET ROUGE "C" " BATOLLE LINE "D" " CABARET ROUGE.	Q.
	23/6/16		Enemy Observation balloons seems to be brought down by our aircraft. a few thousand.	Q.
	25/6/16		Party consisting of 25 'Other Ranks + a/R.S.M. & R.Q.M.S. Cattermole proceeded to the CHATEAU DE LA HAIE to undergo special training.	Q.
	26/6/16		Casualties No 14610 Pte Mand - Wounded. No 18685 Pte Q. Linen Slightly Wounded. (since 26/4/16)	Q.
	24/6/16	8pm	Battalion relieved 1st Kings Regt in SOUTHERN Subsector, BERTHONVAL + 14th Middlesex took over the Subsect Area. No 18358 a/C.S.Mjr & R. Bartley slightly Wounded remained at duty.	Q.

2353 Wt. W2514/1454 700,000 5/15 D. D. & L. A.D.S.S./Forms/C. 2118.

WAR DIARY
or
INTELLIGENCE SUMMARY.
(Erase heading not required.)

Army Form C. 2118.

Place	Date	Hour	Summary of Events and Information	Remarks and references to Appendices
Southern Subsector	28/4/16		Shelling at intervals on both sides. No 18541 Pte H. J. Chase Wounded	d.
	29/4/16		Slight shelling at intervals	d.
	30/4/16		Whilst at howling practice at the CHATEAU DE LA HAIE an accident occurred owing to the premature bursting of a bomb causing the following casualties. **Killed** No 18832 Pte A. E. Sykes **Wounded** No 14661 Pte A. B. Ellis (died 1/5/16) No 18844 Pte R.P. Pogson No 14470 Pte E. Barker No 18351 L/cpl J. J. McKerrell No 21662 Pte A.W. Jacks. **Wounded** No 14136 Pte A.W. Stanton No 18015 L/cpl A.E. Pearce (Remained at duty) L/cpl Gibbons 21 ft + 2/Lieut 13th Essex Regt Shelling on front at intervals.	d.

6th Inf.Bde.
2nd Div.

WAR
DIARY

13th BATTN. THE ESSEX REGIMENT.

J U L Y

1 9 1 6

CONFIDENTIAL

WAR DIARY

of

13th (S) Bn. THE ESSEX REGT

From JULY 1st 1916   To JULY 31st 1916

Southern Subsection
BERTHONVAL
July 1/17

War Diary

A raid was carried out on the enemy's strong point at the junction of VINCENT STREET and German front line.
The raiding party consisted of:-

CAPT A G HAYWARD
LIEUT W W BUSBY
LIEUT F R KEEBLE

and 100 NCOs & Men including No 3/30449 a/RSM. G.E. CATTERMOLE

The whole party crawled out in the dead ground between the two lines to within 60 or 70 yards of the objective and they were in position there by 12.30 am. At Zero hour, 12.30 am an intense fire of Artillery, Trench Mortars and Stokes Guns was started. The artillery and trench mortars forming a box barrage round the objective also firing on suspected emplacements. Mnunuenfer [Minenwerfer] locations and communication trenches in rear, these continued to fire on the same points throughout the raid.
The Stokes guns opened rapid fire on the objective for one minute and instantly the minute was up to slacken was made for the enemy trenches and the whole party succeeded in getting in suffering only one casualty — the strong point was found already to be full of Germans. Some ten or a dozen of whom were attacked immediately by the fire from the Stokes guns. A fierce fight ensued. A party on the left told off to deal with the gap in VINCENT STREET found it unoccupied, men went that

Ref War Diary
St 3/1/H0070
Trench M&P
1/11/000
QM

War Diary

they any more successful with the Subdued Machine Gun Emplacements to the North of it, which was found to be a Mine Shaft a few Germans however, were seen by the party and five of them were killed. The left centre party also found a few Germans of whom one was killed and five of them who took refuge in a dug-out were also killed.
The right centre party found more Germans in their part of the trench. They killed five of them and saw seven to ground in a shallow dug-out. Six of whom they killed and one made prisoner.
The Garrison attempted to withdraw down to Communication Trench leaving Eastward. These were heavily bombed by the right party and twenty were killed and a number wounded.
The raiding party withdrew after being about a quarter of an hour in the enemy's trenches and came under rather heavy shrapnel fire on the way home.
The casualties among the raiding party were as follows:-

Officers   —
Capt   A. G. HAYWARD
Lieut   F R KEEBLE

Other Ranks

War Diary

Other Ranks

Killed
- No 14534 Pte E.W. Clark
- " 80947 " a Newton
- " 188595 " W Mary
- No 18054 Pte 2/Lt Moss
- " 18509 " Lt/ Edwards
- " 14335 " 2/Lt Turner

Wounded
- No 14144 Pte Bree C T
- " 46946 " Peek J
- " 14394 " Keer & Lt
- " 14659 " August & Lt Hartigan Pl.
- " 19849 " Cox & Lt
- " 18994 " Desmond C T
- " 44994 " Simmonds & Lt
- " 14144 " Griffiths G.A
- " 14004 " Edmonds E E
- " 18007 " Hill R.A.M.C
- " 18313 " Clarke & Lt
- " 18494 " Williams T.A
- " 18375 " Carter C & Lt
- " 24468 " Honey T J
- " 88994 " Wilson W.R.
- " 14141 " Page W
- " 18448 " Foulks R &
- " 52457 " Power W
- " 19419 " Raine R
- No 44493 Pte Tomlin C. L.
- " 14242 " Flint B &
- " 14202 " Soaker &
- " 14151 " Minshaw T
- " 14159 " Stretton's a
- " 14819 " Mantle P
- " 14945 " the
- " 14252 " Conlin B
- " 14203 " Cooper & Lt
- " 14094 " Myre & Lt
- " 14456 " Allen's & Lt
- " 41400 " Hood M R
- " 18418 " Kern W
- " 14941 " Abbott W
- " 19465 " Varley J.A
- " 15434 " Frank's a v
- " 18113 " Clayton C
- " 14455 " Pelham & Lt
- " 14404 " Waring Q B
- " 49484 " Cochrane J L
- " 14939 " Sgt Cleese Q Y
   at trenches & of duty

† Subsequently died of wounds

Missing
- No 19226
- " 14600 " Cpl A.E. Batten
- " 14400 " Pte J. Rumney
- " 18054 " Pte O. Henley

War Diary

Souchez Sub-Station BERTHONVAL	2nd	No 19265 Pte F. SAGE was also killed by shellfire during the night 1st/2nd July.
		Slight shelling on both sides at intervals
CAMBLAIN L'ABBE	5th	Battalion relieved by the 1st Kings Regt and took over billets at CAMBLAIN L'ABBE. Relief complete about 3 am
ESTREE CAUCHIE	10th	Battalion marched to ESTREE CAUCHIE and took over billets vacated by the 22nd Royal Fusiliers. The following wire was received from the G.O.C. 1st Army :-

"The G.O.C. 1st Army wishes to congratulate all who took part in the raid carried out on night of 1st/2nd July at about S.15.c.45.1"

The following N.C.O. When were awarded the MILITARY MEDAL by the IV Corps Commander for "gallantry" on the night of 1st/2nd July 1916.

No 18351 A/Sgt C.W.B. Browning W.f
" 18081 Pte a Thenman "
" 14499 Pte Q.L Brown "
" 18059 " W.J Muller "
" 18081 " L. Simmonds

Authy :- IV Corps No I Ref 734 of 13/4/17

ESTREE CAUCHIE 11th

War Diary

Raiding party marched to CAMBLAIN L'ABBÉ and were inspected by General C.C. MONRO, the Army Commander.

The following letter was received from 1st Army. (H.O.A.D. 34) of 2/4/16

"The numerous successful raids carried out along our front during the last few days have undoubtedly been of considerable assistance to the main operations besides having caused appreciable loss to the enemy's casualties.

The Commander-in-Chief desires that his appreciation of the good work done may be conveyed to all who have planned and carried out the raids."

(Sd) L.E. Kiggell Lieut General Chief of the General Staff

The following were awarded the Military Cross for gallantry on the night 1st/2nd July 1916

Capt A.G. HAYWARD
Lieut W.W. BUSBY
Lieut F.R. KEEBLE
Nr 3/3049 R.S.M. (a/RSM) G.E. CATTERMOLE

(Authy:- A.M.S. 1st Army of 11/4/16)

(a)

War Diary

ESTREE CAUCHEE 8pm	13th/14th	Battalion relieved 2nd Oxs. & Bucks L.I. in NORTHERN Sub-Section. CARENCY. **Dispositions** A Coy. RIGHT C Coy CENTRE B " PICQUETS. D " QUARRIES Enemy Trench Mortar Activity about 1 am. Shelling at intervals on both Sides and enemy Trench Mortar activity. **Casualties** <u>Killed</u> No 16545 Pte. G. T. FRANKER <u>Wounded</u> No 14413 Pte E. A. LAMB. No 18140 Sergt F. S. DABBS (at duty)	20l
	14th	Shelling on both Sides at intervals **Casualties** <u>Killed</u> No 9123 Pte R LEE <u>Wounded</u> No 14466 Sergt E. T. F. HAWTIN No 17131 A/ Sgt C H PIDDINGTON (at duty) (at duty)	do.
	15th		do.

War Diary

		Ref. White Sheet 51c.36c 1/40000 512 1/40000 Trench Map
Northern Shelter CAREWCY 10.30 pm Night 16th/17th	Battalion relieved by 2/2nd London Regt. and took over billets vacated by the 2nd Royal Fusiliers at GOUY-SERVINS	
Gouy Servins 18th 10.30am	Battalion marched to BEUGIN - a distance of about 4 Miles arriving at 2.30 pm.	
Beugin 30th 4am	Battalion marched to BRYAS Station - a distance of about 4 Miles arriving at 10.45am. From thence the Battalion - including Transport) entrained and travelled to LONGEAU Station arriving at 5.30 pm. At this Station the Anglers all ranks were started, and the Battalion marched to WELCOME WOOD, VAUX SUR SOMME a distance of about 12 Miles arriving about 12 Midnight. (Bivouac in huts) Battalion transferred to XIII Corps 4th Army with the 2nd Division.	
Welcome Wood 23rd 12.50pm	Battalion marched to BOIS DE TAILLES and were billetted in tents.	
Bois du Tailles 26th 9am	Battalion relieved the 8th Batt. Kings Own (Framework Regt) in Reserve Trenches at R.7.A. (Δ TRIANGLE)	
6am 26th	Battalion stood down "Standby vacated by the 1/4th Middlesex Regt at BRESLAU SUPPORT.	

War Diary

Bernafay Support 6.30pm 28th

Delville Wood 29th

Afternoon 30th

Night

31st

6.30pm

Battalion went into action in DELVILLE WOOD. B & D Coys who were attacking the Hun Staff Regt were repulsed. Intense artillery activity during the whole of the night. 2nd Lieut R.G. NORMAN & 2nd Lieut H.P. DAVIS Wounded. Intense Artillery activity on both sides for which Activity by the enemy

A party of enemy snipers were discovered and a party of about 40 men drove them out. Enemy made an attack which was repulsed. Intense Artillery activity on both sides continuously during the day & night.

Casualties

Lieut Col. P.R. PAPILLON (at duty)
Major A.P. CHURCHILL
2/Lieut a/adjt C.L.B. LYNE (at duty)
Captain T.M. ROUND (at duty)
Lieut L.C. HOLTHUSEN

Artillery activity continued throughout the day on both sides. Battalion relieved by 1st Kings Regt and took over Reserve trenches.

cont

Casualties

Delville Wood
3/9/16

War Diary

Casualties   Wounded
Capt   C G CARSON
Hart   F.T. FOLKARD

Casualties during tour in
DELVILLE WOOD
Other Ranks.

Killed   30
Wounded   138
Shell Shock   20
Missing   119
Wounded at duty   4
                   ___
                   321

Outl OB Carson 3/9/1t T4/9/1t
13th Entre Regt

6th Infantry Brigade.

2nd Division

13th BATTALION

THE ESSEX REGIMENT

AUGUST 1 9 1 6

Report on Operations 8/9th August 1916

Army Form C. 2118.

WAR DIARY
or
INTELLIGENCE SUMMARY.
(Erase heading not required.)

Vol 9

CONFIDENTIAL

WAR DIARY

of

13th (S) Bn. THE ESSEX REGT.

FROM

1st AUGUST 1916 31st AUGUST 1916

Army Form C. 2118.

WAR DIARY
or
INTELLIGENCE SUMMARY.
(Erase heading not required.)

Instructions regarding War Diaries and Intelligence Summaries are contained in F.S. Regs., Part II. and the Staff Manual respectively. Title pages will be prepared in manuscript.

Hour, Date, Place	Summary of Events and Information	Remarks and references to Appendices
1/8/16 Braken Support Trenches.	Continuous shelling by enemy on MINE ALLEY during afternoon. Enemy shell exploded about transport of the 99th Machine Gun Coy which was going towards MONTAUBAN. Killing several men & wounding others. Battalion moved to new trenches, some distance front.	Ref Map:- MONTAUBAN SHEET. 1/20000
2/8/16	In Reserve trenches. Shelling by enemy at intervals and heavy fire by our Artillery during the night	
3/8/16 4/8/16	In Reserve trenches. Shelling on both sides which increased towards midnight	
5/8/16 5pm	Battalion relieved 14th Royal Fusiliers in front line in WATERLOT FARM Section at 5pm. Heavy Shelling on both sides during the night. One Casualty - Wounded.	
Waterlot Farm Section 6/8/16 6.30pm	Battalion relieved by 14th Middlesex Regt and took over trenches vacated by the 1st Kings Regt in MINE ALLEY (A & a)	

(73989) W4141—463. 400,000. 9/14. H.&J.Ltd. Forms/C. 2118/10.

Army Form C. 2118.

WAR DIARY
or
INTELLIGENCE SUMMARY.
(Erase heading not required.)

Instructions regarding War Diaries and Intelligence Summaries are contained in F.S. Regs., Part II and the Staff Manual respectively. Title pages will be prepared in manuscript.

Hour, Date, Place	Summary of Events and Information	Remarks and references to Appendices
Trenches MINE ALLEY 7/8/16	Continuous Shelling by our Artillery and heavy Shelling by enemy on our trenches lasting from 10 pm until about 1 am. No Casualties	Ref. MONTAUBAN Sheet (57c SW)
8 pm to 9/8/16	Orders were received to move up to the trenches at TRONES WOOD & make the attack which had failed earlier in the day. The Battalion got into position at 3.30 am on the night of 8/9th leaving in time for reconnaissance & thorough explanation to officers NCO's & men of the attack which was to take place at 4.10 am. There were four objectives viz:-	GUILLEMONT GINCY & GUILLEMONT Sw Britain
	(i) German front line from Rest Any. ents (inclusive) to BROMPTON ROAD (exclusive)	
	(ii) GUILLEMONT STATION	
	(iii) Line of HIGH HOLBORN to MACHINE GUN HOUSE (inclusive)	
	cont.	

Army Form C. 2118.

WAR DIARY
or
INTELLIGENCE SUMMARY.
(Erase heading not required.)

Instructions regarding War Diaries and Intelligence Summaries are contained in F. S. Regs., Part II. and the Staff Manual respectively. Title pages will be prepared in manuscript.

Hour, Date, Place	Summary of Events and Information	Remarks and references to Appendices
TRONES WOOD 2/9/16	IV Southern portion of Z Z Trench from BROMPTON ROAD (exclusive) including forks running due South and South East of Railway lines to S 3 d B 9 8 inclusive. At 4.10 am C Coy moved up under artillery barrage to within 40 or 50 yards of the 1st objective. When the barrage lifted they pushed on to attack but found that the enemy were there, had not been cut and in attempting to get through were mown down by Machine Gun fire. A Coy followed at an interval of 10 minutes and again attacked this position with a like result. Orders were given to the two remaining Companies to stand fast and assist in getting in the wounded. The matter was then referred to Brigade Headquarters and instructions were sent through not to continue the attack.	GUILLEMONT 1/20,000 GINCHY & GUILLEMONT (2nd Edition)

Army Form C. 2118.

WAR DIARY
or
INTELLIGENCE SUMMARY.
(Erase heading not required.)

Hour, Date, Place	Summary of Events and Information	Remarks and references to Appendices
Trones Wood 8/8/16	Casualties 2nd Lieut G.H.T. ROSS MISSING 2nd Lieut P.R. PAGE MISSING 2nd Lieut E.O. JOHNSON Wounded (at duty) 13 Other Ranks Killed 60 " " Wounded 13 " " Missing 1 " " Died of Wounds	Q. Q.
c. 3.30pm 9/8/16	Battalion returned to trenches at MINE ALLEY Q.8a.	
11 am 10/8/16	Battalion moved to HAPPY VALLEY.	Q.
HAPPY VALLEY 5pm 12/8/16	Battalion marched to MEAULTE, a distance of about 4 Miles and took over billets	Maj G > D ||∠○○○○
MEAULTE 8.50pm 13/8/16	Battalion marched to MERICOURT L'ABBE & ten went entrained at 8pm for SALEUX rest	Q.

Army Form C. 2118.

WAR DIARY
or
INTELLIGENCE SUMMARY.
(Erase heading not required.)

Instructions regarding War Diaries and Intelligence Summaries are contained in F.S. Regs., Part II. and the Staff Manual respectively. Title pages will be prepared in manuscript.

Hour, Date, Place	Summary of Events and Information	Remarks and references to Appendices
BOIS-DU-WARNIMOUNT 10.30am 19/8/16	Battalion marched to COURCELLES where a halt was made for dinner after which we proceeded to relieve the 1st Bn. IRISH GUARDS in the RIGHT Subsection. Casualties 3 Other Ranks Wounded.	Ref M/p 547 1/400000 00h
RIGHT SUBSECTION 6.50pm 22/8/16	Battalion relieved by 14th MIDDLESEX Regt and took over billets vacated by them at COURCELLES	00h
COURCELLES 24/8/16 4.30pm	Battalion relieved 2nd SOUTH STAFFS Regt in LEFT Subsection SERRE Section	00h
25/8/16 26/8/16 27/8/16	Heavy Shelling at intervals Casualties 1 O.R Killed 1 O.R. & 10 Wounded 7 Wounds 4 O.R Wounded	00h 00h
Left Subsection 28/8/16 6.30pm	Battalion relieved by 2nd SOUTH STAFFS Regt and took over billets vacated by them in COURCELLES Cont	00h

(73989) W4141—463. 400,000. 9/14. H.&J.Ltd. Forms/C. 2118/10.

WAR DIARY
or
INTELLIGENCE SUMMARY.
(Erase heading not required.)

Army Form C. 2118.

Instructions regarding War Diaries and Intelligence Summaries are contained in F.S. Regs., Part II. and the Staff Manual respectively. Title pages will be prepared in manuscript.

Hour, Date, Place	Summary of Events and Information	Remarks and references to Appendices
Left Shelter 28/8/16	Lieut - Colonel P.R. PAPILLON proceeded to England on special leave. Capt S.E. COLLIER took over the Command of the Battalion with Capt J.M. ROUND as Second in Command.	
COURCELLES 29/8/16	Information received that the following had been awarded the MILITARY MEDAL for gallantry during operations on July 30/31st and Aug 6/9 4th. No 14698 Sergt COTTON P. No 13144 Sgt TODD F.W. 18061 L/Sgt SONGHURST C. No 18644 Pte ROSCOE H. 18094 Pte JAMES F.A. No 1414 " SAMPSON W. No 14558 Pte SMITH W.H.J. Authy - 1st Army Routine Order No 502 of 24/8/16	
30/8/16 31/8/16	No 12260 Pte C.E. BECK commended in 1st Army Divisional Routine Orders for coolness in stopping a panic & running mules on mules in COURCELLES. Battalion huttled in COURCELLES	

Commanding Offr of 1st Battn Essex Regt

6th. Infantry Brigade.
----

1.   I beg to report that in accordance with verbal instructions given me at 8.30 p.m. on the night of 8.8.16, I moved my Battalion from MINE ALLEY (S.8.a.) to TRONES TRENCH and NEW TRENCH for the purpose of attacking the German Trenches between WATERLOT FARM and GUILLEMONT.

The Communication Trench; MONTAUBAN ALLEY - LONGUEVAL ALLEY, (the only means of approach) was greatly congested and the expected guides were not available, consequently the Battalion was not in position in the Assembly Trenches until 3.30 a.m. on the morning of the 9th instant.

2.   MY dispositions were as follows :-
"C", "D" and "B" Companies in NEW TRENCH and "A" Company in TRONES TRENCH.

The Objectives were four in number as set out in para. 4 of Operation Order No.190 of 8.8.16, and my orders were that :-
"C" Company should sieze and hold 1st Objective.
"D"   "   "   "   "   2nd   "
"B"   "   "   "   "   3rd   "
"A"   "   "   "   "   4th   "

3.   At ZERO hour (4.20 a.m.) - 10, on 9. 8. 16, the first Company was lying out in front of the trench along a tape previously put out exactly parallel to the Objective, and, when the bombardment commenced, they crept forward practically up to the barrage, so that, when the barrage, lifted they were up to the German wire almost at the same moment.

My second Company, "D", aligned themselves along the tape directly "C" Company began to creep forward, i.e., about 4.15. a.m.

4.   At ZERO hour the attack was launched; the first wave, "C" Company, being closely followed by the second wave, "D" Company.

The men were ably led and the attack was made with great dash and courage, but the enemy was fully on the alert and the trenches were strongly held with men and Machine Guns (5 at least of the latter have been located and there were others).

The defences and wire were practically intact, and apparently had suffered no damage from the short bombardment. The result was that the attack was broken up by Machine Gun fire upon reaching the wire and by a perfect barrage of bombs which the enemy had organised.

A few men on the left flank succeeded in entering the enemy's trench, but they were overpowered by superior numbers; elsewhere the attack did not get beyond the wire.

5.   My attack was unsupported on the right, as I had been given to believe that it would be, and on the left the Lewis Gun fire had little effect on the enemy's trenches.

MACHINE GUN HOUSE on my left was still held by the enemy and the fire from this position was very effective.

Further attacks without thorough Artillery preparation could only have resulted in very heavy losses without any likelihood of success, and it did not appear that they could in any way assist operations on my right and left.

I therefore gave orders that the attacks should not be renewed pending your instructions.

6.   Both men and Officers behaved extremely well.
The ground was new to everyone and there had been no

opportunity

opportunity for previous reconnaissance, no intimation of the attack having been given to any of us previous to 8.30.p.m. on the night before.

This had a material influence on the result, as reports on former attacks led me to believe that both wire and parapet were practically non-existent, whereas the reverse was found to be the case.

Had time been given to make a reconnaissance, a patrol would undoubtedly have discovered that <u>the enemy had siezed his opportunity to strengthen considerably both wire and parapet, during the hours of darkness on Night 8th/9th.</u>

The time at disposal was far too short for proper maturing of plans and for making all ranks acquainted with the scheme of attack, in fact it barely sufficed as stated above, to get the men into position for it.

Owing to the configuration of the ground, the four Objectives were invisible from jumping off point and owing to the darkness, these could not be seen until the men were quite close to them.

The Artillery preparation was ineffective and the enemy were more than usually on the alert owing to previous attacks. The Battalion had also lost 12 good Officers and several of the best N.C.Os in recent fighting a day or two before in DELVILLE WOOD.

In spite of these disadvantages the attack was extremely well delivered, both alignment and direction being well maintained and the rush being made with great dash and courage close behind the Artillery Barrage.

It was only broken owing to the strength and alertness of the enemy, to the number of Machine Guns at their disposal and to the strong obstacle afforded by their wire, and having failed, it appeared to me that it would only be a needless and useless sacrifice of men to launch the two remaining waves.

I regret to have to report that both Company Commanders are believed to have been killed and that my other casualties amount to over 90.

Captain Round and Lieut. Brown behaved most gallantly in bringing in the wounded under fire, the latter remaining out all night on the 9th/10th until all the ground had been cleared.

I hope to have the honour of bringing other names to your notice shortly.

10.8.16.

P. R. Papillon   Lieut. Colonel,
Commanding 13th Essex Regiment.

STAR.

SX 2/95   9.   AAA.

I beg to forward attached report just received from Capt. ROUND. at NEW TRENCH. Everything is now very quiet.

(Signed) F.R. Papillon. Lt Col
Cmdg. 13th Essex.

9.55 a.m.

Report.

A rough estimate of Casualties is as follows.

  C. Coy. 62 killed. wounded & missing
  B. Coy. 6 killed
       12 wounded.
       12 missing
  D Coy. 4 wounded
       19 missing.

  A Coy. 5. missing.

Many of the missing should be recovered tonight. I cannot get the exact Lewis gun casualties but there are 3 guns & 16 men lost to B, C & D Coys

3. Brigade bombers wounded – 3 missing. 2/Lt ROSS, PAGE, HONE & JOHNSON have not yet returned.
Total about 138.

With regard to the machine guns one was definitely located on the left of our first objective at the junction of railway & trench & another was located at the right corner of the same trench. There were also at least 2 more firing from the trench in between the two at either flank. There was also fire from either MACHINE GUN HOUSE in HIGH HOLBORN or from another emplacement lower down HIGH HOLBORN. The new ridge of the first objective still presents a considerable obstacle.

(Sgd) T.H. ROSS. Capt.

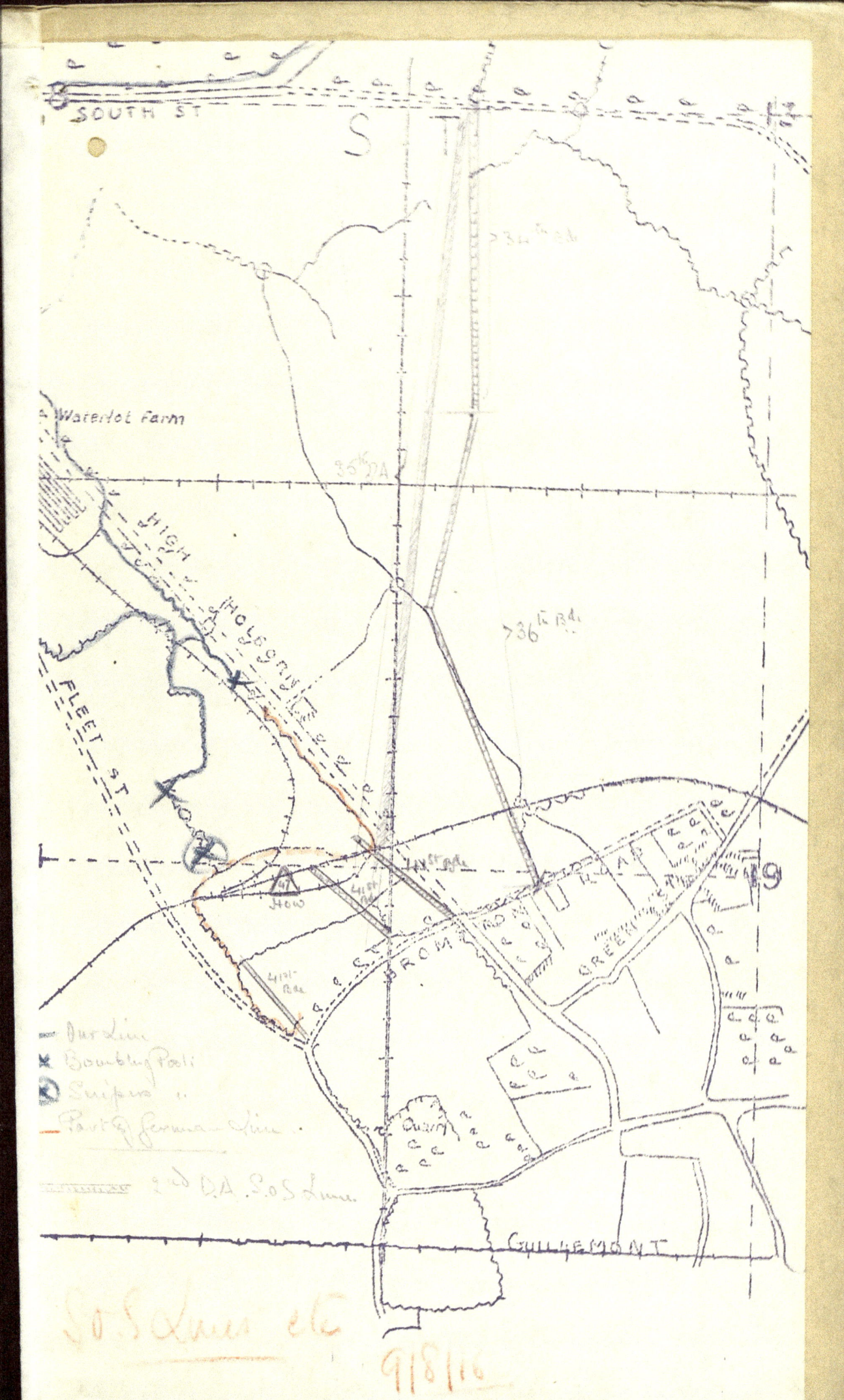

6th Brigade.

2nd Division.

13th BATTALION

THE ESSEX REGIMENT

SEPTEMBER 1916.

WAR DIARY
or
INTELLIGENCE SUMMARY.

Army Form C. 2118.

Vol 10

CONFIDENTIAL
WAR
of
13th (S) Bn The Essex Regt
Salonika
September 1st – 30th 1916.

WAR DIARY
or
INTELLIGENCE SUMMARY.

Army Form C. 2118.

Place	Date	Hour	Summary of Events and Information	Remarks and references to Appendices
Courcelles	1/9/16	6pm	Battalion relieved 2nd South Staffs Regiment in the LEFT Subsection, SERRE Section. Dispositions: "A" Coy Right Front, "B" do Left do, "C" do Right Support, "D" do Left do	Map Sheet 57 1/40.000
Left Sub Section	2/9/16		Heavy bombardment on our front line trenches by enemy Minenwerfers.	
do	4/9/16	11/am	Enemy patrol of 1 N.C.O. + about 8 men came over to our [...] No. 14155 Pte. W. Ware. Wounded No. 18318 Pte S. Branton No. 11164 Pte S. Brennan	

Place	Date	Hour	Summary of Events and Information	Remarks and references to Appendices
Left Sub Section	4/9/16		lines apparently with the view of ascertaining the extent of the damage done by their bombardment on the previous day. The party was seen and bombed, the N.C.O. being killed, one man also killed and another taken prisoner. The patrol belonged to the 168th Jaeger Rifles. Casualties Killed No. 885 L/Cpl A. Miller. No. 18411 L/Cpl T.O. Hunt " 408 Pte H/M Evans. " 24746 Pte W.J. Lee Wounded No. 24780 Pte W. & Bailey. No. 18644 Pte E. Moore " 23493 " C.R. Prater " 47887 " W. Mythen " 3318 " A.E. Bennett " 6119 " S. Branham	☆
to	5/9/16	5 pm	Battalion relieved by 1st South Staffs Regt and took over billets at COURCELLES. Lieut Col. P.R. PAPILLON returned from leave and resumed the Command of the Battalion	

Army Form C. 2118.

WAR DIARY
or
INTELLIGENCE SUMMARY.
(Erase heading not required.)

Instructions regarding War Diaries and Intelligence Summaries are contained in F. S. Regs., Part II. and the Staff Manual respectively. Title pages will be prepared in manuscript.

Place	Date	Hour	Summary of Events and Information	Remarks and references to Appendices
Louvencourt	6/9/16 7/9/16 8/9/16		Battalion in Support - engaged on Working Parties	
Sp 5	9/9/16	5.30pm	Battalion relieved 2nd South Staffs Regt in left Sub-Section SERRE Section. Dispositions: C Coy Right Front D " Left " A " Right Support B " Left Support Casualties No 14140 Pte A Brown. Wounded at duty	
Left Sub Section	10/9/16		Shelling on both sides at intervals.	
	11/9/16	1.30am	Mine sprung by enemy. 2/Lieut P. G. FOUNTAIN rejoins the Battalion and takes over the duties of Acting Adjutant	

WAR DIARY
or
INTELLIGENCE SUMMARY.

(Erase heading not required.)

Army Form C. 2118.

Place	Date	Hour	Summary of Events and Information	Remarks and references to Appendices
Left Sub Section	11/9/16	cont	Heavy Shelling by both Sides at intervals. Casualties Wounded. No 23651 L/Cpl E.J. Steward. No 14340 Pte J. Clark. No 2686 Pte A. Price.	A
Do	12/9/16		Normal. Slight Shelling at intervals.	A M
Do	13/9/16		Battalion relieved by the 2nd South Staffs Regt & took over billets vacated by them at COURCELLES.	A
Courcelles	14/9/16 15/9/16 16/9/16 17/9/16		Working parties found by Battalion. Lieut Col P.R. PAPILLON awarded the D.S.O. Capt J.A. PATERSON awarded the M.C. No 14391 L/Cpl N.W. BELLINGER awarded the D.C.M. The following were awarded the Military Medal. No 14136 Sgt C Burleigh. No 14155 Sgt T.W. White No 14391 L/Cpl N.W. Bellinger. 18108 Pte J. to Plate. No 14192 Pte J.M. Smith. (Authy:- London Gazette 14/9/16.)	A A A A A

Army Form C. 2118.

WAR DIARY
or
INTELLIGENCE SUMMARY.
(Erase heading not required)

Place	Date	Hour	Summary of Events and Information	Remarks and references to Appendices
Courcelles	17/9/16	3·30pm	Battalion relieved by 1st South Staffs Regt in the LEFT Subsection, SERRE Sector.	Relative Secret Map 1/10000 Sa Esquire Ia. Secret Map 1/10000 fs.
Left Sub Section	18/9/16	9pm	Heavy shelling by Enemy Minenwerfers. Our Artillery retaliated which proved effective. Mine sprung by enemy in front of RIGHT Brigade.	
	19/9/16	10am	Battalion relieved by the 16th Rifle Brigade and took over tentage - hut accommodation at BOIS DU WARNIMONT.	
Bois du Warnimont	20/9/16 to 30/9/16		Battalion training including Co-operation with Aircraft, Assault on trenches re.	

Gartsere 2/Lt adjt
13th E.Lan Regt.

6th Brigade.

2nd Division.

13th BATTALION

THE ESSEX REGIMENT

OCTOBER 1916.

Army Form C. 2118.

WAR DIARY
or
INTELLIGENCE SUMMARY.
(Erase heading not required.)

Vol XI

CONFIDENTIAL

WAR DIARY

of

13th (S) Bn THE ESSEX REGT.

FROM 1.10.16 to 31.10.1916

Instructions regarding War Diaries and Intelligence Summaries are contained in F.S. Regs., Part II. and the Staff Manual respectively. Title pages will be prepared in manuscript.

Hour, Date, Place	Summary of Events and Information	Remarks and references to Appendices

Army Form C. 2118.

WAR DIARY
or
INTELLIGENCE SUMMARY.
(Erase heading not required.)

Instructions regarding War Diaries and Intelligence Summaries are contained in F. S. Regs., Part II and the Staff Manual respectively. Title pages will be prepared in manuscript.

Hour, Date, Place	Summary of Events and Information	Remarks and references to Appendices
Bois du Warnimont 1/10/16 10:30 am	Battalion relieves the 11th Bn. Sherwood Foresters in the RIGHT Subsection SAILLY AU-BOIS Section	Map 57/17 1/40000 Secret Trench Map HEBUTERNE 1/10,000
	en route to the above trenches Lieut-Colonel P R PAPILLON DSO the Commanding Officer returned to the Transport lines - Sect-	
	Major W.H. CARTER D.S.O. M.C. 2nd South Staffordshire Regiment attached to the 11th Middlesex Regt. took over the Command of the Battalion & assumed the rank of Lieut Colonel	
Right Subsection Sailly au Bois 4/10/16	Heavy Shelling by Enemy Trench Mortars - minenwerfer. New kicking off trench constructed in No Mans Land.	

Army Form C. 2118.

WAR DIARY
or
INTELLIGENCE SUMMARY.
(Erase heading not required.)

Instructions regarding War Diaries and Intelligence Summaries are contained in F.S. Regs., Part II and the Staff Manual respectively. Title pages will be prepared in manuscript.

Hour, Date, Place	Summary of Events and Information	Remarks and references to Appendices
Right Subsection Sailly au Bois Section 3 p.m. 3/10/16	Battalion relieved by the 1st Bn Gordon Highlanders and took over billets at BERTRANCOURT.	A
Bertrancourt 4/10/16 5/10/16 6/10/16	Battalion found various Working Parties.	A
4.15 pm 7/10/16	Battalion moved to new billets at PUCHEVILLERS a distance of about 8 miles.	A
Puchevillers 8/10/16 to 13/10/16 14/10/16	Battalion engaged in practising Divisional attack on trenches	A
18/10/16	Battalion moved to new billets at BERTRAN COURT.	A
Bertrancourt 19/10/16 20/10/16 9 am 21/10/16	Working parties supplied by Battalion. Battalion moved to MAILLY-WOOD. EAST and took over huts/ments vacated by 2nd Bn Royal Fusiliers.	A A

Army Form C. 2118.

WAR DIARY
or
INTELLIGENCE SUMMARY.
(Erase heading not required.)

Instructions regarding War Diaries and Intelligence Summaries are contained in F.S. Regs., Part II. and the Staff Manual respectively. Title pages will be prepared in manuscript.

Place	Date	Hour	Summary of Events and Information	Remarks and references to Appendices
Mailly Maillet East	22/10/16 23/10/16 24/10/16 25/10/16	3pm	Working Parties supplied by the Battalion. Battalion relieved 1st Kings Regt on the Brigade front. Heavy bombardment of German lines by our Artillery. Slight retaliation by enemy. Casualties 1/Lt S. M. Stuart Killed. No.14194 Sergt H.J. Morrison Killed. 11 Other Ranks Wounded.	A A A
Brigade Front	26/10/16 27/10/16 28/10/16		Heavy Shelling on both sides at intervals. Battalion relieved by the 2nd South Staffs Regt and took over huts vacated by them at BERTRANCOURT.	A A
Bertrancourt	29/10/16 30/10/16 31/10/16		Battalion supplies Working Parties.	A

[signature] 1st Lt & Adjt
13th Essex Regt

6th Brigade.

2nd Division.

13th BATTALION

THE ESSEX REGIMENT

NOVEMBER 1916.

CONFIDENTIAL

WAR DIARY

of

13th (S) Bn THE ESSEX REGT

From November 1st – 30th 1916.

Army Form C. 2118.

WAR DIARY
— or —
INTELLIGENCE SUMMARY.
(Erase heading not required.)

Instructions regarding War Diaries and Intelligence Summaries are contained in F. S. Regs., Part II. and the Staff Manual respectively. Title pages will be prepared in manuscript.

Hour, Date, Place	Summary of Events and Information	Remarks and references to Appendices
Bertrancourt 1/11/16, 2/11/16, 3/11/16, 4/11/16, 5/11/16, 6/11/16	Battalion engaged in Working parties in preparing the trenches for the proposed attack	✓
10 am 7/11/16	Battalion moved to new billets in MAILLY MAILLET Village.	
Mailly - Maillet 8/11/16, 9/11/16, 10/11/16	Battalion engaged in preparing the trenches for proposed attack	✓
10.30am 11/11/16	Battalion relieved the 1st King's Regiment in trenches in the Brigade front. preparatory to attack	
Brigade Front Reserve Sector 12/11/16	On the night 12th + 13th the dispositions of the Battalion in the assembly Trenches was as follows — "A" Coy. from junction of BUSTER and front line to junction BORDEN AVENUE and front line. BORDEN AVENUE inclusive.	✓

Army Form C. 2118.

WAR DIARY or INTELLIGENCE SUMMARY.

(Erase heading not required.)

Place	Date	Hour	Summary of Events and Information	Remarks and references to Appendices
Regan Redr.	12/13 11/11/16		**Instructions continued**	

"B" Coy from left of "A" Coy to 100 yards NORTH MINOR trench and front line.

"C" Coy from junction of BUSTER and CHATHAM, along CHATHAM line to BORDEN AVENUE exclusive.

"D" Coy from BORDEN AVENUE along CHATHAM, WOLF, & MINOR.

Disposition prior to the Assault

No's 1 & 2 platoons of "A" Coy and No's 5 & 6 platoons of "B" Coy formed the 1st WAVE. These were to be followed by No's 3 & 4 platoons of "A" Coy & No's 7 & 8 platoons of "B" Coy immediately in rear of No's 1, 2, 5 & 6 platoons. No's 3, 4, 7 & 8 platoons were to form the "Cleaning up Parties" of the 1st & 2nd German lines. These two lines were to advance at 3 paces interval between each man; the "Cleaning up Parties" keeping as near up as possible to the 1st WAVE.

Two heavy guns were detailed by O.C. heavy guns to go with each Company, ie A & B Coys. These particular

WAR DIARY
or
INTELLIGENCE SUMMARY.
(Erase heading not required.)

Army Form C. 2118.

Place	Date	Hour	Summary of Events and Information	Remarks and references to Appendices
			Lewis guns were to be with the cleaning up parties behind each platoon of the 1st WAVE, the outer ones being immediately on the flank, ie, the right of No 1 platoon and left of No 6 platoon. The whole of No 1 platoon to go with the 1st WAVE into the GREEN LINE. The 2nd WAVE consisted of 1 platoon of C Coy on the Right and 1 platoon of B Coy on the left. Immediately in the rear of these 2 platoons would be the "cleaning up Party" for the 3rd German line, 1 platoon of C Coy on the Right and 1 platoon of B Coy on the left. Two Lewis guns were detailed by O.C., Lewis guns Party, for the 3rd German line "cleaning up" The 3rd WAVE consisted of 1 platoon of C Coy & 1 platoon of A Coy. Two Lewis guns were detailed by O.C. Lewis guns to proceed on the Right & Left flanks of either platoons	

Army Form C. 2118.

WAR DIARY
or
INTELLIGENCE SUMMARY.
(Erase heading not required.)

The 4th WAVE consisted of 1 platoon of C Coy and 1 platoon of D Coy. Two Lewis Guns were detailed by O.C. Lewis Guns to follow on in immediate rear & centre of either platoon. The men in the Intervals were to Kept between each man forming the sections. Platoons Police & Pioneers were to remain with 4 O's under the command of an officer. Platoons commanded for Special Work.

O.C. A Coy. 1 platoon + 1 Lewis Gun to form a Defensive Right Flank.

O.C. B Coy. 1 platoon + 1 Lewis Gun to form a Defensive Left Flank.

These were to deploy in position immediately the objective was taken.

O.C. A Coy. No 15 platoon was detailed to form Working Party under R.E.'s to construct a strong point at a point selected by O.C. A Coy & R.E. officer. K.35.c.1.1. was suggested.

O.C. "A" & "B" Coys were detailed to earmark 4 parties each consisting of 3 bombers + 3 bayonet men to close communication trenches leading from the GREEN LINE and right + left of the Objective, in the event of the Battalions on the RIGHT and LEFT not having reached that point.

Cleaning up parties.

Nos 3 + 4 Platoons were to be the "Cleaning up parties" for the 1st German Line.
Nos 7 + 8 Platoons were to be the "Cleaning up parties" for the 2nd German Line.
Nos 10 + 13 Platoons were to be the "Cleaning up parties" for the 3rd German Line.

Officers in charge of "Cleaning up Parties" were detailed to detail 3 men in each party to remain in the trench to act as relay runners, as soon as they are satisfied that all is clean. The remainder of the many numbers the Officer were to make their way to the objective + join their Companies.

Carrying Parties were to be made up with the runners

WAR DIARY
or
INTELLIGENCE SUMMARY.
(Erase heading not required.)

Army Form C. 2118.

Instructions regarding War Diaries and Intelligence Summaries are contained in F.S. Regs., Part II and the Staff Manual respectively. Title pages will be prepared in manuscript.

Hour, Date, Place	Summary of Events and Information	Remarks and references to Appendices
	Raiding Party.	
	Each Company was detailed to carry the following:-	
	15 Men with Shovels. 5 Men with Picks.	
	10 Men with Sandbags containing 10 bombs	
	5 Men with Sandbags containing 10 Mills	
	Rifle grenades	
	35 flares to be distributed between 1st 2nd & 3rd Waves (not clearing up Parties.)	
	Ammunition. Rations	
	Each man was issued with the following:-	
	100 rounds S.A.A.	
	0 Bombs	
	6 Very Lights	
	6 Sandbags.	
	6 Iron Rations	
	1 Extra days Ration	
	— Cheese Rations	
	— Chocolate Rations	
	Tools for cleaning up Parties.	
	5 Men per Platoon were detailed to carry	

WAR DIARY
or
INTELLIGENCE SUMMARY.
(Erase heading not required.)

Army Form C. 2118.

Hour, Date, Place	Summary of Events and Information	Remarks and references to Appendices
	Shovels & 5 Men to carry Sandbags with 10 bombs. Special. 2 parties of 5 Men each were detailed to help themselves in readiness to carry "Bangalore Torpedoes" These parties were to follow on behind the 2nd WAVE. If the 1st. WAVE was hung up by wire those parties were to be called upon in addition to the small parties told off to bomb the German line in the vicinity of the obstacle, whilst the men with wirecutters - wire breakers try to force their way through. If a gap could be made with wire cutters & wire breakers the torpedo was not to be placed in position as the use of the Torpedo would not only be difficult but would also cause a certain amount of delay from the vicinity of the obstacle have to move away from the vicinity of the obstacle to allow of its being used.	

WAR DIARY
or
INTELLIGENCE SUMMARY.
(Erase heading not required.)

Army Form C. 2118.

Place	Date	Hour	Summary of Events and Information	Remarks and references to Appendices
			Communication
3 Signallers were detailed from each Company by OC Signals to carry wires and shutters and one telephone.
OC Signals was detailed to follow up behind the 4th WAVE with sufficient Signallers to keep up communication with HQ's. As soon as it was possible he was to select spot in the 1m x 3m German lines suitable for Battalion HQ's and AID posts. Telephone lines were to be laid in and moved forward so that he could tap in at any time to addition to this line being laid a roll of wire netting 5 feet wide was to be used – Battalion Runners
The Bombing Platoon was detailed to transfer stores from the old Battalion HQ's to the new HQ's immediately they are selected in the German lines.
Re-organization.
As soon as possible after the objective has been taken Companies were to re-organise and Company formed of the bombers, Very lights & riviers by the men of the Company.	⚐

WAR DIARY
or
INTELLIGENCE SUMMARY.
(Erase heading not required.)

Army Form C. 2118.

Place	Date	Hour	Summary of Events and Information	Remarks and references to Appendices
			One large dump was to be formed with the stores dropped by the 1st KINGS Regt as they passed through the GREEN LINE. These were to be sent up to the YELLOW LINE as soon as it was taken. **Barrages** All ranks were warned that it was most important for WAVES to follow up our barrage as closely as possible. They were also instructed that, in the event of the enemy putting up a barrage, they were to rush it and not to hesitate on the least hesitation would cause a larger number of casualties. They were instructed to keep the old proverb in mind - "he who hesitates is lost" **Objective.** The QUADRILATERAL and H lines of German trenches SOUTH of same. The following report was sent in by the Commanding officer Lieut Col W.H. CARTER, D.S.O, M.C. 1/5 th O.S of Infantry Brigade after the attack, Previous to the attack On the night of the 12th, I sent for the Company Commanders	

WAR DIARY
or
INTELLIGENCE SUMMARY.
(Erase heading not required.)

Army Form C. 2118.

Instructions regarding War Diaries and Intelligence Summaries are contained in F. S. Regs., Part II. and the Staff Manual respectively. Title pages will be prepared in manuscript.

Hour, Date, Place	Summary of Events and Information	Remarks and references to Appendices
	who were in command of the 1st Wave and told them that I thought it was impossible to take the QUADRILATERAL with a frontal attack and gave orders that it should be taken from the flanks. Both the officers disagreed with this and on account of the front they raised (especially (1)" That it was almost impossible to get the men into line again and that the questions would be lost (2) That once the fire was divided they would come under enfilade fire from the QUADRILATERAL) I decided to let my orders for the attack stand as before, although I was still in doubt as to whether I had done right. This consultation took place in the presence of the Adjutant, who heard everything that was said	day of the attack

(73989) W4141—463. 400,000. 9/14. H.&J.Ltd. Forms/C. 2118/10.

Army Form C. 2118.

WAR DIARY
or
INTELLIGENCE SUMMARY.
(Erase heading not required.)

Place	Date	Hour	Summary of Events and Information	Remarks and references to Appendices
	13/11/16		Day of the attack	

At 2.30 am bands moved/leaved to cut of hot covers.
At 3.0 am the WAVES moved into positions in open country
at 4.15 am all WAVES and cleaning up parties were in
position. Orders were given that they should lie in position
by 4 am but on account of the waves not laying in touch
with the Battalion on my LEFT, everyone had to be moved.
The men lay quiet till the barrage commenced at
5.45 am. Then the whole of the waves moved forward followed
by the 1st KINGS.
Immediately the barrage lifted, they assaulted the
FIRST LINE. After that I lost touch with them and got no
information back.
At 8 am I sent 2nd Lieut LOWINGS + 2 efficient
SHERMAN with two men each to gather what information
they could. They reported that the RIGHT could not be seen
but that on the LEFT the men were about the GERMAN
FRONT LINE WIRE, and that a party of about 50 were held
up behind a small bank, 100 yards in front of same, under
very heavy Machine Gun + Rifle fire, and

Army Form C. 2118.

WAR DIARY
or
INTELLIGENCE SUMMARY.
(Erase heading not required.)

Place	Date	Hour	Summary of Events and Information	Remarks and references to Appendices
		✕	It was impossible for them to advance. I gave orders for this party to consolidate the position they held and to await instructions. Reference my X's of the 13th. A Second Officer's patrol was sent out and brought back the same report as the first I had previously given orders that if it were possible the Machine Guns in the QUADRILATERAL should be rushed, but on the Officer's report on the conditions of the ground I decided that it was an impossibility. I came to this decision at about 8.45 am. Up to this time I had received no information from my front whatever. At 3 pm 2nd Lieut PATERSON (Signalling Officer) who had gone to find accommodation for the new H.Q's) returned from the GREEN LINE (the objective), and reported as follows :- the and and/or front HONE of this Regiment with a party of ESSEX and KINGS numbering about 50, had gone through to the GREEN LINE with the OXFORD and BUCKS and 20 ROYAL FUSILIERS. They found no british troops on their left and on marching	✗

WAR DIARY or INTELLIGENCE SUMMARY.

Army Form C. 2118.

Place	Date	Hour	Summary of Events and Information	Remarks and references to Appendices

reconnaissance. They found a party of GERMANS and they immediately made a barricade and strong point with 3 Lewis Guns. 2/Lieut PATERSON was relieved by the Brigadier General Commanding 64 Infantry Brigade at 4.30 am. I was informed that the 22nd ROYAL FUSILIERS were coming up to form a defensive flank facing NORTH, South of the QUADRILATERAL and asking me to give them every assistance. I decided to run out a trench from BUSTER to the small sap in GERMAN FRONT LINE, 300 yards SOUTH of the QUADRILATERAL. This was reconnoitred. During the reconnaissance it was found that CAT TUNNEL ended the new work with great advantage, and I asked permission from the Brigade to allow me to use it. Consent was given. (Later the same night the R.E. officer in charge informed me that this tunnel could not be used by us without express instructions from the Division.) About 6 am I was informed that the construction of the trench was handed over to O.C. 22nd ROYAL

WAR DIARY
or
INTELLIGENCE SUMMARY.
(Erase heading not required.)

Army Form C. 2118.

Hour, Date, Place	Summary of Events and Information	Remarks and references to Appendices
14/11/1	FUSILIERS who decided to nullify my proposed scheme and cut it off from EGG STREET to the QUADRILATERAL. This was stated by the R.E. and 10th D.C.L.I. and a certain amount of progress was made. (The next night the R.E. officer who came up to continue the work came and went and said that during the state of the ground to continue the trenches in that direction was useless and I decided that it should be turned half right to form up with the two craters about S. of the QUADRILATERAL. This was done and the trenches completed. At 9am I received intimation that O.C. 1st KINGS took over command of the RIGHT SUB-SECTION. At 9.30am on the 14th inst I sent Lieut PATERSON back to the GREEN LINE to report on dispositions re the return	⧸

Army Form C. 2118.

WAR DIARY
or
INTELLIGENCE SUMMARY.
(Erase heading not required.)

Instructions regarding War Diaries and Intelligence Summaries are contained in F.S. Regs., Part II. and the Staff Manual respectively. Title pages will be prepared in manuscript.

Hour, Date, Place	Summary of Events and Information	Remarks and references to Appendices
	The following information:- 2/Lt HONE was still holding on the GREEN LINE with the party of ESSEX and KINGS at the junction of GREEN and LAGER. the (2/Lt PATERSON) told 2/Lt HONE to place himself under the orders of the 2nd ROYAL FUSILIERS. During the morning of the 18th inst, I went to Brigade HQ. and was informed that two battalions of the 99th Brigade were attacking the QUADRILATERAL from the SOUTHERN flank with the assistance of two tanks and that I was to watch events and take advantage of any movement made by the enemy. This was to be done in conjunction with the 2nd ROYAL FUSILIERS. I interviewed Colonel BARKER regarding his and my own dispositions and told off two parties, one of 30 men under 2/Lt SHERMAN which included 4 bombers another under 2/Lt PATERSON of 25 men and one	A

(73989) W.4141—463. 400,000. 9/14. H.&J.Ltd. Forms/C. 2118/10.

WAR DIARY
or
INTELLIGENCE SUMMARY.

(Erase heading not required.)

Army Form C. 2118.

Hour, Date, Place	Summary of Events and Information	Remarks and references to Appendices
15/11/16	platoon of the KINGS Regt under Capt JAMESON. These parties were to stand in readiness for eventualities. At 5.30am I went and took up a position in VALLADE to watch and report on progress of the TANKS. At 5:45 am I sent out Capt JAMESON and 3 men to give directions to the TANK Commander. At 6 am they started off and by 6:30am they were both out of action. I sent guides for the personnel of the Tanks and Commanders reported that nothing could be done. I went with one Commander to the Brigade. At about 8 am I ordered Capt JAMESON & 1/Lieut SHERMAN to occupy the new cut trench and get in touch with the ROYAL FUSILIERS & instructed 1/Lieut SHERMAN to make a barricade + bombing post at the junction of CAT TUNNEL and the new cut trench at	#

Army Form C. 2118.

WAR DIARY
or
INTELLIGENCE SUMMARY.
(Erase heading not required.)

Instructions regarding War Diaries and Intelligence Summaries are contained in F.S. Regs., Part II. and the Staff Manual respectively. Title pages will be prepared in manuscript.

Hour, Date, Place	Summary of Events and Information	Remarks and references to Appendices
15/11/16	At 10.30am I asked for artillery barrage to be brought on the 2nd + 3rd GERMAN LINES at a point 100 yards NORTH of the QUADRILATERAL and later asked for the barrage to move on. The ESSEX, KINGS + ROYAL FUSILIERS were in the CHORD. At 11am I sent 2/Lt PATERSON to find Capt JAMESON and report on the progress made, and he reported that Capt JAMESON had worked his way into the QUADRILATERAL in conjunction with the ROYAL FUSILIERS under a Major ADAMS and was working NORTHWARDS successfully. I then sent my last party under 2/Lieut PATERSON to report to Major ADAMS for disposal. I then ordered my party who were holding the new trench to go forward and reinforce Capt JAMESON + again conferred with Col BARKER regarding this and my own disposition. At 3pm I sent out to Major ADAMS to get the disposition of the whole force in	

(73989) W4141—463. 400,000. 9/14. H.&J.Ltd. Forms/C. 2118/10.

WAR DIARY
or
INTELLIGENCE SUMMARY.
(Erase heading not required.)

Army Form C. 2118.

Hour, Date, Place	Summary of Events and Information	Remarks and references to Appendices
16/11/16	QUADRILATERAL. A sketch showing the dispositions was sent to Brigade HQrs. at 3.15 p.m. & was informed that the Battalions would be relieved. During the afternoon of the 15th inst an Officer of the 24th ROYAL FUSILIERS came with a party of 50 men & I sent him to report to Major ADAMS as reinforcements. At 6.10 p.m. I was ordered to arrange relief with Colonel BARKER & I went to confer with him. The remainder of the Battalion was relieved by a Company of the 1st Bn DORSET Regt in the RIGHT SUBSECTION at 8.30 am on the morning of the 16th inst & I handed over with dispositions as follows:- One platoon in MINOR, one platoon in WOLF, one platoon in TOP of EGG, + one platoon in EGG with a post of two Lewis Guns at junction of MINOR and FRONT LINE, a post of two Lewis Guns at junction of BORDEN + FRONT	

WAR DIARY
or
INTELLIGENCE SUMMARY.

(Erase heading not required.)

Army Form C. 2118.

Hour, Date, Place	Summary of Events and Information	Remarks and references to Appendices
16/11/16	LINE and post + Lewis Gun at junction of EGG and FRONT LINE. Report by 2/Lt A.C. HONE. On the morning of the 16th inst I was in charge of 1 platoon of "C" Coy forming the right half of the 1st WAVE. At 5:51am we commenced to move forward to the German line. The lines moved forward with very little opposition with the exception of a few of the enemy who bombed us from the left. We pushed forward over the 2nd + 3rd German lines + arrived at the GREEN LINE a few minutes after our own artillery barrage had lifted. I found myself with two Lewis Gun teams + 40 men of the ESSEX Regt + 2/Lt PATERSON (Signalling officer) also 1 Lewis Gun team + a few men of the 1st KINGS Regt with an officer of the 3rd SOUTH STAFFS Regt.	A

War Diary

On looking round my position I found that the left flanks was exposed owing to the remainder of the waves not reaching the objective & immediately placed & being timed on this flank & commenced consolidating the position. A small party of the enemy attempted to bomb us but were dispersed by having timed fire.

I next visited the THIRD LINE & found that the junction of LAGER ALLEY was a weak point so I placed my Lewis Guns & a post at this point.

I placed myself under the 24th ROYAL FUSILIERS. Later I received instructions to place myself under Major ADAMS of the 22nd ROYAL FUSILIERS.

Report forwarded to Brigade HQ's by the Commanding Officer:-

(1) German bombing post S. of QUADRILATERAL & Machine Gun in S.E. corner of QUADRILATERAL.

On the morning of the 15th inst. the position was as follows:- A new communication trench from our lines had been dug from EGG STREET to a point S. of the S.E corner of the QUADRILATERAL. Between this point & the S.E. corner of the QUADRILATERAL the Germans had established a bombing post in their front line. The 22nd ROYAL FUSILIERS had formed a post about 30 yds

War Diary.

South of its junction with the communication trench. The 13th ESSEX established a post in the communications about 25 yards from its junction with the old German line. (The attached rough sketch marks the junction clearer.) Later on the same morning, the Germans, perhaps thinking themselves threatened by the TANKS, withdrew northwards and apparently took with them the Machine Guns previously at S.E. Corner of QUADRILATERAL. We then advanced into the QUADRILATERAL.

(d) <u>Prisoners</u>

The 13th HONE took 70 or 80 prisoners who were handed over to the 8th ROYAL FUSILIERS and sent down to WHITE CITY. One wounded prisoner was found in a dug-out in the QUADRILATERAL.

<u>Report sent to O.C. 1st KINGS Regt on 18/11/16</u>

On 15th November I was in command of operations against the QUADRILATERAL and a portion of the enemy line South of it. At this time only the Southern portion of the QUADRILATERAL was held by our troops. Capt JAMESON with 50 men of the 1st Kings Regt was sent to reinforce the troops under my command and I instructed him to proceed by the newest communication trench that had been dug from our lines

War Diary

to the QUADRILATERAL, to get into touch with the 2nd ROYAL FUSILIERS, to bomb up the trenches still held by the enemy and establish a strong point in the Northern part of the QUADRILATERAL. This was a task of considerable difficulty which he successfully accomplished later, the position of the line was very heavily shelled by the enemy. Capt JAMESON therefore, with great skill drew his men slightly South, established bombing & strong points about the centre of the QUADRILATERAL in spite of the fact that the enemy was prevented from obtaining a foothold in any part of the QUADRILATERAL. This position he held in spite of very heavy shelling and machine gun fire until relieved next morning.

During the present week, the ground was again in a very bad condition owing to the constant rain. Reference to the attack. The trenches in places were much deeper in mud, and in all trenches the thick mud was at least knee deep. Our "No Mans Land" progress was greatly hampered owing to the shell holes & halted mine. Beyond the German first line was a perfect quagmire due to the heavy shelling from our guns.

War Diary

16/11/16 3am	On the day of the attack (Nov 13th) there was a thick mist + this continued in modification until the afternoon of the 15th inst. On the morning of the 11th inst a thick frost prevailed. On the morning of the 11th inst when the Battalion took over the sector preparatory to the attack until relieved on the 16th inst. The spirit of the officers + Men was excellent on making the attack on the 13th inst. everybody was quite cheerful + confident.
	The Battalion was relieved by the 1st DORSET Regt and took over billets at MAILLY-MAILLET.
Vauchelles-les-Authie 9.30am 19/11/16	The Battalion proceeded to VAUCHELLES-LES-AUTHIE by Motor lorries + new billets at
11am	
Doullens 10.0am 21/11/16	The Battalion moved to DOULLENS, a distance of about 10 Miles arriving about 3pm.
	The Battalion moved to new billets at BERNAVILLE, a distance of about 10 miles, arriving about 3pm.
Bernaville 10.40am 22/11/16	The Battalion moved to new billets at COULONVILLERS, a distance of about 10 miles, arriving about 3.40pm.

War Diary

Coulonvilliers 9am 24/11/16	The Battalion moved to new billets at MARCHEVILLE, a distance of about 10 miles arriving about 2 pm.
Marcheville 10am 25/11/16	The Battalion moved to new billets at LE TITRE, a distance of about 4 miles arriving about 11.30 am. Draft of 147 Other Ranks arrived.
Le Titre 7.50am 27/11/16	The Battalion moved to new billets at GAPENNES, a distance of about 5 miles arriving about 1pm. Draft of 51 Other Ranks arrived.
Gapennes 28/11/16 29/11/16 30/11/16	Company training re. Draft of 447 Other ranks arrived.

Casualties on Battle of the Ancre.

Killed.   Died of Wounds.   Missing

Lt. (T. Capt) E.M CHARRINGTON
Captains C. G. CARSON   do
    "   J M ROUND   do
    "   W. W. BUSBY   do
    "   H. B. WILCOCK.   do
Lieut   G. M. GEMMELL   do
    "   C. N MARSHALL   do
    "   B. W. FINN   do
    "   J G FULKES.   do
    "   F. G. ENGLISH   do

War Diary

Wounded

2/Lieut G. SIMPSON
2/Lieut C. L. B LYNE
" D J REW

Other Ranks

Killed   6
Died of Wounds   6
Wounded   133
Missing   165

[signature]
2/Lieut - a/Adjt
13th Essex Regt

6th Brigade.

2nd Division.

13th BATTALION

THE ESSEX REGIMENT

DECEMBER 1916.

CONFIDENTIAL

WAR DIARY
of
13th (S) Battn. The Essex Regt

December 1st to 31st, 1916.

Army Form C. 2118.

WAR DIARY
or
INTELLIGENCE SUMMARY.

(Erase heading not required.)

13th Essex Regt

Place	Date	Hour	Summary of Events and Information	Remarks and references to Appendices
GAPENNES	1/4/16	-	Battalion Training:- Physical training, Arms drill, Platoon drill, Skirmishing & extensions, Bayonet exercises, Musketry. Erecting wire entanglements, cutting gaps, features by Company Commanders + care of arms. N.C.O's under the R.S.M for Commanding drill. 2/Lieut FOUNTAIN P.G. appointed to the Command of A Coy and granted permission to wear the badges of the rank of Captain. 2/Lieut PATERSON W.B appointed Acting Adjutant	A
Do	2/4/16	-	Battalion Training as carried out on the 1st. Major A.G HAYWARD proceeded on leave to England. Captain J.G.H. KENNEFICK took over the duties of Acting 2/C in Command	A
Do	3/4/16	-	Battalion at Rest (Sunday) Boxing Tournament + Boxing Club formed.	A
Do	4/4/16	-	Battalion Training as carried out on the 1st. A draft of 33 "O.Rcs" Ranks joined.	A
Do	5/4/16	-	Battalion Training. Range practice.	A

Army Form C.2118.

WAR DIARY
or
INTELLIGENCE SUMMARY.
(Erase heading not required.)

Place	Date	Hour	Summary of Events and Information	Remarks and references to Appendices

CAPENNES	5/2/16	cont	Draft of 8 Officers + 19 Other Ranks joined. 2/Lieut J.A. BARRETT. 2/Lieut STEELE. J.Y
			   " C.W RITSON " A.R. WELLS.
			   " C. STOKES. " S.F. VOWLES
			   " A.R. SACRÉ " E.G. MUNDAY
				A

"	6/2/16		Battalion Training :- Range Practice Draft of 148 "Other Ranks" joined.	A
"	7/2/16		Battalion Training :- Range Practice. Trench Warfare + preliminary night march.	A
"	8/2/16		General Recreations during the afternoon Battalion Training :- Arms + Company drill.	A
"	9/2/16		Battalion paraded for Ceremonial Parade on the occasion of presentation of awards by the General Officer Commanding 2nd Division, Major General W.G. WALKER V.C., C.B.	A
"	10/2/16		Battalion Sports	A

WAR DIARY
or
INTELLIGENCE SUMMARY.

(Erase heading not required.)

Army Form C. 2118.

Place	Date	Hour	Summary of Events and Information	Remarks and references to Appendices
GAPENNES	11/5/16		Battalion Training - Open Warfare. 3 Companies in attack and one fighting a Rearguard action. Draft of 56 Other Ranks joined.	A
do	12/5/16	5pm	(Evening) Battalion engaged in cleaning Clothing, Equipment re Battalion disciplinary night march.	A
do		9am	Major A.G. HAYWARD rejoined from leave & resumed duties as 2nd in Command of the Battalion. Draft of 20 Other Ranks joined.	A
do	13/5/16	9:30am	Battalion Training - Practising bombing up trenches.	A
		2pm	Battalion Sport	
do	14/5/16	9am	Battalion Training - Physical training & bayonet fighting. Boxing & Running Competitions.	A
		5:30pm	Inter Coy sport held in the ARGENVILLERS - GAPENNES Rd. Major General W.G. WALKER, VC, CB was present	
do	15/5/16	9am	Battalion Training. Tactical Scheme.	A

Army Form C. 2118.

WAR DIARY
or
INTELLIGENCE SUMMARY.
(Erase heading not required.)

Instructions regarding War Diaries and Intelligence Summaries are contained in F. S. Regs. Part II. and the Staff Manual respectively. Title pages will be prepared in manuscript.

Place	Date	Hour	Summary of Events and Information	Remarks and references to Appendices
Lafermes	13/12/16	9.30am	Training under Company Officers. Lieut Colonel W H CARTER, DSO, MC, proceeded on leave to England. Major A G HAYWARD, MC, assumed the Command of the Battalion. Capt E G H KENNEFICK exchanged the duties of Second in Command with Wing Service. One officer - 50 Wing of Seconds present.	
"	14/12/16	10 am		
"	18/12/16	9 am	Battalion Training. Sword Mounting. Duties of Sentries, exchange of Swords, Saluting with & without arms. 2nd Lieut D H MASON joined & posted to "B" Coy.	
"	19/12/16	9.30am	Battalion Training. Physical training. Bayonet fighting, Smoke helmet drill. Arms drill Platoon drill Company drill. 2/Lieut J.J.G. CLARKE & 2/Lieut H.E. MANN joined the Battalion from the Oxford & Bucks Regiment & posted to "A" & "B" Coys respectively. Battalion Training as on 19th inst.	
"	20/12/16	9.30am	do do	
"	21/12/16	9.30am	do do	
"	22/12/16	9.15am	Battalion Training. Field of operations. Scouts, Bombers & Wiring Squads under Coy arrangements.	

WAR DIARY
or
INTELLIGENCE SUMMARY.
(Erase heading not required.)

Army Form C. 2118.

Place	Date	Hour	Summary of Events and Information	Remarks and references to Appendices
Sittingbourne	22/12/16	9.15am	Battalion Training. Physical Training + Bayonet fighting. Smoke helmet drill, arms - platoon & company drill. Company will. 2/Lieut J.P. ROBINSON proceeded on leave to England. 2/Lt H.E. MANN assumed the command of "B" Coy. 2/Lieut - Adjt W.B. PATERSON proceeded on leave to England. 2/Lieut E.C. MUSSON assumed Adjutancy.	
	24/12/16	11am	Divine Service. 4 officers + 100 men per Coy paraded. Capt P.G. FOUNTAIN returned from leave and took over the duties of 2nd in Command + Adjutant.	
	25/12/16		Christmas Day. The Men of all B.O.R.s + each Coy were provided with a Christmas dinner which they all enjoyed. All officers of the Battalion had dinner together.	
	26/12/16	9.30am	Route March	
	27/12/16	9.30am	Battalion Training. Scheme of attack on Trenches re. Physical Training, Bayonet fighting, Smoke helmet drill, arms - platoon & company drill &c.	
	28/12/16	9.30am		

Army Form C. 2118.

WAR DIARY
or
INTELLIGENCE SUMMARY.
(Erase heading not required.)

Instructions regarding War Diaries and Intelligence Summaries are contained in F. S. Regs., Part II. and the Staff Manual respectively. Title pages will be prepared in manuscript.

Place	Date	Hour	Summary of Events and Information	Remarks and references to Appendices
Lahoussoye	29/12/16	9.30am	Battalion training. Relief of trenches - trench routine - leave granted to various ranks, sports, winning teams v runner respective officers.	
			The undermentioned awarded the "Military Medal" for bravery in the field during the "Battle of the Ancre"	
			No 18169 Sgt PIERCY H No 14348 Sgt TOZER T	PRO No 331
			" 18025 L/Cpl COX G " 31761 A/Cpl WRIGHT G V	
			" 21519 L/Cpl SPICER A F	
			" 18741 Cpl E H RAYMENT (attached to L.T. Trench Mortar Battery) awarded the "Military Medal".	PRO No 385
			Jigging Competition - Tactical Exercise for officers - NCOs enter the Commanding officers. Reforming billets re-marking huts. Trees.	
	30/12/16	9.30am		
	31/12/16		Divine Service. 1 Officer + 100 Men for Cy funeral. Lieut Col W.H. CARTER, D.S.O., M.C. rejoined from leave + assumed the Command of the Battalion.	

2353 Wt. W2514/1454 700,000 5/15 D. D. & L. A.D.S.S./Forms/C. 2118.

Army Form C. 2118.

WAR DIARY
or
INTELLIGENCE SUMMARY.
(Erase heading not required.)

Instructions regarding War Diaries and Intelligence Summaries are contained in F. S. Regs., Part II. and the Staff Manual respectively. Title pages will be prepared in manuscript.

Place	Date	Hour	Summary of Events and Information	Remarks and references to Appendices
Salonica	3/1/1916		Major A. G. HAYWARD assumed 2nd in Command of the Battalion.	

C. B. Hampton Capt. Adjt.
13th Essex Regt.

2nd Division

6th Infantry Bde,

13th Essex Regt.

January To June,

1917

6th Brigade.

2nd Division.

13th BATTALION

THE ESSEX REGIMENT

JANUARY 1917.

Army Form C. 2118.

WAR DIARY
or
INTELLIGENCE SUMMARY.
(Erase heading not required.)

Vol /4

CONFIDENTIAL

WAR DIARY

of

13th (S) Battn. The Essex Regt

January 1st to January 31st 1917.

WAR DIARY
or
INTELLIGENCE SUMMARY.
(Erase heading not required.)

Army Form C. 2118.

Place	Date	Hour	Summary of Events and Information	Remarks and references to Appendices
Béthune	1/1/17	9 am	Battalion formed up on Parade Ground in strong up parade for the purpose of re-arranging Platoons. One Section of each Platoon was formed into a Bombing Section.	
Do	2/1/17	9 am	Battalion Training. Practice Trench attack 2/Lieut E.H SHERMAN took over the duties of Acting Adjutant	
Do	3/1/17	9 am	Battalion Training. Physical training. Bayonet fighting. Smoke helmet drill. Company drill re Capt S E COLLIER awarded the Military Cross for distinguished Service in the Field. (Chapman Gazette Supplement dated 1/1/17)	
Do	4/1/17	8.40 am	Battalion Training. Attacking trenches. Extended order, Platoon & Section drill re	
Do	5/1/17	9.45 am	Brigade Training. Field Operations. Attacking trenches protected by Artillery barrage. Cleaning trenches + dug-outs. Consolidating positions. Lieut J D ROBINSON returned from leave + assumed command of "B" Coy.	

WAR DIARY
or
INTELLIGENCE SUMMARY.

Army Form C. 2118.

(Erase heading not required.)

Place	Date	Hour	Summary of Events and Information	Remarks and references to Appendices
Lapeume	6/1/19	9 am	Battalion Training. Physical training, Sword Mounting, & duties of sentries & Bayonet fighting, saluting with and without arms. Extract from Supplement to the London Gazette 21/1/19 Mentioned in Dispatches for distinguished service and devotion to duty. Lieut Col. PAPILLON P.R. Wharton CARTER W.H (now Lieut Col) No 14318 Sergt WINDSOR L. " 14516 Sergt ALEXANDER J. The following Officers were awarded the "Meritorious" for having in the field. 2/Lieut W.B. PATERSON 2/Lieut A.C. HONE. Sunday. Voluntary divine Services	
Do	7/1/19			

WAR DIARY
or
INTELLIGENCE SUMMARY.
(Erase heading not required.)

Army Form C. 2118.

Place	Date	Hour	Summary of Events and Information	Remarks and references to Appendices
Lapurnes	4/1/14		The following were unofficially reported prisoners of war about C E N Marshall. No 18114 A/CSM Todd S.W. No 14114 Sgt Foreman L. No 43118 Pte Rush & No 43094 Pte Pollard E. No 43105 " Trundell W. Cooper J. No 43103 Pte Clarke T.E.	
To	8/1/19	9 am	Battalion Training. Physical training, bayonet fighting, smoke helmet drill. Platoon drill. Company drill. No 18010 C.Q.M. Sgt CAULFIELD. RCF proceeded to England as candidate for commission. T/Capt E.C. LOWINGS proceeded to England on Special leave 2/Lt A.R. SACRE took over the command of 'D' Coy 2/Lt W B PATERSON MC resumed the duties of A/Adjutant 2/Lt R.C.H. MAY tories for duty & posted to 'C' Coy.	
To	9/1/19	11.15am	Battalion moved to new billets at BOISBERGUES - distance of 15 miles arriving at 6.1pm after moves at 1pm for dinner.	

Army Form C. 2118.

WAR DIARY
or
INTELLIGENCE SUMMARY.
(Erase heading not required.)

Instructions regarding War Diaries and Intelligence Summaries are contained in F. S. Regs., Part II. and the Staff Manual respectively. Title pages will be prepared in manuscript.

Place	Date	Hour	Summary of Events and Information	Remarks and references to Appendices
Bauberque	10/1/17	10.30am	Lectures by the Commanding Officer & Company Commanders on March discipline.	
Do	11/1/17	1.30am	Battalion marched to new billets at RAINCHEVAL, a distance of 15 miles, arriving about 2pm.	
Raincheval	12/1/17	9.35am	Battalion moved into new billets at BOUZINCOURT, a distance of 15 miles, arriving at 4pm. Halt made for dinner en route at 12 noon. (Battalion in Brigade Reserve)	
Bouzincourt	13/1/17		Cleaning billets, Roads &c.	
Do	14/1/17		Do	
Do	15/1/17		Working parties found by Battalion.	
Do	16/1/17		Working parties found. Remainder of Battalion in bombing drill & Company in attack.	
Do	17/1/17		Do	
Do	18/1/17		Do Lectures under Company arrangements	
Do	19/1/17		Do	
Do	20/1/17	8	Battalion moved to Huts (WOLFE HUTS) OVILLERS in Brigade Support. 450 men & all officers found for Working Parties	

WAR DIARY
or
INTELLIGENCE SUMMARY.
(Erase heading not required.)

Army Form C. 2118.

Place	Date	Hour	Summary of Events and Information	Remarks and references to Appendices
Mailly Maillet	21/1/17		Working parties found.	
OVILLERS	22/1/17	6.45am	Battalion start to entrain huts for half an hour	
"	23/1/17	9.0am	Physical training. Box Respirator drill. Arm drill in	
"	24/1/17	4pm	Battalion relieved the 1st Kings Regt in the Right Sub-sector, COURCELETTE Sector.	
			Disposition:-	
			"A" Coy } Posts on RIGHT front	
			"B" Coy } Posts on LEFT front	
			H.Q.s Aug. out. WEST MIRAUMONT Road	
			Supporting Platoon. DYKE Road COURCELETTE dug-outs	
			"C" Coy } RIGHT SUPPORT	
			"D" Coy } LEFT SUPPORT	
Right Subsector	25/1/17		Improved Shelters, Headquarters + Strengthened posts, new wire put out.	
			Patrolling carried out	
	26/1/17		"A" & "B" Coys relieved in front line by "C" + "D" Coys respectively. "A" Coy RIGHT Support, "B" Coy LEFT Support	

Army Form C. 2118.

WAR DIARY
INTELLIGENCE SUMMARY.
(Erase heading not required.)

Instructions regarding War Diaries and Intelligence Summaries are contained in F. S. Regs., Part II. and the Staff Manual respectively. Title pages will be prepared in manuscript.

Place	Date	Hour	Summary of Events and Information	Remarks and references to Appendices
Right Subsctr	29/1/17		Improving posts, wiring &c &c.	
	30/1/17	6pm	Battalion relieved by the 1st BERKS Regt and took over billets at BOUZINCOURT. (Brigade Reserve)	
Bouzincourt	30/1/17	9am	Company training. Physical training, Bayonet fighting, Boxing &c.	
		4pm	All officers under the Lewis Gun officer in Lewis Gun instruction	
		6pm	all officers under the Commanding Officer marching on Compass bearings by night.	
Ho	31/1/17	9.30am	Battalion training on 30th inst. Lewis Gunners under their own officers - firing on Range. Bombers under bombing officer.	

M.A. Grover
Lieut m/Adjt
1st (S) Bn. Essex Regt.

6th Brigade.

2nd Division.

13th BATTALION THE ESSEX REGIMENT

FEBRUARY 1917.

Army Form C. 2118.

WAR DIARY
or
INTELLIGENCE SUMMARY.
(Erase heading not required.)

Vol/5

CONFIDENTIAL

WAR DIARY

OF

13th (S) Battn. THE ESSEX REGT.

FEBRUARY 1st to 28th 1917.

Army Form C. 2118.

WAR DIARY or INTELLIGENCE SUMMARY.

(Erase heading not required.)

Instructions regarding War Diaries and Intelligence Summaries are contained in F. S. Regs., Part II. and the Staff Manual respectively. Title pages will be prepared in manuscript.

Place	Date	Hour	Summary of Events and Information	Remarks and references to Appendices
BOUZINCOURT	1.2.17		Battalion in Reserve Brigade. Commanding Officers Ceremonial Parade 9.30 am to 12 noon. Battalion Parade Ground. Lewis Gunners paraded at 9.30 am. Batt. H/qo for instruction under Lewis Gun Officers. Lieut C.W DUNSCOMBE took over command of A Coy from today (2/Lieut J.J.G CLARKE relinquished same on 31.1.17)	
Do	2.2.17		Battalion bathing at Batho. SENLIS. Lieut AIRWELLS appointed Battalion. Telegrams and Sniping Officers from 2.2.17. Officers Shooting Competition at 2 pm.	
Do	3.2.17		Battalion paraded at 9.30 am for drill under the Commanding Officer. Ceremonial Parade. Lewis Gunners, Bombers, Snipers, Signallers paraded under their respective instructors. Capt. J.G.H. KENNEFICK (at "C" Coy) admitted to Hospital sick. 3.2.17. 2/Lieut J.J.G CLARKE took over command of "C" Coy. Working Party of 60 O.R. supplied.	
Do	4.2.17		Sunday. All Officers, 100 men & proportionate number of NCOs paraded for divine service in Drocourt Cinema at 11 am. Lewis Gunners paraded under Lewis Gun Officers. 85 O.R. supplied for working Party.	

WAR DIARY or INTELLIGENCE SUMMARY

Army Form C. 2118.

Place	Date	Hour	Summary of Events and Information	Remarks and references to Appendices
BOUZINCOURT	5.2.17		Battalion moved into new billets at OVILLERS HUTS, a distance of about three miles, arriving there about 11 a.m.	
OVILLERS HUTS	6.2.17		Rifle Kit & Feet inspections. Supplied parties of 150 OR for work. Special attention paid to men's feet which were inspected by the Medical Officer. 275 OR were supplied as working parties. Battalion in Support Brigade. Lieut Col. W.H. CARTER DSO., MC. proceeded to 5th Army Infantry School to attend a Commanding Officers Conference. Major A.G. HAYWARD MC. assumed command of the Battalion during the absence of Lieut Col. W.H. CARTER, DSO., MC.	
Do.	7.2.17		Rifle Inspection by Company Commanders. Feet Inspection by the Medical Officer. Capt. P.G. FOUNTAIN struck off strength from 1.2.17. having been invalided to England sick. 425 OR supplied for Working Parties.	
Do.	8.2.17		Companies paraded under Company Commanders at 9.30 am for Physical Training Bayonet fighting, Rifle Exercises, section drill, Saluting. Lewis Gun Class paraded at 9.30 am under Lewis Gun Officer. Snipers paraded at 9.30 am. Stores to the value of £53.3.6 were solved by the Battalion for the	

Army Form C. 2118.

WAR DIARY
or
INTELLIGENCE SUMMARY.
(Erase heading not required.)

Instructions regarding War Diaries and Intelligence Summaries are contained in F. S. Regs., Part II. and the Staff Manual respectively. Title pages will be prepared in manuscript.

Place	Date	Hour	Summary of Events and Information	Remarks and references to Appendices
OVILLER'S HUTS	8.2.17		Month ending Jany. 31st 1917.	
Do.	9.2.17		Companies paraded under Company Commanders for training as yesterday. All Specialists paraded at 9.30 a.m. that respective instructors. 425 O.R. were supplied for Working Parties. Lieut Col W.H. CARTER D.S.O., M.C. returned from Conference at Fifth Army Infantry School & resumed Command of the Battalion. Major A.G. HAYWARD, M.C. resumed the duties of 2/I.C. in Command. 595 O.R. supplied for Working Parties.	
Do.	10.2.17		Companies paraded under Company Commanders for training as yesterday. All Specialists paraded at 9.30 a.m. under their respective instructors. Draft of 2 Officers and 20 Other Ranks joined. Posted to A Coy Lieut. A.H. CREASY to A Coy Lieut. H.B. BABONEAU to D Coy. Lieut. C.C. COLE returned from Hospital. 465 O.R. were supplied as Working Parties. 395 O.R. supplied for Working Parties.	
Do.	11.2.17		Sunday. Voluntary Church Service held.	
Do.	12.2.17		Companies paraded at 9.30 a.m. for Rifle Inspection, Equipment Inspection & Foot Inspection by Section Commanders. Snipers & Scouts paraded at 9.30 a.m. Still were carried out by Working Parties. 546 O.R. were supplied to Working Parties.	

WAR DIARY or INTELLIGENCE SUMMARY

Army Form C. 2118.

Place	Date	Hour	Summary of Events and Information	Remarks and references to Appendices
6 VILLERS HUTS	13.2.17		All men except those on necessary duties, paraded at 9.30 am for parades in Grand mounting. 2/Lieut C.W. DUNSCOMBE granted permission to wear the badge of the rank of Captain, whilst in Command of a Company (A Coy). 2 O.R. wounded whilst on Working Party (1 at duty). 390 O.R. supplied for Working Parties. The Commanding Officer brought to the notice of the Battalion the fact that "A" Coy subscribed £51.3.0 to the War Loan.	
Do.	14.2.17		An Inspection at 9.30 am. was made of the Fighting Order of the Battalion by the Company Commanders. The Major General Commanding 2nd Division sent a letter to the Commanding Officer complimenting 2/Lieut RITSON C.W. & the working party under him on their work at Keeness. Working parties up of 286 O.R. supplied. 2/Lieut. E.H. SHERMAN appointed Assistant Adjutant & also Battalion musketry Officer.	
Do.	15.2.17		"A" Coy paraded at 9.30 am for musketry under musketry officer. "B" Coy paraded at 10 am for Commanding Officers Inspection. "C" Coy & "D" Coy at 9.30 am for arms drill under Section Commanders. 302 O.R. were supplied for Working Parties.	

WAR DIARY or INTELLIGENCE SUMMARY.

Army Form C. 2118.

(Erase heading not required.)

Place	Date	Hour	Summary of Events and Information	Remarks and references to Appendices
OVILLERS HUTS No.2 ?) WOLFE HUTS			The Battalion moved into new billets at WOLFE HUTS arriving about 12 midnight. Battalion in support of remainder of 6th Brigade. 2nd Lieut. W. LAVINGTON and 2nd Lieut. H.L. BALL joined and were posted to "B" Coy. 157 OR as Working Parties. Battalion "Stood to" at 5.45 am in consequence of active operations by the 6th Brigade in the COURCELETTE Sector. Statements of camps were cleaned up by the Battalion. Stood to from 2pm onwards in readiness to proceed into the line. Commanding Officer proceeded to Bde Hqrs in the line to confer with B.G.C. with a view to making an attack on our front. 2nd Lieut J.D. STEELE admitted to Hospital. Ration party of 50 or supplies.	
Do	17.2.17			
Do	18.2.17		Sunday. Battalion carried out Foot Drill. Carried on with cleaning up camps & huts ents. Battalion relieved the 99th Brigade in the Left front sector COURCELETTE Sector. Disposition RIGHT DEFENSIVE FLANK B Coy RIGHT FRONT A Coy LEFT FRONT D Coy SUPPORT C Coy. W. MIRAUMONT DUGOUTS. Bn. Headquarters 2nd Lieut. F.J. SOUTHERN joined for duty & posted to C Coy	

Army Form C. 2118.

WAR DIARY
or
INTELLIGENCE SUMMARY.
(Erase heading not required.)

Instructions regarding War Diaries and Intelligence Summaries are contained in F.S. Regs., Part II. and the Staff Manual respectively. Title pages will be prepared in manuscript.

283c

Place	Date	Hour	Summary of Events and Information	Remarks and references to Appendices
LEFT SUB-SECTOR.	19.2.17		Deepened & strengthened posts. Ground in a terrible state. 9 many became sick in the mud. The Commanding Officer conferred with the B.G.C. with the object of carrying out an attack on (CREST TRENCH - R.11.9.94 - R.n.a.0.6) Strengthening posts - Construction of Splinter proof shelters.	
Do.	20.2.17		"A" & "C" Coys relieved by 17th Middlesex about midnight. "B" Coy to COURCELETTE DUG-OUTS. "C" Coy to WOLFE HUTS. "A" Coy unable to move from the front line owing to daylight breaking. Lieut W.D. HARVEY & 2Lt W.N. FREEMAN joined for duty & posted to D & A Coys.	
Do.	21.2.17		"A" returned from line to COURCELETTE DUG-OUTS. "D" Coy relieved by 17th Middlesex	
Do.	22.2.17		returned to W. MIRAUMONT DUG-OUTS.	
Do.	23.2.17		Battalion relieved by 2nd H.L.I. & took over Lulles in ALBERT about 2am on 24.2.17. Casualties during tour from 18.2.17 to 23.2.17 killed in action Lieut. C. STOKES. 18.2.17 2Lieut E.G. MUNDAY. 20.2.17 12 O.R. 1 O.R. 30 O.R. (including 5 O.R wounded 1 O.R. (S.I.W) at duty)	
ALBERT			Died of Wounds. Wounded	

WAR DIARY
or
INTELLIGENCE SUMMARY.

(Erase heading not required.)

Army Form C. 2118.

Place	Date	Hour	Summary of Events and Information	Remarks and references to Appendices
ALBERT	23.2.17		Casualties (cont'd) Missing 6 O.R. Sent to Hospital (with T.F.) 80 O.R.	
Do.	24.2.17		Working Party of 110 O.R. supplied. Battalion cleaning up & generally resting as yesterday. Continued work & forming a permanent working party of 100 O.R. no yesterday. Fort Drill carried out.	
Do.	25.2.17	Sunday	Battalion inspected by Commanding Officer by companies. Voluntary Church Service held. Lieut R. HORTH proceeded to transfer to M.G. Corps (Heavy Branch) Permanent Working Parties of 295 O.R. supplied.	
Do.	26.2.17		Battalion (less W. Parties) engaged in cleaning Kit & Equipment, & carrying out Fort Drill under the C.S.Mjr & Senior N.C.O.	
Do.	27.2.17		Working Parties (permanent) now total 335 O.R. Lieut OR SACRÉ admitted to Hospital. Battalion (less Working Parties 335 O.R.) generally smartening up. Commanding Officer Inspection. All Officers under Commanding Officer on kit, bedding & teaching Compass. Lieut F.H. AUSTIN and Lieut R.B. TONKIN joined for duty. Lieut H.L. BALL to duty.	
Do.	28.2.17		All available NCOs then paraded at 9.30 a.m. under Lieut H.P. TURNER for Arms Drill, Platoon Drill & extended Order Drill. All Officers & Signallers	

Army Form C. 2118.

WAR DIARY
or
INTELLIGENCE SUMMARY.
(Erase heading not required.)

Instructions regarding War Diaries and Intelligence Summaries are contained in F. S. Regs., Part II. and the Staff Manual respectively. Title pages will be prepared in manuscript.

Place	Date	Hour	Summary of Events and Information	Remarks and references to Appendices
ALBERT	28.2.17		Attended demonstration of High Power Buzzet in ground behind HQs. Gifts received (O+O) from Queen Alexandra's Field Force Fund and distributed among the men of the Battalion. Working Parties of 335 OR. Lieut. A.C. LEACH reported for duty & posted to "C" Coy.	XW G

WRaven Lieut Col
Cmdg: 13th Essex Regt.

13th ESSEX REGIMENT

2853

6th Brigade.

2nd Division.

13th BATTALION THE ESSEX REGIMENT

MARCH 1917

Army Form C. 2118.

WAR DIARY
or
INTELLIGENCE SUMMARY.

(Erase heading not required.)

6/2

Vol 16

4.17

CONFIDENTIAL

WAR DIARY
OF
THE
13TH (S) BN. ESSEX REGT

MARCH 1ST 1917 to MARCH 31ST 1917

Place	Date	Hour	Summary of Events and Information	Remarks and references to Appendices

Instructions regarding War Diaries and Intelligence Summaries are contained in F. S. Regs., Part II. and the Staff Manual respectively. Title pages will be prepared in manuscript.

Army Form C. 2118.

WAR DIARY
or
INTELLIGENCE SUMMARY.
(Erase heading not required.)

Instructions regarding War Diaries and Intelligence Summaries are contained in F. S. Regs., Part II. and the Staff Manual respectively. Title pages will be prepared in manuscript.

Place	Date	Hour	Summary of Events and Information	Remarks and references to Appendices
ALBERT	1st	9.30am	All available Officers met the Commanding Officer at W.27.b.8.8 for the purpose of Distinction in hap Reading marching on Compass Bearings etc. All other ranks available were occupied in cleaning Arms, Kit & Equipment. Notification received that Major W.A. WINTHROP having relinquished his Commission on account of ill-health, was struck off the Establishment of the Battalion from February 23rd 1914. (A/) T/Capt J.D. ROBINSON relinquished the Command of "B" Coy & the temporary rank of Captain from today. Lieut. J.V.G. CLARKE transferred from B Coy to C Coy. Working Parties of 6 Officers and 335 other Ranks supplied.	
ALBERT	2nd	9.30am	All available Officers, N.C.Os & men paraded at 9.30 am. for Commanding Officers inspection. Lieut. C.V. RITSON was transferred to & took over command of "B" Company. Lieut. D.H. MASON transferred from "B" Coy to "D" Coy. 1.TR died of Epilepsy. Working Parties of 6 Officers & 346 other ranks supplied.	
ALBERT TO OVILLERS HUTS	3rd	3.30pm	Having occupied in general cleaning up. special attention being paid to Fillets. The Battalion (in Support Brigade) moved into near Fillets at OVILLERS	

Army Form C. 2118.

WAR DIARY
or
INTELLIGENCE SUMMARY.
(Erase heading not required.)

Instructions regarding War Diaries and Intelligence Summaries are contained in F. S. Regs., Part II. and the Staff Manual respectively. Title pages will be prepared in manuscript.

Place	Date	Hour	Summary of Events and Information	Remarks and references to Appendices
OVILLERS HUTS	3rd	2.30 p.m.	HUTS a distance of about 3 miles arriving at 5.15 p.m. & relieving the 1st KINGS ROYAL RIFLE CORPS. Six Officers and 300 other ranks as working Parties.	
OVILLERS HUTS	4th	6.30 a.m.	SUNDAY The whole Battalion paraded as a working party at 6.30 a.m. proceeded to COURCELETTE where roadmaking work was carried out. The following memo was received from the 2nd Division :- "The Major General Commanding was much impressed by the splendid work done by the 13th Bn. Essex Regt. in the road through COURCELETTE. The progress made was little short of astonishing in so short a time. The Major General Commanding congratulates the Battalion on their achievement." Lieut. A.R. WELLS proceeded for course of Instruction at Fifth Army Sniping School.	
OVILLERS HUTS	5th	9 a.m.	Battalion bathing proceeded from 9 am to 1pm, each Company being allowed two hours. "A" Coy commencing. "B", "C" & "D" Coys paraded at 9.30 a.m. & were split up into small squads for instruction in Musketry, etc. A Coy carried on after bathing parade. Bomber paraded under the Bombing Officer at 9.30 a.m. Snipers, Scouts, & Lewis Gunners paraded under	

WAR DIARY
or
INTELLIGENCE SUMMARY.
(Erase heading not required.)

Army Form C. 2118.

Place	Date	Hour	Summary of Events and Information	Remarks and references to Appendices
OVILLERS HUTS	5		their respective Instructors at 9.30 a.m. 1 O.R. formerly reported "Wounded" died of Wounds.	
OVILLERS HUTS	6	9.30 a.m.	Companies paraded to listen to a lecture for the organisation of Platoons. Lieut. J.D. STEELE returned from Hospital. Lieut. J.J.G. CLIBORNE and Lieut. C.W. RITSON were granted permission to wear the badge of the rank of Captain whilst commanding Companies. Lieut. W. LAVINGTON proceeded on leave to England. Four Officers & 300 O.R. supplied for Working Party.	
OVILLERS HUTS	7		Battalion paraded at 9.30 a.m. Three Officers and 110 O.R. supplied for the Working Parties. 1 O.R. died today. Commanding Officers Inspection. M.R. SACRE returned from Hospital.	
OVILLERS HUTS	8	9.30 a.m.	Battalion paraded for Company Drill Rifle Exercises &c. Lewis Gunners paraded with their platoons. All other Specialists paraded under their respective Instructors. All Section Commanders paraded for a lecture on "musketry" by the Second in Command. Working Parties of 9 Officers and 356 O.R.s supplied.	
OVILLERS HUTS	9	9.30 a.m.	Battalion paraded (less Section Commanders) for Commanding Officer Inspection. Section Commanders attended lecture by the 2nd in Command on "Fire Control".	

Army Form C. 2118.

WAR DIARY
or
INTELLIGENCE SUMMARY.
(Erase heading not required.)

Place	Date	Hour	Summary of Events and Information	Remarks and references to Appendices
OVILLERS HUTS	9ᵗʰ		(A/T) Lt. Col. W.H. CARTER, D.S.O., M.C. promoted Captain in ROYAL WARWICKSHIRE REGT. Lieut. C.C. COLE Commanded "C" Coy from 28.2.17 to today when he proceeds on Leave. Divisional Course of Instruction. Lieut. R.C.H. MAY admitted to Hospital today. Draft of 18 O.R. joined. Draft of 4 O.R. rejoined. The undermentioned were awarded the Military Medal for Bravery in the Field. London Gazette dated 19.2.17. No. 17528 Sergt. VALENTINE. J. "B" Coy. K/A. 30.7.16 " 17225 " WATERMAN. C. "A" Coy. K/A. 30.7.16 " 17231 Pte. SAIT J.H. "D" Coy. K/A. 30.7.16 Casualties. 1 O.R. reptd missing now reptd. Prisoner of War. 14.11.16. 1 O.R. reptd missing now reptd. killed in action 14.11.16. Eight Officers and 281 O.R. subjected to Gas. Commanders for musketry and Rapid Loading. Battalion paraded under Lieut. J.P. BARRETT at 9.30 am for firing. All available Lewis Gunners paraded under the parade of fired. Bombers paraded under Lieut. "C" Coy for today. Officers attended the parade a field. Lieut. A.R. SACRE took over Command of "C" Coy from today.	
OVILLERS HUTS	10ᵗʰ	9.30 am		

WAR DIARY
or
INTELLIGENCE SUMMARY.
(Erase heading not required.)

Army Form C. 2118.

Place	Date	Hour	Summary of Events and Information	Remarks and references to Appendices
OVILLERS HUTS	10th		Supp of 9 OR rejoined from Hospital. Draft of 6 OR joined. Seven Officers & 285 OR supplied as working parties.	

OVILLERS HUTS to LINE	11th		SUNDAY. the Battalion relieved the 1st K.R.R.C. and no part of the 1st R. Berks in the LEFT SUB-SECTOR, LOUPART SECTOR today. Battalion Headquarters.
			
			 Disposition
			
			    A Coy. AQUEDUCT ROAD
			    B Coy. FRONT LINE
			    C Coy. LADY'S LEG
			    D Coy. RESERVE COY
			          SUPPORT COY
			
			 Casualties. Capt. C.W DUNCOMBE wounded. 1 OR. wounded	

LOUPART SECTOR	12th	night of 12/13	Battalion holding line - LEFT SUB-SECTOR LOUPART SECTOR. Enemy commenced re-building LOUPART WOOD. He was followed by our patrols who established a line by 12 mn 13th from N. point of LOUPART WOOD to G.28.C. (LOUPART WOOD Major B.I.I (?)) Lieut. D.H. MASON. took over Command of "A" Coy from today 2nd Lieut. A.R. WELLS returned from Fifth Army Sniping School. 2 OR. wounded. Casualties	

WAR DIARY
or
INTELLIGENCE SUMMARY.
(Erase heading not required.)

Army Form C. 2118.

Place	Date	Hour	Summary of Events and Information	Remarks and references to Appendices
LOUPART SECTOR	Sept 13th	13/14	Battalion holding advanced line of posts in LEFT SUB-SECTOR, LOUPART SECTOR. Enemy continued retirement & Battalion pushed forward & established line on the SUNKEN ROAD about 2 p.m. on the 14th. Lieut F.C. MUSSOTT admitted to Field Ambulance. T/Lt Col. P.R. PAPILLON assumed the establishment of Battalion from today. No. 18025 L/Cpl. COX G. awarded the Bronze Medal for Military Valour (Italian Decoration). Lieut P.H. CREASY wounded. Casualties. 5 OR killed in action. 12 OR wounded.	
LOUPART SECTOR	14th		Battalion holding line in SUNKEN RD. Relieved on night of 14/15th by 2/9 Bn. S. STAFFS. REGT. and proceeded to Reserve Battalion of DYKE VALLEY CAMP. Lieut W.A. HARVEY proceeded to 5th Army Trench Mortar School. 7/Capt. C.W. DUNSCOMBE wounded on 11.3.19. died of wounds today. Casualties. 1 Other Rank killed in action. 5 Other Ranks wounded.	
DYKE VALLEY CAMP	15th		Battalion (in Reserve) arrived DYKE VALLEY CAMP at 4 a.m. All ranks occupied in drying clothes & generally cleaning up. General Inspection by the Commanding Officer & Medical Officer.	

WAR DIARY or INTELLIGENCE SUMMARY

Army Form C. 2118.

Place	Date	Hour	Summary of Events and Information	Remarks and references to Appendices
DYKE VALLEY CAMP	15th		5 rs and 150 other Ranks proceeded as Working Party. Duckboard Track from AQUEDUCT ROAD to LOUPART WOOD commenced.	
DYKE VALLEY CAMP	16th		Battalion (in Reserve) occupied in cleaning up clothing arms & equipment. Special care was taken with arms. The Commanding Officer placed on record his appreciation of the conduct of all Officers, NCOs & men during the recent advance, especially T/Major A.G. HAYWARD.M.C. and T/Capt. C.W. RITSON. The advance itself was a great strain as all ranks who had already undergone a severe strain in holding the posts. There is no doubt that all ranks in the Unit at the present time are not only trying to keep up the tradition of the Regiment but are trying to go ONE BETTER. Nine Officers and 360 OR. were supplied as Working Party. Casualties 1 OR (Transport) wounded.	
DYKE VALLEY CAMP	17th		Battalion (in Reserve) continued general cleaning up. Physical Training for Conference not on Working Parties, from 9.30 - 12.30. Salvaging 2pm to 4 pm. Lieut. J.D. ROBINSON proceeded to ETAPLES for the purpose of training reinforcements.	

Army Form C. 2118.

WAR DIARY
or
INTELLIGENCE SUMMARY.
(Erase heading not required.)

Instructions regarding War Diaries and Intelligence Summaries are contained in F.S. Regs., Part II. and the Staff Manual respectively. Title pages will be prepared in manuscript.

Place	Date	Hour	Summary of Events and Information	Remarks and references to Appendices
DYKE VALLEY CAMP	17th		Working parties of 12 Officers and 433 other Ranks supplied. Laying of duckboard tracks to LOUPART WOOD continued.	
DYKE VALLEY CAMP to LOUPART WOOD	18th		SUNDAY. Battalion (in Reserve) moved up to LOUPART WOOD arriving about 4 p.m. Lieut A.C. LEETCH proceeded to 5th Army Sniping School for Course of Instruction. Six Officers and 210 other Ranks supplied for Working Parties. Duckboard Track from AQUEDUCT ROAD to LOUPART WOOD completed and named ESSEX TRACK.	
LOUPART WOOD to SAPIGNIES	19th	9 a.m.	Battalion (in Reserve) advanced as enemy retreated and at about 10 a.m. commenced to consolidate on first line of trenches, 800 yds S.W. of SAPIGNIES - about 3½ miles distant from LOUPART WOOD. The 2nd Division troops having been withdrawn by the 18th Division, the Battalion left position before SAPIGNIES & proceeded to COURCELETTE CAMP. 2nd Lieut D.H. MASON relinquished command of A Company & 2nd Lieut A.W. KAYE assumed command of A Coy.	
COURCELETTE CAMP	20th	3 a.m.	Battalion arrived in COURCELETTE CAMP. Capt. J.G.H. KENNEFICK rejoined from Hospital. 2nd Lieut W. LAVINGTON returned from leave. Battalion engaged in drying clothes & cleaning arms & equipment.	
COURCELETTE CAMP	21st	2:30 p.m.	Battalion moved from COURCELETTE CAMP to OVILLERS HUTS arriving there at 2:30 p.m.	

Army Form C. 2118.

WAR DIARY
or
INTELLIGENCE SUMMARY.
(Erase heading not required.)

Instructions regarding War Diaries and Intelligence Summaries are contained in F. S. Regs., Part II. and the Staff Manual respectively. Title pages will be prepared in manuscript.

Place	Date	Hour	Summary of Events and Information	Remarks and references to Appendices
OVILLERS HUTS	21st		Lieut A.W. KAYE relinquished Command of "A" Coy	
OVILLERS HUTS to WARLOY	22nd	11.50 am	The Battalion moved in to new billets at WARLOY, a distance of 8½ miles arriving there at 4.30 pm. Capt. J.G.H. KEMMEFICK assumed command of A Coy from today.	
WARLOY	23rd		The Battalion was engaged in cleaning up clothing arms & equipment. Sergeant tailors & Sergeant Shoemaker commenced refitting the men with clothes & boots. The Commanding Officer placed on record that he was pleased with the march discipline exhibited by the Battalion from OVILLERS HUTS to WARLOY, but there was still room for improvement.	
WARLOY	24th		The Battalion paraded at 10 am for Commanding Officers inspection. Platoons were organised. Lewis Gunners paraded with their embusses. Men were selected at random & their kits, clothing & equipment was inspected as follows:— T/Major A.G. HAYWARD MC T/Capt E.C. LOWINGS Hon. Lieut & Qr M. H. LANG	
		10.0 am	An audit board constituted as follows:— assembled at HQrs mess at 10 am & audit accounts placed before them.	

2353 Wt W2544/1454 700,000 5/15 D. D. & L. A.D.S.S./Forms/C. 2118.

Army Form C. 2118.

WAR DIARY
or
INTELLIGENCE SUMMARY.
(Erase heading not required.)

Instructions regarding War Diaries and Intelligence Summaries are contained in F. S. Regs., Part II. and the Staff Manual respectively. Title pages will be prepared in manuscript.

Place	Date	Hour	Summary of Events and Information	Remarks and references to Appendices
WARLOY	25th	9am	SUNDAY The Battalion bathed from 9am to 1pm. Ranks for Company paraded for Church Service.	
WARLOY to BEAUVAL	26th	9am	The Battalion moved into new billets at BEAUVAL a distance of 13 miles. Arriving there at 3pm.	
BEAUVAL to HAUTE VISEE	27th	8 noon	Battalion moved into new billets at HAUTE VISEE, a distance of about 6 miles. Arriving at destination at 3.15pm. Major A.G. HAYWARD M.C. proceeded to ALDERSHOT for Senior Officers' Course. T/Capt E.C. LOWINGS assumed the duties of 2/Second in command. Lieut. D.W. KAYE took over the command of "D" Company.	
HAUTE VISEE to SIBIVILLE	29th	11 am	The Battalion moved into new billets at SIBIVILLE, a distance of 9½ miles. Arriving there at 2.50 pm.	
SIBIVILLE	29th		Battalion cleaning up clothes, arms & equipment.	
SIBIVILLE to CONTEVILLE & HUCLIER	30th	6.30 am	Battalion moved into new billets at CONTEVILLE and HUCLIER a distance of about 12 miles arriving 12.25 pm. Headquarters and two Companies (A & B) billeted in CONTEVILLE and two Companies (C & D) in HUCLIER. T/Capt J.J.G. CLARKE returned from Fifth Army Infantry School. Lieut. A.R. SPERE	

WAR DIARY
or
INTELLIGENCE SUMMARY.
(Erase heading not required.)

Army Form C. 2118.

Place	Date	Hour	Summary of Events and Information	Remarks and references to Appendices
CONTEVILLE & HUCLIER	30th		relinquished the command of "C" Coy from today.	
CONTEVILLE & HUCLIER	31st	9.30 am	The Battalion paraded under Company arrangements for organization as follows:- 1 Section Riflemen, 1 Section Bomb Throwers, 1 Section Bombers, 1 Section Rifle Grenadiers. Cleaning & fitting of equipment was carried out. Special attention being paid to the latter. All Signallers not on Strength of Signalling Section paraded under the Signalling Officer at 10 am.	
		10 am	The Commanding Officer placed on record that he was very pleased with the march discipline and general appearance of the Battalion during the march from SIBIVILLE to CONTEVILLE.	
		10 am	The Commanding Officer attended a Divisional Conference at Marqueslis PERNES at 10 am when the following men items were discussed:- Operations (Past & Future), Organization, Discipline, & General items	

CCParson Lieut Colonel

Cmdg: 13th (S) Bn. Essex Regt.

"A" Form.
MESSAGES AND SIGNALS.

Army Form C.2121

TO: 6th Bde

Sender's Number.	Day of Month.	In reply to Number.	
OR 7/40	12	GS 658/7	AAA

Herewith detailed instructions issued to Coys concerned. O C Reserve Coy instructed verbally as to supplying platoon for work with Left Front Coy

From: OC 13th Essex Rgt

O C A Coy

Para I. The 17th Middlesex will dig a front line in front of our present posts tonight. As soon as they start work the garrison of the present posts will assist them in digging and will then establish posts in the new trench - the old posts will be vacated. He must arrange this with the O C Middlesex party.

II. No 5 Strong point will be improved by its garrison. You will provide covering parties on your company front.

III. The garrison of GREVILLERS TR will improve it as much as possible working Westwards to meet B Coy

H.H.Carter Lt Col
Cmdg 13th Essex Regt

O.C B Coy   A.11

Para I You will tonight dig new communication
        trench which has already been taped out
        from No 6 Strong point in "the Toe of the
        ladies leg" to the new front line which
        is being dug tonight by the 17th Middlesex
        it is to be dug to a depth of 6 feet
        at least.
        1 platoon of the reserve coy will
        report to you as soon as possible
        after dusk for this work and
        you should make use of any available
        men from your own Company.
        It is of the utmost importance
        that this work should be
        completed tonight.

II   The Strong point No 6 should be
        improved by its garrison.

III   As soon as the 17th Middlesex
        commence work on the new front
        line the garrison of the posts in
        advance of No 6 Strong point should
        move forward and assist them
        in digging the new front line
        the old posts will then be vacated
        and their garrison will establish
        posts in the new trench you
        should arrange this work with

O.C working party of Middlesex.
You will provide the necessary
"covering parties" for the above work
on your Company front

IV The Officer and 25 men forming garrison
of GREVILLERS TR at the bottom of
the LADYS LEG will improve the
trench as much as possible working
Eastwards.

J.W.Carter H Col
Cmdg 13th Green. Ry

O C D Coy

Para I
The 17th Middlesex will dig a new front line in front of our present posts tonight. As soon as they start work the garrison of the forward posts will assist them in digging and will then establish posts in the new trench. The old posts will be vacated. You should arrange this with O C 17th Middlesex party.

II No 4 Strong point will be improved by its garrison as much as possible. You will provide the necessary covering parties for the above work on your Coy front.

III The platoon in the E end of GREVILLER TR near its junction with COULEE TR will improve it as much as possible working Westwards Towards A Coy.

M B Carter Lt Col
Cmdg 13th Essex R[gt]

6th Brigade
A Coy in Brown Line
B " Strong Points
C " in the wood
D " South edge of wood
Bn Hdqrs G 28 d 5 1

Herewith rough Sketch shewing
dispositions of the Battalion
under my Command.

[signature] Lt Col
Comdg 13th Essex Regt

Dispositions.
Batt HQ   G 28 d 5 1

"A" Coy HQ   G 28 d 7 2
"B" Coy HQ   G 34 b 20 65
C + D " HQ   G 34 b 4 0

scale 1/10000

"A" Form.
MESSAGES AND SIGNALS.
Army Form C.2121 (in pads of 100).

TO: 6th Bn

Sender's Number.	Day of Month.	In reply to Number.	
OR 7/141	12	BM 699	AAA

Dispositions

Right Front Coy

1 complete platoon with additional Lewis Gun in N° 4 Strong point.

1 Section of Rifle men 1 section of Bombers 1 Section of Lewis Gunners in N° 1 forward post.

1 Section of Rifle men & 1 section of Bombers in N° 2 forward post.

1 Complete platoon in Eastern end of Junction GREVILLERS COULEE TRENCHES

2 Sections of Bombers in COULEE TRENCH NORTHERN end also Headquarters of Coy as power Buzzer & Telephone is there.

"A" Form.
MESSAGES AND SIGNALS.

Army Form C.2121
(In pads of 100).
No. of Message ....

Prefix .... Code .... m.	Words	Charge	This message is on a/c of :	Recd. at .... m.
Office of Origin and Service Instructions	Sent		.... Service.	Date ....
....	At .... m.			From ....
....	To		(Signature of "Franking Officer.")	By ....
	By			

TO { Code

| Sender's Number. | Day of Month. | In reply to Number. | A A A |

CENTRE FRONT COY

1 Complete platoon with additional Lewis
gun in N° 5 Strong post
1 Section of riflemen 1 Section of Bombers
& 1 Section of Lewis Gunners in N° 1 forward
post
1 Section of Riflemen 1 Section of Bombers
in N° 2 forward post
1 Section of Riflemen 1 Section of Bombers
& 1 Lewis Gunners in N° 3 post
1 Section of Riflemen & 1 Section of Bombers
in N° 4 forward post
2 Section of Riflemen in GREVILLERS TR
NB 1 Lewis gun lent from Reserve Coy

From
Place
Time

"A" Form.
MESSAGES AND SIGNALS.

Army Form C.2121 (in pads of 100).

TO: Comd

AAA

LEFT FRONT COY

1 Complete Platoon with additional Lewis Gun in No 6 Strong Post

1 Section Riflemen 1 Section Bombers in No 1 Forward Post

1 Section Riflemen 1 Section Bombers 1 Section Lewis Gunners in No 2 Forward Post

1 Officer & 25 at bottom of Ladys Leg in GREVILLERS TR

Remainder with Hd quarters in Ravine

"A" Form.
MESSAGES AND SIGNALS.

Army Form C.2121 (in pads of 100).

Prefix ...... Code ...... in.	Words	Charge	This message is on a/c of:	Recd. at .... m.
Office of Origin and Service Instructions.	Sent		.... Service.	Date ....
	At .... m.			From ....
	To			
	By	(Signature of "Franking Officer.")	By ....

TO { Comd }

| Sender's Number. | Day of Month. | In reply to Number. | A A A |

Reserve Coy less 1 Lewis Gun Section
in dugouts and Funk holes near
Bn Hdqrs & 1 complete in BELOW TRENCH

From
Place
Time

"A" Form.
MESSAGES AND SIGNALS.

Army Form C.2121 (in pads of 100).

TO — 6th Bde

Sender's Number: OR 7/142

AAA

Please note.
Herewith dispositions as requested

From: OC 13th Econ Regt

6th Brigade
2nd Division.

13th BATTALION

THE ESSEX REGIMENT

A P R I L 1917.

Appendices :-

Report on Operations 28.4.17.

Battalion Operation Order.

Army Form C. 2118.

WAR DIARY
or
INTELLIGENCE SUMMARY.
(Erase heading not required.)

Vol 17

CONFIDENTIAL

WAR DIARY
— of —
13th (S) BN. ESSEX REGT

April 1st 1917 <u>to</u> April 30th 1917

Army Form C. 2118.

WAR DIARY
or
INTELLIGENCE SUMMARY.
(Erase heading not required.)

Instructions regarding War Diaries and Intelligence Summaries are contained in F.S. Regs., Part II. and the Staff Manual respectively. Title pages will be prepared in manuscript.

Place	Date	Hour	Summary of Events and Information	Remarks and references to Appendices
CONTEVILLE & HUCLIER	April 1st		Battalion paraded as strong as possible & carried out training in Arms Drill, Bayonet fighting, Musketry. Specialists paraded under their respective instructors. Proprietors & Companies of billets Rifles, Equipment & Clothing took place during the afternoon. Lieut A.R. WELLS proceeded to 5th Squadron R.F.C. for course of instruction.	⅟
do	2nd		Battalion paraded as strong as possible & carried out training as yesterday. At 2 p.m. the Battalion paraded for inspection by Battalion Drill under the Commanding Officer. Specialists paraded under their respective instructors. Lieut A.M. KAYE admitted to Field Ambulance.	⅟
do	3rd		Battalion paraded for training in accordance with programme. Draft of 24 O.R. joined Battalion. Capt. R.S.B. PINCHARD (Bde. Transport Officer) proceeded on leave. Capt. & Adjt. Ed. TRUMBLE struck off Establishment.	⅟
do	4th		Battalion paraded from 9.35 am and 12.30pm and 2 p.m. to 4 p.m. for training in accordance with programme. Sents & Signallers carried out night work from 7pm to 9pm.	⅟
do	5th		Battalion paraded from 9am to 12.45 pm and 2pm to 4 pm. & carried out in accordance with training programme. Lieut A.R. WELLS returned from 5th Squadron R.F.C.	⅟

2353 Wt. W2544/1454 700,000 5/15 D.D. & L. A.D.S.S./Forms/C. 2118.

Army Form C. 2118.

WAR DIARY
or
INTELLIGENCE SUMMARY.
(Erase heading not required.)

Instructions regarding War Diaries and Intelligence Summaries are contained in F. S. Regs., Part II. and the Staff Manual respectively. Title pages will be prepared in manuscript.

Place	Date	Hour	Summary of Events and Information	Remarks and references to Appendices
CONTEVILLE & HUCLIER	6.		Good Friday. Voluntary Church Parade at 11 a.m. Lieut Col. W.H. CARTER D.S.O., M.C. relinquished command of the Battalion & proceeded to the Senior Officers School Infantry School ALDERSHOT, were struck off the strength of the Battalion.	
CONTEVILLE to OURTIN	7.		Lieut Col. C.T. MARTIN assumed command of the Battalion from today. Capt. A.D. DERVICHE-JONES MC joined. The Battalion moved into new billets at OURTIN, a distance of about 9½ miles, moving off at 2.30 p.m. & arriving at OURTIN at 7 p.m. 1/Capt. E.C. LOWINGS relinquished the duties of 2nd in Command of the Battalion.	
OURTIN	8.		Sunday. Voluntary Church Service was held at 10 a.m. & 6 p.m. by R.C. at 8.30 a.m. Capt. J.G.H. KENNEPICK went J.D. STEELE and 4th O.R. proceeded at the XII Corps Depot training school for the purpose of training reinforcements. Lt R B TOMLIN returned from leave & Capt. A.D. DERVICHE-JONES M.C. resumed the duties of 2ᵈ in Command.	
OURTIN	9.		The Battalion paraded for training in accordance with programme, and fatigues.	
OURTIN	10.		Battalion paraded as strong as possible for training in accordance with programme.	

WAR DIARY
or
INTELLIGENCE SUMMARY.
(Erase heading not required.)

Army Form C. 2118.

Place	Date	Hour	Summary of Events and Information	Remarks and references to Appendices
OURTIN to "X" Huts	11th		The Battalion moved to "X" Huts ECOIVRES a distance of about 12 miles, leaving OURTIN at 10.20 am and arriving at destination at 5pm. Dinner was served on line of march. Route :- LA COMTE - HOUDAIN - PREVILLERS - VILLERS BRULIN - then ARRAS-ST.POL. Rd.	
ECOIVRES X Huts to ROCLINCOURT	12th		The Battalion moved into Reserve Brigade Area (Dugouts around ROCLINCOURT) relieving a Battalion of the 152nd Infantry Brigade. Route :- BRAY - MAROEUIL - ANZIN - ST. AUBYN	
ROCLINCOURT (OPPY SECTOR)	13th		Battalion in Reserve Brigade Area. Battalion layeng duckboard track from ROCLINCOURT to MAISON DE LA COTE and COMMANDANT'S HOUSE (OPPY SECTOR)	
do	14th		Battalion in Reserve Brigade Area. Battalion laying duckboard track as yesterday. The Divisional Commander expressed his satisfaction with regard to the progress made on the duckboard track yesterday by the Battalion.	
do	15th		Battalion in Support Brigade Area. Laying of duckboard track continued and completed. Permission granted for Capt P.O. DERVICHE-JONES MC to wear the badges of the rank of Major.	
do	16th		Battalion in Support Brigade Area. Battalion feet inspection. Practice gas attack & gas helmet inspection. The following message was received from	

WAR DIARY
or
INTELLIGENCE SUMMARY.

(Erase heading not required.)

Army Form C. 2118.

Place	Date	Hour	Summary of Events and Information	Remarks and references to Appendices
RICLINCOURT	16th		6th Infantry Brigade "Coys Commands" & O.E. of Corps hqs much interested with Organization works being carried out by 6th Brigade in our Communication and roads. 2/Lieut F.A. JENNIS and 2/Lieut R IBBOTSON joined for duty & were posted to "C" and "D" Coy respectively. 2/Lieut F.B. JONES being appointed Assistant Adjutant.	
to	17th		Battalion in Support Brigade Res. The Company officers made a Tour of Inspection of all dugouts occupied by the Battalion. 2/Lieut H.E. MORRIS was admitted to Field Ambulance.	
RICLINCOURT to H.C.	18th		Battalion relieved the 14th Bn. Royal Fusiliers in the LEFT SUB-SECTOR, OPPY SECTOR. Dispositions. RIGHT COMPANY "D" Coy. LEFT Do "C" Coy. SUPPORT COMPANIES "A" & "B" Coys Battalion HQs in Railway Embankment at B.5.d.5.6 (ROCLINCOURT 51.B.N.W.1 1/10000) 2/Lieut F.J. SOUTHERN was admitted to Hospital sick. Consolidation of Front Line Rob. & Support Trench carried out.	

WAR DIARY
or
INTELLIGENCE SUMMARY.

(Erase heading not required.)

Army Form C. 2118.

Place	Date	Hour	Summary of Events and Information	Remarks and references to Appendices
LINE	19"		Battalion holding the LEFT SUB-SECTOR, OPPY SECTOR. A connecting trench between front line posts was commenced & posts & support trench were consolidated. Casualties 5 O.R. Killed 4 O.R. Wounded. Our front line posts and support trench were heavily shelled throughout the morning. Lieut. F.H. AUSTIN returned from 2nd Divisional Course. Lieut C.O.F. proceeded direct to XIII Corps Scout-Training Depot from 2nd Divisional Course. HONOURS & AWARDS. The undermentioned were awarded the Military Medal for gallantry & devotion to duty in action. 13363 Cpl PEARTREE T "A" Coy 15110 Pte UPCHURCH W "B" Coy	
LINE	20"		Battalion holding the LEFT SUBSECTOR, OPPY SECTOR. Consolidation continued. Our front line posts & support trench heavily shelled from 9am to 10 am. Shelling was kept up in a desultory manner & practically ceased between 3pm & 3.30pm. Casualties 1 O.R. Wounded.	
LINE	21"		Battalion holding the LEFT SUB-SECTOR, OPPY SECTOR. Support trench deepened, & taping of posts carried out. Casualties 1 O.R. Killed.	

Army Form C. 2118.

WAR DIARY
or
INTELLIGENCE SUMMARY.
(Erase heading not required.)

Place	Date	Hour	Summary of Events and Information	Remarks and references to Appendices
LINE	22nd		Battalion holding the LEFT SUB-SECTOR, OPPY SECTOR. About 9pm preceded by a heavy barrage the enemy raided our front line. A party of about 20 bombers advanced round the LEFT FLANK and in rear, and a smaller party on the LEFT FRONT. In response to our S.O.S. our Artillery opened fire, probably enemy about 9.15 pm. Enemy entered our trench at B.11.b.7.5. (RICLINCOURT 51.B.N.W.1 /10000) A company went out forward to retake the trench & strongly occupy it which they did. A German officer party was in the trench badly wounded, and belonging to the 46th Bavarian Regt. Casualties 5 OR killed. 3 OR wounded. 22 OR missing.	
LINE to RICLINCOURT	23rd		Battalion relieved on night of 23rd by 24th & 17th Royal Fusiliers & retired to Reserve Brigade Area (Argyris) around RICLINCOURT arriving at 6 am on the 24th. Casualties. 1 OR killed. 1 OR wounded.	
RICLINCOURT	24th		Battalion in Reserve Brigade Area. In consequence of an impending German counter attack in the OPPY SECTOR the Battalion occupied the Support Brigade line (RUDLEMPH STERLING RICLINCOURT 51.B.N.W.1. /10000) about 3pm returning to the Reserve Brigade Area about 4pm.	

Army Form C. 2118.

WAR DIARY
or
INTELLIGENCE SUMMARY.
(Erase heading not required.)

Instructions regarding War Diaries and Intelligence Summaries are contained in F.S. Regs., Part II. and the Staff Manual respectively. Title pages will be prepared in manuscript.

Place	Date	Hour	Summary of Events and Information	Remarks and references to Appendices
ROCLINCOURT	25th		Battalion in Reserve Brigade Area. The Commanding Officer attended a conference at Brigade Headquarters re impending operations.	
ROCLINCOURT TO MAROEUIL	26th		The Battalion moved to huts at MAROEUIL. Orders received to prepare for attack on the RIGHT of OPPY VILLAGE. Conference of Company Commanders held. Detailed Operation Orders prepared & issued for attack.	
MAROEUIL to ROCLINCOURT and LINE.	27th		Battalion moved to ROCLINCOURT, leaving MAROEUIL at 11 a.m. and practising the attack en route, arriving at ROCLINCOURT at 2 p.m. where dinners were served etc, which men rested until dusk. Battalion then moved up to assembly trenches beyond BAILLEUL (OPPY SECTOR) and formed up ready for attack. All ranks appeared confident of success & cheerful. Each man carried chocolate & 2 cheese sandwiches & was given a rum ration before moving off. The following is a copy of Operation Orders issued by the Commanding Officer to the Company Commanders, & others concerned:— The Battalion will carry out an attack as marked on sketch map (see attached) on "Z" Day. "Z" Day will be notified later.	Ref. Maps. OPPY 1/5000.

WAR DIARY or INTELLIGENCE SUMMARY

Army Form C. 2118.

(Erase heading not required.)

Place	Date	Hour	Summary of Events and Information	Remarks and references to Appendices
LINE	27th		The attack will be carried out by the 2nd Division - the 6th Brigade on the RIGHT & the 5th Brigade on the LEFT. The 63rd (Royal Naval Division) will be on the RIGHT and the 1st Canadian Division on the LEFT of the 2nd Division respectively. Dividing line with the Battalion of the Division on the RIGHT will be from enemy front line at B.24.B.3.8 & C.14.a.0.1. Dividing line with 14th Middlesex on the LEFT will be from SOUTH EDGE of OPPY WOOD & VILLAGE to C.14.a.0.2. 13th Essex on the RIGHT. 14th Middlesex on the LEFT. Disposition of the 6th Brigade. Disposition of Battalion RIGHT to LEFT. "B" "C" "D" "A". Each company will have a frontage of 120 yds. Method of carrying out attack. Companies will be organized in three platoons and the Battalion will advance in three waves. One platoon from each company will form the 1st WAVE. do do do do 2nd WAVE do do do do 3rd WAVE	

WAR DIARY or INTELLIGENCE SUMMARY

Place	Date	Hour	Summary of Events and Information	Remarks and references to Appendices
LINE	27"			

1st WAVE will be the First OBJECTIVE
2nd WAVE   do   Second OBJECTIVE
3rd WAVE   do   GREEN LINE

First wave will advance at ZERO other at 50 yds distance.

Objective. First OBJECTIVE. SOUTH of OPPY VILLAGE at C.13.a.+1. to C.19.a.8.9.
Second OBJECTIVE from trench at C.13.b.3.3. to C.13.d.4.0.
BROWN LINE from C.14.a.0.2. to C.14.c.0.1.

One company of 2nd SOUTH STAFFS will be attached to the Battalion from 12 noon "Y/Z" Day. This company will supply garrison for the Strong Points and "Moppers-up". Carrying parties are detailed from 1st KINGS and 2nd SOUTH STAFFS.

Moppers up. "Moppers up of various waves will follow up twenty yds in rear of their respective waves. They will join their companies in which they were originally attached after mopping up. 1 Officer and 40 O.R. 10 men will be specially told off for communication trenches running from B.18.d.4.3 to B.18.d.6.2.

1st WAVE. German front line.

WAR DIARY or INTELLIGENCE SUMMARY

Army Form C. 2118.

Place	Date	Hour	Summary of Events and Information	Remarks and references to Appendices
LINE	27th		Six men at B.18.d.4.6. Six men at B.18.d.8.8. 2nd WAVE. Twenty men for groups of practice trenches running in B.13.d. Six bombers under an N.C.O. to follow communication trench running N.E. through B.13.d. **Artillery Barrage.** The artillery barrage is the guiding factor as to the pace of infantry advancing. It must be impressed on all ranks taking part in the attack that it is absolutely essential to advance close up to the barrage, so that they must assemble any portion of the enemy trench or portion opposite them immediately the barrage lifts off it. Barrage lifts will be towards later. The protective barrage will lift 500 yds EAST of the BROWN LINE. Companies will consolidate 100 yds in front of trench. This consolidation will take the form of strong points. **Patrols.** On gaining the BROWN LINE, patrols will be sent forward to NEUVIREUIL immediately. The protective barrage lifts. All ground gained must be consolidated immediately, + no closed everything men will be carried too	↓

WAR DIARY
or
INTELLIGENCE SUMMARY

Army Form C. 2118.

Place	Date	Hour	Summary of Events and Information	Remarks and references to Appendices
LINE	27"		The purpose in all waves Stokes Mortars. Two Stokes mortars will join in with the artillery barrage on enemy front line at ZERO. Two mortars will be attached to the Battalion and will move forward with 4th WAVE and proceed to a point where track crosses trench at B.13.B.8.1. Strong Points. Strong points will be made as follows:— Arsenal Boundary at C.13.d.5.0. and C.13.B.4.1. Garrison of each Strong point will be two Vickers Guns and an Officer and 16 O.R. from the 2nd S. STAFFS Regt. Parties will carry two extra Stores. These garrisons will move with 4th WAVE and will present checks to then bobs & comma counter-attacks. Formation of Assault Pats. On reaching the line of the Final Objective (BROWN LINE) Strong points will be established in touch with and supporting each other 100 yds. in front of enemy trench. Relay posts will be established as follows:— (1) B.19.C.4.6. (2) B.19.d.8.5. (3) C.13.C.8.5. Communication.	

Army Form C. 2118.

WAR DIARY
or
INTELLIGENCE SUMMARY.
(Erase heading not required.)

Place	Date	Hour	Summary of Events and Information	Remarks and references to Appendices
LINE	27th		Each post will be established under Battalion arrangement and will consist of 4 Runners and 2 Signallers. Posts will be marked by blue flag on ground. A rifle shuttle will be set up for guiding purposes. Every effort is to be made to obtain visual signalling. O.C. Companies will send in Hourly reports from ZERO onwards. All Company Commanders or platoon commanders in reading their objective will forward field message cards + sketch maps showing position + whether they have seen gained with flanks. A contact aeroplane will fly over our line at 4 am, 4 am when the contact aeroplane sounds the KLAXON HORN or fires a VERY LIGHT, this will be the sign that troops are to show their location. The marking of Contact Patrol Aeroplanes of No 5. Squadron R.F.C. (attached to XIII Corps) is as follows:— Two black bands under each bottom plane. Four streamers, one on each rear interplane strut, on both right + left pairs of Battalion Headquarters. Brigade Headquarters B.21.a.6.8. Posts of Headquarters. Road Junction B.19.d.3.4.	

WAR DIARY
or
INTELLIGENCE SUMMARY.
(Erase heading not required.)

Army Form C. 2118.

Place	Date	Hour	Summary of Events and Information	Remarks and references to Appendices
LINE	27th		Food & Water Supply. Reserve ration dumps will be at B.26.a. Iron rations will be issued on "Y" Day, consisting of two cheese sandwiches per man. Rations will be brought up to BAILLEUL Stn. for consumption on day after ZERO. Guides will meet ration parties at the Station. Reserve water will be drawn from front line at the rate of 50 petrol tins per Battalion. Watches. Watches to be synchronized on "Y" Day. Carrying Parties. One NCO & 16 men per Company. Os. C Companies will ensure that these men are sent back to fetch more material. Dress. Fighting Order. One days ration and Iron Ration to be carried. Water bottles filled. The following will also be carried. 3 Bombs per man (No 5 hells) Rifle Bombers 10 No. 23 Grenades Bombers 10 Bombs (Mills) 2 Sandbags per man. Every man to carry one flare & 120 rds. S.A.A. 32 Magazines per Lewis Gun will be carried. Four Lewis Guns from 2nd SOUTH STAFFS. Two will be attached to "D" Coy and two to "B" Coy.	✓

WAR DIARY
or
INTELLIGENCE SUMMARY.
(Erase heading not required.)

Army Form C. 2118.

Place	Date	Hour	Summary of Events and Information	Remarks and references to Appendices
LINE	27-		Every man to have a round in chamber when advancing. Special parties will be told off to deal with enemy machine gun emplacements behind enemy's front line and enemy traverses. **Wounded** All walking wounded must bring down their equipment. **Prisoners** Prisoners to be sent forage in RUCLINCOURT at Cross Roads A.22.a (about 5 Bn. HQrs). All Officers will be searched & all documents etc at once to be allowed. It will demand. An escort of one man per 10 prisoners will be allowed. A receipt on landing over to Divisional cage. **Aid Posts** Regimental Aid Posts at Bn. HQs. the following Aid Posts will be established. B.16.a.3.8. (SUGAR FACTORY) B.15.c.8.4. (SUNKEN ROAD) B.21.c.7.7. (BAILLEUL STN) **S.O.S.** The SOS signal for barrage fire will be RED, on GREEN, one RED light fired in rapid succession. This signal will be repeated at short intervals until the artillery comply with the signal. A succession of WHITE lights remains the signal for lengthen range.	

Army Form C. 2118.

WAR DIARY
or
INTELLIGENCE SUMMARY.
(Erase heading not required.)

Instructions regarding War Diaries and Intelligence Summaries are contained in F. S. Regs., Part II. and the Staff Manual respectively. Title pages will be prepared in manuscript.

Place	Date	Hour	Summary of Events and Information	Remarks and references to Appendices
LINE	21st		The 1st WAVE will consist of TRENCH MORTARS, five VICKERS GUNS, a garrison of sling bombs. On arrival at objectives O.S.C. Coys will form Company dumps of bombs. (Sgd) E. Hatton Lt Col. Cmdg. 13th Bn. Scot. Regt.	
LINE	22nd			
LINE	23rd	2 am	The Battalion was formed up in their jumping off position without any hitch occurring about 2 am in spite of heavy shelling. Companies were organized in three platoons, one platoon of each company representing 1st, 2nd & 3rd WAVES, each had snashing [?] of two lines. 1st Line. Bombers & Riflemen. 2nd line. Lewis Gunners & Rifle Bombers. Troops up but each wave were formed up in rear of the 2nd y Line. Carrying parties & garrison for slung bombs were formed up in rear of the 3rd wave. Close touch was gained with the Highland Light Infantry, the 14th Yorkshires and the Royal Marine Light Infantry	
		4.25am	At 4.25 am our our barrage came down and at 4.38 am the 1st wave crossed the enemy's front line trench, with the exception of the extreme right of	

Army Form C. 2118.

WAR DIARY
or
INTELLIGENCE SUMMARY.
(Erase heading not required.)

Place	Date	Hour	Summary of Events and Information	Remarks and references to Appendices
LINE	24th		The Battalion, which was held up by heavy wire and lost heavily from hostile Gun fire in endeavoring to get through it. At the period their was entirely lost with the Royal Fusiliers Light Infantry on our RIGHT. It was maintained between the 13th Essex & 14th Middlesex but was lost with the Stafford Light Infantry who were on the LEFT of the 14th Middlesex. The advance continued under the barrage to the line of the practice trenches to C.13.d. Eastern end of OPPY WOOD and trench in C.Y.C. At this period, a party of German tanks attacked our RIGHT FLANK. Heavy machine gun fire & rifle fire took place from OPPY VILLAGE and large numbers of the enemy were advancing down the SUNKEN ROAD at the extreme	
	5.50am	At 5.50 am I ordered one Company of the Kings Royal Rifle Corps (which company had been sent by the 6th Infantry Bde as support) to advance and form a defensive flank from B.13.d.3.5 & southern end of practice trenches. The enemy was made to pause further than the British front line owing to hostile barrage and machine gun fire. About this line the Battalion on our LEFT (17th Middlesex) were heavily attacked	

WAR DIARY or INTELLIGENCE SUMMARY

Army Form C. 2118.

Place	Date	Hour	Summary of Events and Information	Remarks and references to Appendices
LINE	24th		From the front & on the LEFT flank a large number of the enemy advanced through EPPY WOOD, got in rear of the line & reoccupied parts of the German front line. A patrol that was sent forward to clear up the situation about 7.30 am but did not return, & no message was received from him. The heavy fighting continued and at 9 am the troops who were in front held & consolidated the German front line. Small detached parties only succeeded in doing this & were unable to cope with the enemy who were then holding the trench. All the Officers of the Battalion had become casualties and the majority of the N.C.O.'s & what was left of the Battalion was quite disorganized and exhausted. Small parties held out but eventually retired to the old British Line, running from shell hole to shell hole as chance offered. Casualties Killed (Present) T/Capt J.J.G. CLARKE O.C. 'C' Coy. (Wound) T/Capt C.W. RITSON O.C. 'B' Coy. 3 O.R.	

WAR DIARY
or
INTELLIGENCE SUMMARY.

Army Form C. 2118.

Place	Date	Hour	Summary of Events and Information	Remarks and references to Appendices
	23rd		Gravelle (cont'd)	

Wounded

(2nd) Capt F.C. JENNINGS   a/ "D" Cy
Lieut   F.H. SHEPPARD   Asst Gas Officer
Lieut   D.R. SPERS
Lieut   W. ADDINGTON
         99 OR.

Missing.

Lieut   R.C. LEACH
Lieut   W.B. FREDERICK   Injured
2 Lieut D.R. MASON   O.C. "B" Cy
2 Lieut J.A. BARNETT
2 Lieut S.F. YOWLES
2 Lieut H.P. TURNER
2 Lieut W. FREEMAN
2 Lieut R. IBBOTSON
         240 OR.

WAR DIARY
or
INTELLIGENCE SUMMARY.
(Erase heading not required.)

Army Form C. 2118.

Instructions regarding War Diaries and Intelligence Summaries are contained in F. S. Regs., Part II and the Staff Manual respectively. Title pages will be prepared in manuscript.

Place	Date	Hour	Summary of Events and Information	Remarks and references to Appendices
LINE to ROCLINCOURT	28th		The remainder of the Battalion & the same troops holding the British line were relieved on the night of the 28th by the 22nd Royal Fusiliers in the front line and a company of the 93rd Royal Fusiliers in the support line, returning to dugouts near ROCLINCOURT, & arriving there about 5 a.m. on the 29th. The undermentioned officers joined the Battalion for duty. Draft of 159 O.R. joined. Lieut R.G. TREBILCO Lieut R.G. BOX Lieut H.V. COOK Lieut W.S. McLAREN Lieut C.C. COLE rejoined the Battalion from XIII Corps Staff Learners Report Lieut F.P. JERVIS Battalion cleaning up and resting. The undermentioned officers assumed command of Companies as under:— Lieut R.G. TREBILCO "A" Coy Lieut R.G. BOX "B" Coy Lieut C.C. COLE "C" Coy Lieut H.V. COOK "D" Coy Lieut W.D. HORLEY proceeded for a course of Lewis Gunnery at LE TOUQUET.	
ROCLINCOURT to ECURIE	29th		Battalion moved into tents at ECURIE, a distance of 1½ miles, leaving dugouts ROCLINCOURT at 6.30 p.m. & arriving at ECURIE at 9 p.m. Information received that Capt. J.D. PATERSON to strike off the Establishment from 12.2.14	

Army Form C. 2118.

WAR DIARY
or
INTELLIGENCE SUMMARY.
(Erase heading not required.)

Instructions regarding War Diaries and Intelligence Summaries are contained in F. S. Regs., Part II. and the Staff Manual respectively. Title pages will be prepared in manuscript.

Place	Date	Hour	Summary of Events and Information	Remarks and references to Appendices
ECURIE	29th		Lieut F.H. AUSTIN transferred from "D" Coy to "B" Coy. Draft of 25 O.R. joined. Battalion cleaning up & resting. Lieut R.G. TRESILICO (Lieut G Coy) & Lieut. F.H. AUSTIN.	
ECURIE to MARŒUIL	30th		Lieut R.B. TONKIN and 120 O.R. proceeded for attachment to 1st Anzac Regt. to make that Battalion up to strength for active operations, so sent to the Rabaul Comp'd. Battalion moved to H'Q'rs at MARŒUIL, arriving there about 7 pm. Lieut Col C.T. MARTIN assumed command of the 6th Infantry Brigade during the absence of Brigadier General WALSH DSO. on leave. Major A.D. DERUCHE-JONES MC. assumed command of Battalion whilst Lieut Col C T MARTIN is in command of the 6th Infantry Brigade.	

A. Westerbrooker
Major
a/dy. 13th Bn. Essex Regt.

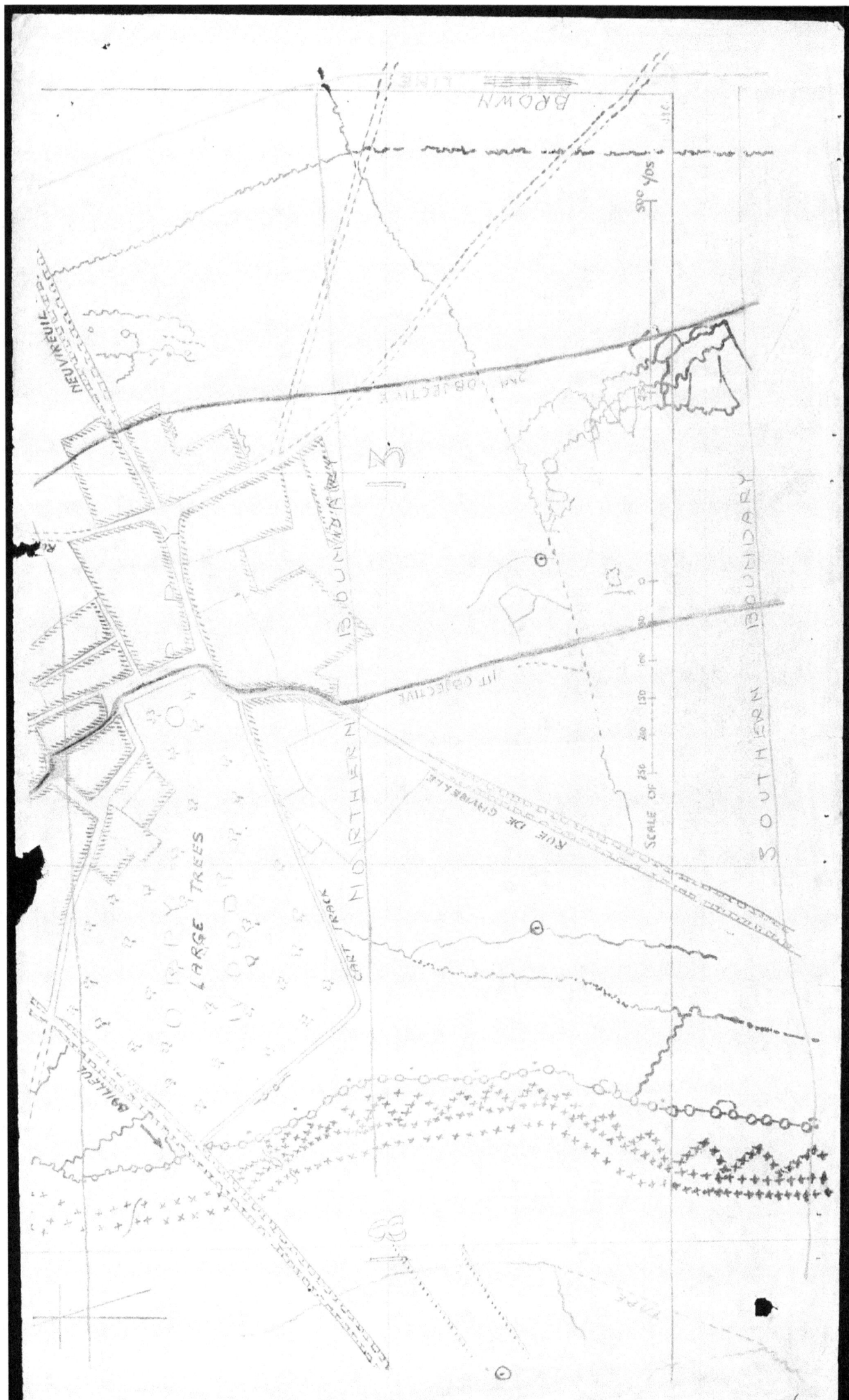

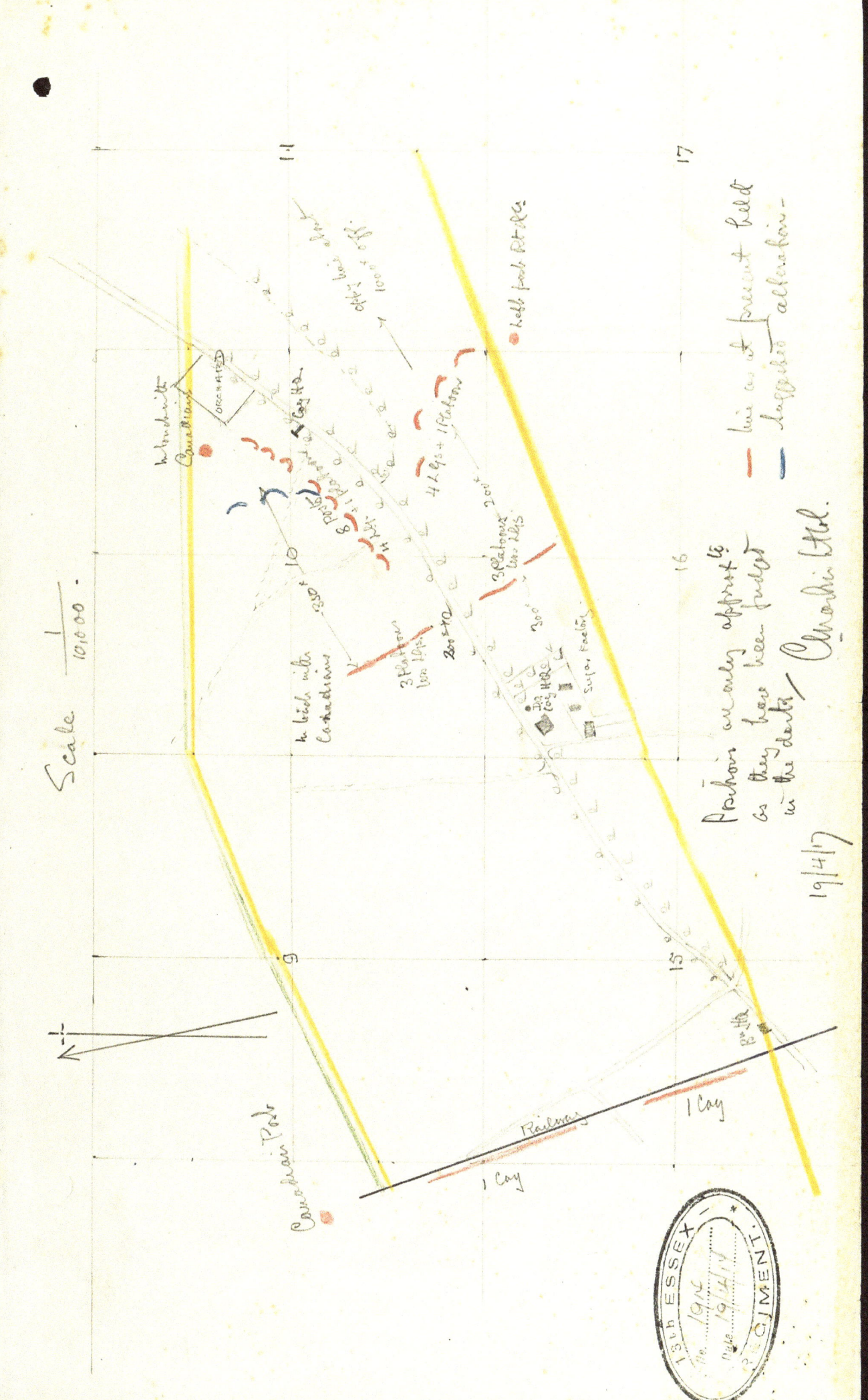

SECRET   Operation Orders No. 100   Copy. No. 1
                 by Lieut. Col. C. MARTIN
Map.   Cmdg: 13th Bn. Essex Regt.   April 27th 1917
OPPY 1/5000.

The Battalion will carry out an attack as marked on Sketch Map, on "Z" Day.

"Z" Day will be notified later.

The attack will be carried out by the 2nd Division, the 6th Brigade on the RIGHT, & the 5th Brigade on the LEFT.

The 63rd (ROYAL NAVAL DIVISION) will be on the RIGHT and the 1st CANADIAN DIVISION on the LEFT of the 2nd Division respectively.

DIVIDING LINE. Dividing line with the Battalion of the Division on the RIGHT, will be from enemy front line at B.24.b.5.8. to C.14.d.0.1.

Dividing line with 17th MIDDLESEX on the LEFT will be from SOUTH EDGE of OPPY WOOD and VILLAGE to C.14.a.0.2.

DISPOSITIONS OF THE 6th BRIGADE. 13th ESSEX on the RIGHT. 17th MIDDLESEX on the LEFT.

DISPOSITIONS OF BATTALION
RIGHT to LEFT.

"B"   "C"   "D"   "A"

Each company will have a frontage of 120 yds.

METHOD OF CARRYING OUT ATTACK

Companies will be organized in three platoons and the Battalion will advance in three WAVES.

One platoon from each Company will form the first wave.
           Do.   Do.   2nd WAVE
           Do.   Do.   3rd WAVE

First WAVE   1st OBJECTIVE
Second WAVE   2nd OBJECTIVE
Third WAVE   GREEN LINE

First WAVE will advance at ZERO, others at 50 yds distance.

OBJECTIVES.
1st OBJECTIVE.   SOUTH of OPPY VILLAGE, at C.13.a.4.1. to C.19.a.8.9.
2nd OBJECTIVE   From track at C.13.b.3.3 to C.13.d.4.0.
GREEN LINE.   From C.14.a.0.2. to C.14.c.0.1.

One company of 2nd SOUTH STAFFS will be attached to the Battalion from 12 noon "Y/Z" day.

This company will supply garrison for two strong points and "moppers up."

Carrying parties are detailed from 1st KINGS and 2nd SOUTH STAFFS.

MOPPERS UP. "Moppers up" of various waves will follow up twenty yds in rear of their respective waves. They will join their companies to which they were originally attached after mopping up.

(1)

MOPPERS UP (Cont'd)   1st WAVE. GERMAN FRONT LINE, 1 Officer and 40 other ranks.
10 men will be specially told off for communication trench running from B.18.d.4.3. to B.16.d.6.2.
Six men at B.18.d.7.6.
Six men at B.18.d.8.8.
2nd WAVE. Twenty men for group of practice trenches running in B.13.d.
Six bombers under an N.C.O. to follow communication trench running N.E. through B.13.d.

ARTILLERY   <u>The Artillery barrage is the guiding factor as to the pace of infantry advancing.</u> It must be impressed on all ranks taking part in the attack that it is absolutely essential to advance close up to the barrage, & that they must assault any portion of the enemy trench or position opposite them, immediately the barrage lifts off it.
Barrage tables will be forwarded later.
The protective barrage will halt 500 yds EAST of the GREEN LINE and companies will consolidate 100 yds in front of trench. This consolidation will take the form of strong points.

PATROLS.   On gaining the GREEN LINE, patrols will be sent forward to NEUVIREUIL immediately the protective barrage lifts.
All ground gained must be consolidated immediately, & one shovel every fourth man will be carried for this purpose in all waves.

STOKES MORTARS   Two Stokes mortars will join in with the Artillery barrage on enemy front line at ZERO.
Two mortars will be attached to the battalion & will move forward with 4th WAVE and proceed to a point where track crosses trench at B.13.B.8.1.

STRONG POINTS   Strong points will be made as follows:-
DIVISIONAL BOUNDARY at C.13.a.5.0. and C.13.B.4.1.
Garrison of each strong point will be two Vickers Guns and an officer & 16 other ranks from the 2nd SOUTH STAFFS REGT.
These garrisons will move with 4th WAVE and will proceed direct to their posts & commence consolidation.

FORMATION OF FORWARD POSTS.   On reaching the line of the final objective (GREEN LINE) strong points will be established in touch with & supporting each other 100 yds in front of enemy trench.

COMMUNICATIONS   Relay posts will be established as follows:-
(1) B.18.c.7.6.
(2) B.18.d.8.5.
(3) C.13.c.2.5.
Each post will be established under Battalion arrangements and will consist of 4 Runners & 2 Signallers.
Posts will be marked by BLUE FLAG on the ground.
A rifle shutter will be set up for guiding purposes.
Every effort is to be made to obtain visual signalling.
O.S.C. Companies will send in hourly reports from ZERO onwards.
All Company Commanders or Platoon Commanders on reaching their objectives will forward Field Message Cards with sketch maps showing position & whether touch has be obtained with flanks.

(2)

COMMUNICATIONS (Cont'd)   A contact aeroplane will fly over our line at 4 am.
Flares will be lit and mirrors flashed. This will be done when the contact aeroplane sounds his KLAXON HORN or fires a VERY LIGHT.

The marking of Contact Patrol machines of No. 5. Squadron R.F.C. (attached to XIIIth Corps) is as follows:—

Two black bands under each bottom plane.

Four streamers, one on each inner inter plane strut, on both right & left planes.

POSITION OF HEADQUARTERS   Brigade Headquarters B.21.a.6.8.
Battalion Headquarters. ROAD JUNCTION B.17.d.3.4.

FOOD & WATER SUPPLY   Reserve ration dump will be at B.16.a.

Iron rations will be issued on "Y" day, consisting of two cheese sandwiches per man.

Rations will be brought up to BAILLEUL Stn. for consumption on day after ZERO.

Guides will meet ration parties at the Station.

Reserve water will be drawn from front line at the rate of 50 petrol tins per Battalion.

WATCHES.   Watches to be synchronized on "Y" day.

CARRYING PARTIES.   One N.C.O & 16 men per company. O.C. companies will ensure that these men are sent back to fetch more material.

DRESS.   Fighting Order. One days rations & Iron Rations to be carried & water bottles filled. The following will also be carried.

  2 Bombs per man, (No 5. Mills)
  Bombers 10 bombs. (Mills)
  Rifle Bombers. 10 No. 23. Grenades
  Every man to carry one flare & 120 rounds of S.A.A.
  2 Sandbags per man.
  32 magazines per Lewis Gun will be carried.

Extra Lewis Guns from 1/5 SOUTH STAFFS. Two will be attached to 'A' Coy & two to 'B' Coy.

Every man to have a round in chamber when advancing.

Special parties will be told off to deal with enemy machine gun emplacements behind enemy's front line & enemy traverses.

WOUNDED.   All walking wounded must bring down their equipment.

PRISONERS.   Prisoners to be sent to cage in ROCLINCOURT at Cross Roads A.28.a.

All officers will be examined and all wounded etc at once taken to Bn. HQs.

An escort of one man per ten prisoners will be allowed. He will demand a receipt on handing over to Divisional cage.

AID POSTS.   Regimental Aid Post at Battalion HQs. The following Aid Posts will be established:—

  B.16.a.3.8. (SUGAR FACTORY)
  B.15.c.8.7. (SUNKEN ROAD)
  B.21.c.7.7. (BAILLEUL STN)

(3)

S.O.S. The S.O.S. signal for barrage fire will be as under, one GREEN, one RED lights fired in rapid succession.

The signal will be repeated at short intervals until the Artillery comply with the signal.

A succession of WHITE lights remains the signal for lengthen range.

NOTES. The 4th WAVE will consist of TRENCH MORTARS, five VICKERS GUNS and garrison of strong points.

On arrival at objectives O.C. Coys will form Company dumps of bombs.

       (sgd) C. Martin Lieut-Col.
       Cmdg: 13th Bn. Essex Regt.

Copy No 1. Commanding Officer
   2. 2nd in Command.
   3. O.C. "A" Coy.
   4. O.C. "B" Coy.
   5. O.C. "C" Coy.
   6. O.C. "D" Coy.
   7. Signalling Officer
   8. Lewis Gun Officer.
   9.
   10.
   11.
   12.
   13. Orderly Room.

NARRATIVE of OPERATIONS on 28th April, 1917.

13th Bn. ESSEX Regt. & 17th Bn. MIDDLESEX Regt.

Battalions were formed up in their jumping off positions about 2 a.m., without any hitch occurring, in spite of steady shelling of the front area. Companies were organized in three platoons, one platoon of each company representing 1st, 2nd and 3rd waves, each wave consisting of two lines -
    1st line - Bombers and Riflemen.
    2nd line - Lewis Gunners & Rifle Bombers.
'Moppers Up' for each wave were formed up in rear of the 2nd line.

Carrying parties and garrisons for strong points were formed up in rear of the last wave.

Close touch was gained with the H.L.I., the 17th MIDDLESEX and the R.M.L.I.

At 4.25 a.m. our own barrage came down and at 4.33 a.m. the 1st wave crossed the enemy's front line trench, with the exception of the extreme right of the 13th ESSEX, who were held up by uncut wire, and lost heavily from Machine Gun fire in endeavouring to get through it. At this period touch was entirely lost with the R.ML.I. on our Right, who had apparently failed to cross the German front line. It was maintained between the 13th ESSEX and 17th MIDDLESEX, but was lost with the H.L.I. on our Left, their right being held up at about the Trench Junction B.12.d.2.0.

The advance continued under the barrage to the line of the practise trenches in C.13.d. - LINK TRENCH - EASTERN End of OPPY WOOD. A small party of the MIDDLESEX gained a footing in the trench and Strong Point at C.7.c.5.3., but failed to hold it.

At this period strong parties of German Bombers were attacking our right flank from the direction of the enemy's front line trench and the SUNKEN ROAD in B.24.b. Heavy Machine Gun and Rifle Fire was enfilading the 13th ESSEX Regt. from the direction of OPPY VILLAGE; Machine Guns were seen being placed in position on the roofs of the houses and firing through loop-holes in the walls, also enemy snipers were observed in the trees in OPPY WOOD. The 17th MIDDLESEX Regt. were under heavy M.G. and Rifle Fire from direction of OPPY VILLAGE.

At 5.50 a.m. I ordered one Company - 70 strong - with 4 Lewis Guns, to advance and form a defensive flank from B.18.d.5.0. - Sunken Road - Southern End of Practise Trenches - to organize bombing parties and bomb South down enemy's front line trench in conjunction with the R.M.L.I. on our Right, who were bombing North up this trench Two Trench Mortars were sent forward to assist in this enterprise.

The greatest determination was to be displayed to clear the area in rear of the advanced troops and secure the right flank. This Company was apparently unable to proceed further than the British front line owing to hostile barrage and M.G. fire. A Senior Officer from each Battalion was sent forward to report on the situation, only one of them returned.

Between 6 and 7 a.m. the situation was as follows :-
Right flank. Enemy had gained a footing in their front line trench, but were held on the line of the Sunken Road.
Front. Strong parties of the enemy were observed crossing the Ridge in C.14.a. and c. advancing S.W. and shortly afterwards the advanced troops were heavily attacked on the right front and from OPPY VILLAGE.
Left Flank. About 2 Companies of the enemy advanced from the direction of the CRUCIFIX into OPPY WOOD, part attacking through the Wood West and part advancing South and attacking the rear of the troops holding the Sunken Road.

1 Company 1st R.BERKS were sent forward to secure the left flank of 17th MIDDLESEX, but did not succeed in reaching the German front line; very severe hand to hand fighting ensued and owing to lack of ammunition and bombs, the troops were forced to retire on the German front line.

At about 9 a.m. I ordered both Battalions to hold and consolidate the German front line. Parties of the enemy were already in occupation of this line and the elements of the advanced troops

= 2 =

who succeeded in reaching it were apparently unable to clear it. Small detached parties held on till dark, when they retired on the British Front Line.

                                                 Lieut. Colonel,

1/5/17.   Commanding, 13th Essex Regiment.

6th Brigade.

2nd Division.

13th BATTALION

THE ESSEX REGIMENT

M A Y 1917.

Battalion Orders attached.

Army Form C.

WAR DIARY
or
INTELLIGENCE SUMMARY.
(Erase heading not required.)

Vol 8

CONFIDENTIAL
WAR DIARY
OF
13TH BN ESSEX REGT.
FROM
MAY 1ST 1917 — MAY 31ST 1917

WAR DIARY
or
INTELLIGENCE SUMMARY.
(Erase heading not required.)

Army Form C. 2118.

Place	Date	Hour	Summary of Events and Information	Remarks and references to Appendices
ECURIE to MARŒUIL	May 1st	5pm	Battalion moved to huts at MARŒUIL (Companies in billets) arriving there about 6.30 pm. Distance about 4 miles. Capt R.S.B. PINCHARD rejoined a Medical Board of 1 month & strength from 26.4.17 and Lieut. W.S. McLAREN. Lieut. R.C.H. MAY proceeded for course at the Corps Infantry School. Reorganisation of Battalion proceeded with. Training in Close Order Drill.	
MARŒUIL	2nd	9am & 3pm	Musketry, Lewis Gunnery, Bombing &c.	
do	3rd	9am & 3pm	Battalion carried out training as yesterday Lieut H.L. BROOKE joined for duty reported to "D" Coy. Lieut F.J. SOUTHERN rejoined from hospital today. Reorganisation proceeded with. Lieut R.G. TREBILCO (O.C. "D" Coy) Lieut F.H. AUSTIN & Lieut R.B. TONKIN & the 120 O.R. who proceeded on 30.4.17 to make 1st KINGS REGT. up to strength, made, as part of the Composite Brigade attacking, an attack in the OPPY SECTOR The Brigade failed to hold the ground gained. 5 OR Killed, 1 OR Died of Wounds, 16 OR Wounded. 6 OR Missing. Cionallis to detachment.	

WAR DIARY
or
INTELLIGENCE SUMMARY.
(Erase heading not required.)

Army Form C. 2118.

Place	Date	Hour	Summary of Events and Information	Remarks and references to Appendices
MARŒUIL to ROCLINCOURT	4	9 am from	Battalion training carried out, also company organization under their respective instructors. Battalion moved into Tent Camp near ROCLINCOURT arriving about 3 p.m. into Tent Camp. Being erected by the Battalion on arrival. Lieut/Col. C. MARTIN relinquishes temporary command of 6th Infantry Brigade from today, & returns to 2nd Bn. H.L.I. & resumes temporary command of the Battalion from today & Major A.E.F. HARRIS D.S.O. is attached to the 6th Infantry Brigade.	ROCLINCOURT Sketch Hereto G.I.O.B. O.O. 107
ROCLINCOURT	5	9 am from	Training carried out — Box Respirator Drill, Company organization parade & tests, there being Specialist under their respective instructors. 2/Lieut. A.P. CHURCHILL in charge of establishment from 12.2.17. 2/Lieut. H.E. MANN has evacuated to England sick on 25.4.17.	Information received Also
Do.	6		Sunday. Church Parade held at 10 a.m. The Battalion (less two Gunners undergoing training, & necessary special duty men) paraded at 12.15 p.m. & proceeded for bath to BAILLEUL light Railway. Lewis Gunners practice under their instructor at 3pm. For Lewis Gunnery.	(Also two Gunners Lewis Gunners practice

Army Form C. 2118.

WAR DIARY
or
INTELLIGENCE SUMMARY.
(Erase heading not required.)

Instructions regarding War Diaries and Intelligence Summaries are contained in F. S. Regs., Part II. and the Staff Manual respectively. Title pages will be prepared in manuscript.

Place	Date	Hour	Summary of Events and Information	Remarks and references to Appendices
ROCLINCOURT	7"	9.30 am	Battalion (Lewis Gun Teams undergoing instruction, 9 nursery camp duties) paraded for work in Light Railway BAILLEUL. Lewis Gunners paraded for instruction under their instructors. Battalion returned from work about 3 p.m. 3 O.R. reported "missing" 28.4.17 was reported "wounded" 28.4.17. 1 O.R. previously reported "missing" 28.4.17 was reported died of wounds. Information received that R.A.P. FORKHARD is struck off establishment from 12.2.17.	
do	8"	9.30 am	Battalion paraded for work as yesterday, returning to camp about 3 p.m. Lewis Gunners & Snipers paraded for instruction under their respective instructors.	
	6.30 pm		Inspection of the Battalion by the Medical Officer.	
do	9"	9.30 am	3 O.R. not reported "missing" 28.4.17 are now reported wounded & 1 sick. Battalion paraded for work as yesterday. (The Signallers, Lewis Gunners, Bombers & Snipers) Specialists paraded under their respective instructors. the Battalion during the month of April salvaged dues to the value of £ 531.1.0 - the highest in the Brigade & third highest in the Division.	
do	10"	9.30 am	Battalion paraded for work as Light Railway as yesterday. Specialists paraded under their respective instructors for training.	

Army Form C. 2118.

WAR DIARY
or
INTELLIGENCE SUMMARY.
(Erase heading not required.)

Instructions regarding War Diaries and Intelligence Summaries are contained in F. S. Regs., Part II. and the Staff Manual respectively. Title pages will be prepared in manuscript.

Place	Date	Hour	Summary of Events and Information	Remarks and references to Appendices
ROLLANCOURT	11th	9.30am	Battalion paraded for route march & right training as yesterday, returning about 3 p.m. Specialists paraded from 9am to 3.30pm for training under their respective instructors.	
do	12th	9.30am	Woke in right training carried out by Battalion as yesterday, returning about 3pm. Specialists paraded for instruction under their respective instructors from 9am to 3pm.	
do	13th	10 am.	Battalion paraded for Divine Service in the open. The Commanding Officer inspected the Battalion.	
do	14th	9.15am	The Battalion, less all specialists & one platoon of "D" Coy, paraded for route march on BAILLEUL Road & Tréléo. The platoon of "D" Coy paraded with the 17th Middlesex Regt. for route march under their orders. All specialists paraded for training under their respective instructors.	
	6.30pm	The Battalion paraded by companies for half an hour voluntary arms drill & Bayonet fighting.	
		# OR not previously reported was reported "missing" 28.4.17.	
do	15th	9.30am	Battalion paraded for route march on BAILLEUL Road & Tréléo returning to Camp about 9.30 pm. Specialists paraded for training under their respective instructors. One platoon of "D" Coy paraded for route march with the 17th Middlesex Regt. as yesterday. Information received that (Hon.) /Capt. H.T. SAVINGS was evacuated to England wounded on 9.5.17.	

Army Form C. 2118.

WAR DIARY
or
INTELLIGENCE SUMMARY.
(Erase heading not required.)

Instructions regarding War Diaries and Intelligence Summaries are contained in F. S. Regs., Part II and the Staff Manual respectively. Title pages will be prepared in manuscript.

Place	Date	Hour	Summary of Events and Information	Remarks and references to Appendices
ROCLINCOURT	15th 16th	4.30am	Lt. Col. D.F.F. HARRIS DSO relinquished temporary command of the 6th Infantry Brigade. Battalion (less Specialists & 1 Platoon of "D" Coy) paraded for work on BAILLEUL Road at 3 p.m. Specialists paraded for training under their respective instructors. The Platoon of "D" Coy were attached to 17th Middlesex Regt. for work as yesterday. One Platoon of "B" Coy attached 2nd I Staffs for work as rado. A/Lt. Col. A.F.F. HARRIS DSO. Assumed Command 8th Battalion. 2/Major B.D. DERVICHE-JONES. MC. Resumed the duties of 2nd in Command.	
do.	17th	4.30am	Battalion paraded as yesterday for work on rado, one platoon of "D" Coy and one platoon of "C" Coy being attached to the 17th Middlesex & 9th S Staffs respectively. Specialists paraded for training under respective instructors. 2/Major P.D. DERVICHE-JONES MC. proceeded to take over command of the 1st King's Regt. relinquishing the appointment of 2nd in Command of this Battalion. Lieut. C.C. COKE (O.C. "C" Coy) granted permission to use the Badges of the rank of Captain from 16.5.17.	
ROCLINCOURT to CAMBLAIN-CHATELAINE	18th	11am	The Battalion proceeded by buses to billets in CAMBLAIN-CHATELAINE arriving there about 4 p.m. Distance about 22 miles.	L/43 Sheet 11 1/40000 C.O. 102

Army Form C. 2118.

WAR DIARY
or
INTELLIGENCE SUMMARY.
(Erase heading not required.)

Instructions regarding War Diaries and Intelligence Summaries are contained in F.S. Regs., Part II. and the Staff Manual respectively. Title pages will be prepared in manuscript.

Place	Date	Hour	Summary of Events and Information	Remarks and references to Appendices

CAMBRAIN - CHATELAINE	18th		The following Officers were granted permission to wear the Insignia of the rank of Captain whilst commanding Companies.
			
			    Lieut. R.G. BOX. "B"
			    Lieut. H.V. COOK. "D"
			    Lieut. R.J. TREBILCO. "A"	

do	19th		Battalion training carried on as per attached programme. Following receiving 6pm (a) of the notes. Draft of 25 OR signed. Draft of 21 OR joined. Lieut & A/Capt F.D. JEANS proceeded on leave to England. This being of per schedule M. LANG assumed the duties of A/Capt during the absence of Lieut F.D. JEANS. Lieut C.W. PHILIPS joined the Battalion for duty, & is posted to "B" Coy.	
do	20th		Battalion training carried out as per attached programme of training, & according to para (A) - 7th note.	
do	21st		Battalion training carried out as per attached programme recovering para (b) of the note. Lieut. F.R KEEBLE rejoined the Battalion from England & took over command of "B" Coy. (A/Capt) Capt R.G. BOX relinquished the acting rank of Captain. Capt J.G.H. KENNEFICK returned from XIII Corps Draft training Depot & resumed	

Army Form C. 2118.

WAR DIARY
or
INTELLIGENCE SUMMARY.
(Erase heading not required.)

Instructions regarding War Diaries and Intelligence Summaries are contained in F. S. Regs., Part II. and the Staff Manual respectively. Title pages will be prepared in manuscript.

Place	Date	Hour	Summary of Events and Information	Remarks and references to Appendices
CAMBLAIN-CHATENAIE	21st		Command of "A" Coy. Lieut (a/Capt) R.J. TREBILCO relinquished the acting rank of Captain. Lieut H.T. JESSOP and Lieut J.D. STEELE rejoined from XIII Corps Staff Training Depot.	
do	22nd		Battalion training as programme attached. For the purpose of training the Battalion was organised in two Coys area — "A" & "B" forming No 1 Coy under Capt J.G.H. KENNEDY and "C" & "D" forming No 2 Coy under a/Capt. C.C. COPE. Lieut F.A. PATTERSON joined for duty and is posted to "B" Coy.	
do	23rd		Training carried out by the Battalion as per programme. Draft of 12 OR joined.	
do	24th		Training carried out as programme attached. Companies paraded under their respective Commanders and not as on the 22nd & 23rd.	
CAMBLAIN-CHATELAINE to ROCLINCOURT	25th	4.15am	Battalion moved to Hut Camp ROCLINCOURT Area, by train, a distance of almost 22 miles, arriving at 10.30 am. Lieut R.G. BOX admitted to hospital. Lieut H.T. JESSOP (W) a/Capt. C.C. COPE proceeded on leave to England.	HENS Sheet 11/10000. O.O. 103.
ROCLINCOURT	26th		Assumed command of "C" Coy during the absence of a/Capt C.C. COPE. Battalion training carried out from 9am to 8pm. Speciatists under their respective instructors. Working party of 21 OR supplied for frozen huts.	

2353 Wt W3544/1454 700,000 5/15 D. D. & L. A.D.S.S./Forms/C. 2118.

Army Form C. 2118.

WAR DIARY
or
INTELLIGENCE SUMMARY.
(Erase heading not required.)

Instructions regarding War Diaries and Intelligence Summaries are contained in F. S. Regs. Part II. and the Staff Manual respectively. Title pages will be prepared in manuscript.

Place	Date	Hour	Summary of Events and Information	Remarks and references to Appendices
ROCLINCOURT	26th		The following Officers & O.R. were "mentioned in Despatches." (Supplement to London Gazette 25.5.17).	
			Capt. (A/Major) A.G. HAYWARD MC.	
			Capt. S.E. COLLIER MC.	
			Lieut. G. SIMPSON	
			4th Lieut. of Yorks & Lancs. H. LANG.	
			18498 A/Cpl HORNSBY J. "D" Coy.	
			43076 Pte NOBLE A.M. "C" Coy.	
	27th	9.30am	A Court of Enquiry, composed of undermentioned, assembled, to investigate the cause of the loss of three Guns belonging to this Unit during recent operations in the OPPY SECTOR.	
			Lieut. F.R. KEEBLE. MC — President	
			[Lieut. A.R. WELLS] Members	
			[Lieut. R.J. TREBILCO.]	
Do.	27th	11.45am	Sunday. Divine Service on Bn. Parade Ground.	
Do.	28th		Battalion Training carried out. Specialist parading under their respective instructors.	

WAR DIARY
or
INTELLIGENCE SUMMARY.
(Erase heading not required.)

Army Form C. 2118.

Place	Date	Hour	Summary of Events and Information	Remarks and references to Appendices
ROUNDCOURT.	28th		Lieut F.R. KEEBLE admitted to Hospital. 2/Major A.D. DERVICHE-JONES, MC proceeded to Fifth Army with a view to taking over Command of the Battalion. Woking Party of 21 OR supplied.	
Do.	29th		Training carried out by the Battalion from 9am to 3.30pm. Specialists under their respective instructors. Lieut. N.B. BABONEAU was admitted to Hospital.	
Do.	30th		Battalion training from 9am to 3.30pm. Specialists paraded under their respective instructors. 2/Capt. H.V. COOK is transferred from "D" Coy to "C" Coy & Lieut H.T. JESSOP is transferred from "C" Coy to "D" Coy & takes over Command of same. Lieut F.H. AUSTIN	
Do.	31st		Training carried out as per programme issued. Returned from Corps Lewis Gun School.	

Attn: Lieut Colonel
Cmdg. 13 Bn. Essex Regt.

2353 Wt W2544/1454 700,000 5/15 D.D. & L. A.D.S.S./Forms/C. 2118.

13th Bn. ESSEX REGT   COPY No. 13

SECRET   OPERATION ORDER No. 101   May 5th 1917

Ref. Map. 51.B. N.W.

(1) The Battalion will move to Tent Camp in ROCLINCOURT area today 5th inst.

(2) (a) Parade on Battalion Parade Ground in column of companies facing N.E.
DRESS. Full marching order. Steel Helmets to be worn.
   (b) ROUTE. MAROEUIL - Cross Country Track to A.29.c.5.4.
   (c) Parade 1.45.pm. ready to move off.
   (d) Order of March.
Headquarters., "B" Coy., "C" Coy., "D" Coy., "A" Coy.
   (e) Intervals between companies 300 yds.

(3) Blankets (tightly rolled in bundles of ten) Officers Kits, Mess Canteens, to be stacked at the Quartermasters Stores at once, ready for loading.
Lewis Guns, Spare Parts, Ammunition, etc., to be at same place at once.

(4) Dinners to be served at 12.15 pm.
Teas to be served on arrival.

(5) Billets and Huts to be left scrupulously clean and certificates to this effect to be rendered to Orderly Room before moving off.

(6) Completion of move to be reported personally by Company Commanders.

(sgd) F.A.JENNS 2/Lt & A/Adjt.

Issued at 11.15.am.   13th Bn. ESSEX REGT.

Copy No. (1) Commanding Officer
         (2) Adjutant
         (3) O.C. "A" Coy.
         (4) O.C. "B" Coy.
         (5) O.C. "C" Coy.
         (6) O.C. "D" Coy.
         (7) Quartermaster
         (8) Transport Officer.
         (9) Medical Officer
         (10) Signalling Officer
         (11) R.S.M.
         (12) & (13) War Diary.

SECRET.
OPERATION ORDERS.
13th Bn. ESSEX REGT.   No. 107.

Ref.Map. LENS Sheet 11 1/100000.

(1) **DESTINATION.**   The Battalion will move to "D" Camp ROCLINCOURT by buses tomorrow 28th inst.

(2) **PARADE.**   Parade on Battalion Parade Ground at 4.15.am. in the following order :-
H.Qs "A" "B" "C" "D" Coys.
DRESS. Full Marching Order, with Blanket and steel helmet carried on pack.
ROUTE. DIVION - HOUDAIN - ESTREE CAUCHIE - ANZIN

(3) **EMBUSSING & DEBUSSING.**   Troops for embussing will be distributed along the roadside as follows:-

For seated lorries.   6 Groups (of 20 men each) per 80 yards of road space.

For Omnibuses   6 Groups (of 25 men each) per 80 yards of road space)

Company Commanders will send an Officer to Bus rendezvous at 4.45.am. to secure buses for their respective Companies.

Companies will rest on Parade Ground until arrival of buses.

Officers will be distributed among the buses and no one vehicle will be reserved for Officers only.

Two N.C.Os per bus to be detailed to sit in front of same and warn occupants of overhead wire.

Buses will be at the T road 50 yards SOUTH of Battalion Headquarters.

(4) **KITS etc.**   Officers Kits, Mess Canteens, Lewis Guns, Spare Parts, Ammunition, etc., to be stacked at the Q.M. Stores at 4.30.am. WITHOUT FAIL, ready for loading.

Orderly Room boxes at the same time and same place.

(5) **TRANSPORT.**   Will be under the arrangements of the Transport Officer.

2/Lieut. R.J. TREBILCO will act as Assistant Transport Officer.

(6) **BILLETS.**   All billets to be left scrupulously clean and certificates to this effect together with "No damage" certificates will be rendered to Orderly Room at 4.30.am.

(7) **MEALS.**   Breakfast will be served on the Battalion Parade Ground (if fine) at 4.15.am. and all cooking pots, dixies, etc., must be off the Ground by 4.30.am.

Dinners will be cooked on the line of march and will be served at 2.30.pm. in "D" Camp ROCLINCOURT. Haversack Rations will be carried.

(8) **COMPLETION of MOVE.**   To be notified personally by Company Commanders.

REVEILLE 3.15.am. BREAKFAST and SICK PARADE 4.15.am.

(Sgd) NORMAN LANG.
Hon Lt.& A/Adjutant,
13th ESSEX REGT.

Issued at 6.45.pm.

Copy No.1 Commanding Officer.   Copy No.7 Quartermaster.
" No.2 Adjutant.   " No.8 Transport Officer.
" No.3 O.C."A" Coy.   " No.9 Medical Officer.
" No.4 O.C."B" Coy.   " No.10 R.S.M.
" No.5 O.C."C" Coy.   " Nos.11 and 12 War Diary.
" No.6 O.C."D" Coy.

Copy No 12.

13th Bn. The ESSEX REGT

SECRET   OPERATION ORDER No.102   Dec 19th 191
                      MOVE BY BUSES

Ref: Map. IRON Sheet 11. 1/40000

(1) DESTINATION   The Battalion will move to BOUBLAIN-CHATEAUX
                   by buses tomorrow 19th ins. ('C' bus).

(2) PARADE   Parade on Battalion Parade Ground at 11.a.m.
                   in column of companies facing West.
                   ORDER   HQrs., "A", "B", "C", "D" Coys.
                   DRESS   Full Marching Order, with blankets and steel
                   helmet carried on pack.
                   ROUTE   ANZIN - ESTREE-CAUCHIE - WILLIER - DIVION.

(3) EMBUSSING   Troops for embussing will be distributed
    & DEBUSSING   along the roadside as follows :-
                   For Seated Lorries   Six Groups (of 20 men each)
                                           per 80 yds of road space.
                   For Omnibuses   Six Groups (of 25 man each)
                                           per 80 yds of road space.
                   Embussing will begin from the front of each section
                   of the Convoy, unless the embussing point is of
                   sufficient length to fill all vehicles of a section
                   simultaneously.
                   Officers will be distributed among the vehicles, &
                   no one vehicle will be reserved for Officers only.
                   Two N.C.Os per bus to be detailed to sit in front
                   of same, to warn occupants of overhead wires.
                   Rendezvous for buses will be the Cross Roads E. of
                   HOUDIN (A.29.a.6.3.) and will leave that point at
                   12 noon.
                   Company Commanders will send an Officer or C.S.M.
                   to rendezvous at 11.45.am. to secure buses for their
                   respective companies. He will also reconnoitre a
                   place for his Coy to rest until buses arrive and
                   will await the arrival of his company.
                   Eighteen buses are reserved for this Battalion.

(4) KITS, etc.   Officers Kits, Mess Canteens, Lewis Guns, Spare
                   Parts, Ammunition, Orderly Room Boxes, to be stacked
                   at the Q.M.Stores at 8.am. WITHOUT FAIL, ready for
                   loading.   Cycles to be carried by the Transport
                   and will be at same place at same time.

(5) TRANSPORT   1st Line Transport (including Cookers) will
                   march tomorrow under orders of the Bde. T.O. They
                   will pass the Starting Point N.29.a.6.8.(Sheet 51.b
                   just E. of MAROEUIL at 9.am.
                   ORDER 2nd ARTISTS, 13th ESSEX - ROYAL W.Q.
                   1st KINGS, 17th MIDDLESEX.

(6) CAMP   The whole camp to be left scrupulously clean
                   and tidy, and certificates to this effect to be
                   rendered to Orderly Room by 10.30.am.

(7) MEALS   Dinner will be taken in the form of Haversack
                   Rations.   Tea to be served as soon as Cookers arrive

(8) COMPLETION   Completion of move to be reported personally
    OF MOVE   by Company Commanders.

                   REVEILLE   6.am.
                   BREAKFAST   7.am.
                   SICK PARADE   8.am.

                                       (sgd) G.A.BYRNE 2/Lt & a/Adjt.
Issued at 9.30.am.   13th Bn. ESSEX REGT.

       Copy No (1) Commanding Officer   (2) Adjutant
              (3) O.C. "A" Coy   (4) O.C. "B" Coy
              (5) O.C. "C" Coy   (6) O.C. "D" Coy
              (7) Quartermaster   (8) Transport Officer
              (9) Medical Officer   (10) 2/Lieut A.R.ROSS
             (11) R.S.Major   (12) War Diary
                      (13) War Diary

1st DAY

½ hour	Close Order Drill
½ hour	Open Order Drill
2 hours	Musketry: Use and Caring solutions, Sighting, Aim, Trigger, Rapid Loading
1 hour	Specialist Training (Elementary)
	Bombers
	Snipers
	Scouts
	Observers
	Grade Gunners
½ hour	Physical Training and Bomb Throwing
½ hour	Bayonet Fighting
In evening	Small exercise for N.C.O's

2nd DAY

½ hour	Close Order Drill (Platoon)
½ hour	Open Order Drill (Platoon)
2 hours	Musketry, Rifle Exercises, Sighting, Rapid Loading
1 hour	Specialist Training (Elementary)
½ hour	Bayonet Fighting
1 hour	Night Patrolling

3rd DAY

½ hour	Close Order Drill
½ hour	Open Order Drill (Platoon)
2 hours	Musketry, Rifle Exercises, Rapid Loading
1 hour	Specialist Training (Elementary)
½ hour	Physical Training and Bomb Throwing
½ hour	Use of cover, and advancing under cover
In evening	Small exercise for N.C.O's

4th DAY

½ hour	Close Order Drill (Section)
2 hours	Musketry, Rifle Exercises, Sighting, Rapid Loading
2 hours	Scheme - Platoon in attack or defence, for Bombers, Snipers, Scouts
1 hour	Specialist Training (Night)

5th DAY

½ hour	Close Order Drill (Company)
½ hour	Open Order Drill (Company)
2 hours	Musketry, Rifle Exercises, Sighting, Rapid Loading
1 hour	Specialist Training (Elementary)
½ hour	Bayonet Fighting
½ hour	Physical Training and Bomb Throwing
In evening	Small exercise for N.C.O's

1st DAY

½ hour	Close Order Drill } Company
½ hour	Open Order Drill }
2 hours	Musketry. Use Fred...th Rules, Range...
1½ hours	Specialist Training (Tren...)
1 hour	Administration and Command Arrangem Platoon(?)
Remaining	Small Exercise for Battalion Company Commdrs.

2nd DAY

½ hour	Close Order Drill } Company
½ hour	Open Order Drill }
2 hours	Musketry. Firing and Parties on Range
½ hour	Bayonet Fighting
1 day	Specialist Training (Atta...
4 hours	(Attack on Trench.
	(Infiltration and Forming Advanced Posts...(?)
	Defence of Flanks.

3rd DAY

½ hour	Close Order Drill } Company
½ hour	Open Order Drill }
2 hours	Musketry. Bay... for Drill, Judging Distance
½ hour	Physical Training and Bomb Throwing
½ hour	Bayonet Fighting
4½ hours	(Firing on ...
	(Attack on T... ... ...

4th DAY

1 hour	Battalion Drill
4 hours	(Trench Attack
	(Defence of Flank
	(Holding Pts...
	(Infiltration and Advanced Posts...

5th DAY

1 hour	...
4 hours	...

6th Brigade.
2hd Division.

13th BATTALION

THE ESSEX REGIMENT

JUNE 1917.

WAR DIARY
or
INTELLIGENCE SUMMARY.

(Erase heading not required.)

Army Form C. 2118.

CONFIDENTIAL

WAR — DIARY

OF

13TH BN ESSEX REGT

FROM

JUNE 1ST 1917 — JUNE 30TH 1917

WAR DIARY
or
INTELLIGENCE SUMMARY.

Army Form C. 2118.

Place	Date	Hour	Summary of Events and Information	Remarks and references to Appendices
ECURIE	JUNE 1st		Training according to programme issued last month carried out under their respective instructors. Working parties of 280 OR supplied. Lieut. H.T. JESSOP took over command of "D" Coy on 30/5/17 vice a/Capt H.V. COOK transferred to "C" Coy. 2/Lieut. 6vt. over command of same. 2/Lieut F.H. AUSTIN assumed command of "B" Coy. 2/Lieut E.H. SHERMAN (Wounded 26/4/17) transferred to England.	
Do.	2nd		The Battalion carried out training as yesterday, the Specialists parading under their own instructors. Working parties of 230 OR supplied. 2/Lieut R.B. TOMKIN returned from Lewis Gun Course. 2/Lieut F.A. JENNS relieved from leave. Hon Lieut & Quartermaster N. LANG relinquished the duties of a/Adjutant. Casualties :- 1 OR. (belonging to advance party sent to line) wounded. 1 OR. previously reported wounded died of wounds.	
Do.	3rd	9.45am	Sunday. The Battalion paraded for Divine Service in Cinema hut ECURIE. 2/Lieut E.A. PATTERSON proceeded on course at Corps Infantry School. The following awarded the MILITARY MEDAL for conspicuous bravery in	

WAR DIARY
or
INTELLIGENCE SUMMARY.
(Erase heading not required.)

Army Form C. 2118.

Instructions regarding War Diaries and Intelligence Summaries are contained in F.S. Regs., Part II. and the Staff Manual respectively. Title pages will be prepared in manuscript.

Place	Date	Hour	Summary of Events and Information	Remarks and references to Appendices
ECURIE & LINE	3d		In Field.	
			A/Major A.B. McFARLANE GRIEVE joined for duty & is appointed 2/I end in Command. Casualties:- 1 OR wounded by airplane bomb. The Battalion relieved the 2nd Bn. A.I.F. in the RIGHT Sub-Sector, ARLEUX SECTOR. Dispositions:- "A" Company RIGHT FRONT "B" " LEFT FRONT "C" " RIGHT SUPPORT "D" " LEFT SUPPORT Bn. Hqrs. near ARLEUX.	38673 L/Cpl MANNING A. "D" 2390 Pte. WOOD H.E. "C" 19914 " PEACOCK W.J. "D" O.O. 105. Ref.map. 51.B. NW 1/20,000.
LINE	4th		Battalion holding line as above. Enemy very quiet. Capt. J.G.H. KENNEFICK relinquished command of "A" Coy. He having Q[uar]termaster H. LANG proceeded on leave. Lieut N.B. BABONEAU evacuated to England sick. Draft of 51 OR joined.	
Do	5th		Battalion holding line, ARLEUX SECTOR. Enemy very quiet, except for occasional	

Army Form C 2118.

WAR DIARY
or
INTELLIGENCE SUMMARY.
(Erase heading not required.)

Place	Date	Hour	Summary of Events and Information	Remarks and references to Appendices
LINE	5ᵈ		Shelling of ARLEUX. Lieut R.J. TREBILCO assumed command of "A" Coy. Casualties:— 1 OR. Wounded. 3 OR. Wounded at Duty. 1 OR. Killed by aeroplane bomb at ETURIE 1 OR. Wounded at duty by aeroplane bomb.	✓
LINE	6ᵈ		Battalion holding line as above. Inter-company relief carried out. dispositions being as follows:— "C" Company — RIGHT FRONT "D" Company — LEFT FRONT "A" Company — RIGHT SUPPORT "B" Company — LEFT SUPPORT The following are extracted from the London Gazette of today. "(Major) A/Lt.Col A.E.F. HARRIS DSO awarded BAR to DSO for gallantry in the field". "Capt. A.A. MACFARLANE-GRIEVE awarded the MILITARY CROSS for gallantry in the field" "Capt. D.W. MURRAY awarded the MILITARY CROSS for gallantry in the field"	✓

WAR DIARY
or
INTELLIGENCE SUMMARY.
(Erase heading not required.)

Army Form C. 2118.

Place	Date	Hour	Summary of Events and Information	Remarks and references to Appendices
LINE	7th		Battalion holding line ARLEUX SECTOR. Enemy very quiet, accordingly our patrols active in case of enemy retirement. Casualties :- 1 OR Wounded.	
			Orders:- 32 OR joined. 4 OR returned from Hospital. a/Capt. C.C. COLE returned from leave.	
do	8th		Battalion holding line ARLEUX SECTOR.	
			Lieut F.H. AUSTIN relinquished command of "B" Company & proceeded on leave to England. Lieut R.B. TONKIN assumed command of "B" Company.	
LINE to SUPPORT LINE	9th		Battalion holding line ARLEUX SECTOR. Battalion relieved by 1st KINGS REGT and moved into SUPPORT AREA, RED LINE, WILLERVAL. Relieved by 1st KINGS REGT.	O.O. No 106. Ref. Maps 51 B. N.W. 1/20m.
			Casualties :- 3 OR accidentally wounded. 2 OR accidentally wounded at duty. Lieut F.R. KEEBLE returned from Hospital. (Lieut) a/Capt H.H. COOK relinquished command of "C" Coy.	
SUPPORT LINE	10th		Sunday. Battalion in Support Line (RED LINE) Battalion Headquarters WILLERVAL. a/Capt. C.C. COLE resumed command of "C" Coy. Lieut R.J. TREFRISCO relinquished command of "A" Company Lieut R.B. TONKIN relinquished command of "B" Coy.	

WAR DIARY
or
INTELLIGENCE SUMMARY.
(Erase heading not required.)

Army Form C. 2118.

Place	Date	Hour	Summary of Events and Information	Remarks and references to Appendices
SUPPORT LINE	10th	(contd)	Lieut F.J. SOUTHERN proceeded for course at First Army Sniping School.	
do	11th		Battalion holding RED LINE, ARLEUX SECTOR. Orders issued in case of Enemy retirement.	C.O. 107 & 108. Attack practice
			Lieut F.R. KETTLE assumed command of "B" Company	
			relinquished command of "A" Company.	HUDD forres.
do	12th		Battalion holding RED LINE ARLEUX SECTOR	
			Lieut. W.S. McLAREN assumed command of "A" Company.	
			24 O.R. (draft) joined for duty. 10 O.R. rejoined from hospital	
do	13th		Battalion holding RED LINE, ARLEUX SECTOR	C.O. 109
do	14th		Battalion holding RED LINE, ARLEUX SECTOR. Battalion relieved by 1st D.C.L.I. and moved	Rd Arb 51 B.
to ROCLINCOURT			to HULL CAMP, ROCLINCOURT, arriving about 1/30 a.m 15.2	
ROCLINCOURT	15th		Battalion in Corps Reserve. Day spent in rest, & cleaning up.	N.W. forres.
			Lieut R.B. TOTHILL proceeded on leave to England.	
do	16th		Training carried out. Training. Specialists paraded under their respective instructors.	
			Lieut G. SMYTHE joined for duty & posted to "A" Company. 2nd Lieut Quartermash	
			H. LANG returned from leave.	
do	14th		Sunday. Divine Service held in the open immediately South of HULL CAMP at 11 a.m.	

WAR DIARY
or
INTELLIGENCE SUMMARY.

Army Form C. 2118.

(Erase heading not required.)

Place	Date	Hour	Summary of Events and Information	Remarks and references to Appendices
ROCLINCOURT	17th (contd)		Lieut. E.L. CORPS joined for duty & posted to "A" Coy. The undermentioned Officers awarded the MILITARY CROSS for gallantry in the field. Lieut. F.A. SHERMAN Lieut. A.R. WELLS. The undermentioned awarded the DISTINGUISHED CONDUCT MEDAL. 17348 Corpl ASH J.J. 43080 Pte HARVEY A.J. (TO ENGLAND for Commission)	Notification through 2nd Div R.O
ROCLINCOURT TO MONT ST ELOY	18th	11.30 p.m	The Battalion moved to billets at MONT ST ELOY, starting at 9.30 p.m and arriving about 11.30 p.m.	C.O. 110 Ref/make SI.B.NW 9/ St. C.N.E. 1/2000
MONT ST ELOY to BETHUNE	19th		Battalion proceeded by lorries to BETHUNE, leaving MONT ST ELOY at 10.30 a.m. and arriving at BETHUNE about 1 p.m. Lieut W.S. McLARTY relinquished command of "A" Company. 2nd Division transferred from XIII Corps to XI Corps.	
BETHUNE to GORRE	20th		Battalion moved into Reserve Billets GIVENCHY SECTOR at GORRE arriving about 6.30 p.m relieving the 2/6th LANCS FUSILIERS (197th INFY. BRIGADE). Lieut R.C.H. MAY assumed command of "A" Company. Lieut E.L CORPS transferred from	G.O. III. Ref Map/o. 36 B/Ypres

WAR DIARY
or
INTELLIGENCE SUMMARY.
(Erase heading not required.)

Army Form 2118.

Instructions regarding War Diaries and Intelligence Summaries are contained in F.S. Regs., Part II. and the Staff Manual respectively. Title pages will be prepared in manuscript.

Place	Date	Hour	Summary of Events and Information	Remarks and references to Appendices
GORRE	20"	(Contd)	"A" Coy & "D" Coy. Lieut C.W. PHILIPS returned from L.G. Course LE TOUQUET.	
do	21st		Lieut H.H. GLEN joined for duty & posted to "C" Company. Strength of 21 OR joined. Training carried out by the Battalion, specialist parading under their own instructors. Capt. S.E. COLLIER MC (Transport Officer) proceeded on leave to England. Capt. J.G.H. KENNEDION assumed the duties of A/Transport Officer. Casualties :- 1 OR died in hospital.	
do	22nd		Battalion carried out training. Specialist training and supplied working parties. Lieut G. SMYTHE proceeded on leave to TOURNEHEM.	
do	23rd		Training carried out, & working parties supplied. Lieut W.A. HARVEY and 9 Instructors returned from XIII Corps Staff Training Depot. Lieut A.G. TIMMS joined for duty and is posted to "A" Company. A draft of 7 OR, 53 OR, and 60 OR joined.	
do	24th		Sunday. Working parties supplied at night by the Battalion. Divine Service (Parade) held in Y.M.C.A. Hut at 10 a.m.	
do	25th		Lieut R.C.A. MAY (of "A" Coy) and Lieut H.L. BROOKE proceeded on leave to PARIS. Training carried out & working parties supplied. Lieut F.H. BUSTIN assumed command of "A" Company.	

Army Form 2118.

WAR DIARY
or
INTELLIGENCE SUMMARY.
(Erase heading not required.)

Instructions regarding War Diaries and Intelligence Summaries are contained in F. S. Regs., Part II. and the Staff Manual respectively. Title pages will be prepared in manuscript.

Place	Date	Hour	Summary of Events and Information	Remarks and references to Appendices
GORRE to LINE	26th		Half days training carried out, & working parties employed in afternoon. The Battalion relieved the 19th MIDDLESEX REGT in the LEFT SUBSECTOR, GIVENCHY SECTOR relief being complete at 1.15 am 27th. Dispositions :— A Company .... RIGHT FRONT B Company .... CENTRE FRONT C Company .... LEFT FRONT D Company .... SUPPORT Bn. Hqrs. .... O.B.L.	
LINE	27th		Battalion holding line as above. Enemy very quiet, except snipers & MGs active at night. Casualties 1 OR killed. 2 OR wounded.	
do.	28th		Battalion holding line as above. Consolidation & repairs to line carried during day and night. Out patrols active.	
do.	29th		Consolidation & repairs to line (including support and O.B.L.) carried out. Working parties up to 1 Officer and 68 OR supplied, and worked under R.E. direction. Inter-company relief carried out — "D" Coy relieving "A" Coy in RIGHT FRONT, and "A" Coy	

Army Form C. 2118.

WAR DIARY
or
INTELLIGENCE SUMMARY.
(Erase heading not required.)

Instructions regarding War Diaries and Intelligence Summaries are contained in F. S. Regs., Part II. and the Staff Manual respectively. Title pages will be prepared in manuscript.

Place	Date	Hour	Summary of Events and Information	Remarks and references to Appendices
LINE	29th		Occupying the Support line.	
S.O.	30th		Battalion holding line GIVENCHY SECTOR. Consolidation and repair carried out. Working parties supplied – 1 Officer and 65 OR.	
			Battalion strength Officers 29. Other Ranks 920.	

Askew
Lieut Colonel
Cmdg. 13th Bn Surrey Regt.

SECRET   13th ESSEX REGT. ORDER No.105.   COPY No.

Ref Map.51.B.NW. 1/20000.   June 2 1917.

RELIEF.   The Battalion will relieve the 2nd. Battalion HIGHLAND LIGHT INFANTRY in the front line, RIGHT SECTION of BRIGADE FRONTAGE known as L.3.ARLEUX SECTOR tomorrow night the 3/4 June.1917.

DISPOSITIONS and ORDER OF RELIEF.

         "A" Coy.   RIGHT FRONT.
         "B" Coy.   LEFT FRONT.
         "C" Coy.   RIGHT SUPPORT.
         "D" Coy.   LEFT SUPPORT.
         Headquarters.

         The leading Company will reach the TUNNEL at RAILWAY EMBANKMENT, B.15.c.6.3. at 9.45.pm. where guides will be stationed, ready to lead them to their company front.

STARTING POINT.
         EAST end of camp. Leading platoon of "A" Coy. to pass starting point at 8.pm.

ROUTE.   DUCKBOARD TRACK and TOMMY TRENCH.
         Intervals of five minutes to be maintained between companies as far as TUNNEL,RAILWAY EMBANKMENT,at B.15.c.6.3. and one minute between platoons after leaving TUNNEL.

DRESS.   Fighting Order. Overcoats in ground sheets on back of belt. Steel helmets to be worn. Water bottles filled with tea. Rations for the 4th inst. to be carried in the haversack and canteen.
         Rifle Bomb Sections will carry 50 rounds S.A.A. and 4 No.23 Rifle Bombs per man.
         Bombing sections will not carry any bombs, but will be equipped with the usual 120 rounds of S.A.A.

KITS etc.   Trench Kits, Mess Canteen, etc., will be carried up under company arrangements.
         Kits etc., not required for the trenches, and packs to be handed in at the Q.M. Stores by 6.pm.

POSITIONS.   Every care is to be taken that all positions, posts, etc., are taken over correctly.

TRENCH STORES.   List of trench stores (if any) taken over, to reach Battalion Headquarters by 9.am. 4th inst.

COMPLETION
OF RELIEF.   To be notified to Battalion Headquarters as follows " Battalion Order No.105 complied with"

HUTS etc.   All huts and surroundings to be left scrupulously clean, and certificates to this effect to be rendered to Battalion Headquarters before moving off.

         The Battalion will remain in the line till about the 14th inst.

                        (Sgd) F.A.JENNS.
                            2/Lieut.& A/Adjutant.
                               13th ESSEX REGT.

No.1 Commanding Officer.
No.2 Adjutant.
No.3 O.C. "A" Coy.   Issued 9.pm.
No.4 O.C. "B" Coy.
No.5 O.C. "C" Coy.
No.6 O.C. "D" Coy.
No.7 Quartermaster.
No.8 Transport Officer.
No.9 Medical Officer.
No.10 2/Lieut.A.R.WELLS.
No.11 R.S.M.
Nos.12 & 13. War Diary.

SECRET   13th Bn. Scot: Rif:
                            Order No. 101.
                                                    9/6/17

Ref. Map. Sh. 3. Map. 9420.

RELIEF. (1) The Battalion will be relieved by 1st King's Regt. on night 9/10th & on relief will take over RED LINE vacated by 1st KINGS REGT.

GUIDES. (2) Following guides will be provided & will be sent to Bn. HQs. to arrive at 10.30 p.m. (9th/10th)

"C" Coy. { 1 guide for RIGHT FLANK PIQUET
         { 1 guide for LEFT FLANK PIQUET

"D" Coy. { 1 guide for RIGHT FLANK PIQUET
         { 1 guide for LEFT FLANK PIQUET

(Note. The Officers commanding relieving companies for FRONT LINE merely require to be shewn the position of the Flank Piquets of the above two companies, and these Officers will then make their own dispositions along their company fronts.)

(3) "A" and "B" Coys will provide 1 guide per Half Company to rendezvous at Battalion HQs at 10.30 p.m. (9th/10th). Each guide will be able to point out the night positions of the two Lewis Guns of his Half Company, & also the centre of his Half Company.

NEW POSITIONS. (4) Directly O.C. relieving Company has stated he is satisfied, Companies will march off independently to their positions in RED LINE accompanied by the two guides mentioned in this Office O.R.637. O.C. Coys reporting previously at Bn. HQs.

RATIONS. (5) Two days rations will be issued tonight & no rations will be issued tomorrow night.

TRENCH STORES (6) heads of Trench Stores to be handed over to reach Bn. HQs. (by the guides) at 10.30 p.m. (9th/10th).

LEWIS GUNS & RIFLE BOMBERS. (7)(a) Transport will NOT be provided for Lewis Guns, etc., these will be carried by Lewis Gun Sections.
Equipment ammunition of Lewis Gun Section will be reduced from 120 to 50 rounds per man.

(b) Equipment ammunition of RIFLE BOMB Sections will be reduced to 50 rounds per man. They will carry away four No.23 Mills bombs per man.

                              (sgd) F. AVENNS. Lieut & Adjt.
Issued at 4 p.m.   13th Bn. Scot. Rif.

Copy No. 1. Commanding Officer   7. O.C. "D" Coy
         2. Second in Command   8. Signalling Officer
         3. Adjutant   9. Medical Officer
         4. O.C. "A" Coy   10. 1st KINGS REGT
         5. O.C. "B" Coy   11. Transport Officer
         6. O.C. "C" Coy   12. R.S.M.
              13. & 14. War Diary.

13th Bn. ESSEX REGT ORDER No.127   Copy No...13

Ref.Map.CHESTER WOOD 1/20000.
(Marked 1st and 2nd Bounds).

INTENTION 1. In event of enemy falling back from his present position the battalion (1st KINGS REGT) occupying the front trenches, will move forward and occupy line of 1st Bound, i.e. about 300 yds E.of RUPERT TRENCH on frontage FOOT ALLEY (inclusive) - U.x.b.x.x.

ADVANCE 2. The 13th ESSEX will, if ordered, advance from present position (RED LINE) in artillery formation and occupy position vacated by 1st KINGS as follows :-
(a) FRONT LINE.   "C" Coy...R.x.a.4.5.(road inclusive)
                          - R.x.b...0.(road excl).
                  "D" Coy...R.x.b.x.x. - R.x.x.x.x.
                                         (bank incl).
(b) SUPPORT LINE "A" Coy...R.x.d.x.x. - R.x.d.x.x.
                                         (bank incl).
                  "B" Coy...R.x.d.x.x. - R.x.x.x.x.
(c)   BN. HQs...R.x.c.x.x.

COMMUNICATION 3.(a) All companies will then immediately obtain touch with Coy HQs of Units on their outer flanks, and report having done so to Battalion HQs.
(b) From this time onwards close touch will be maintained with troops on flanks.
(c) An Officers patrol will be sent forward from each front line Coy to establish touch with 1st KINGS and will maintain touch until 13th ESSEX have passed through them on advance to 2nd Bound.
(d) Battalion Signalling Officer will act in accordance with Bde Special Instructions already issued.

STRONG PATROLS 4. "A" & "B" Coys will each furnish a strong patrol (1 Sgt., 1 Cpl.,15 Ptes). These patrols will consist of specially active men, armed with rifle, bayonet and 220 rds and will report to Battn HQs on receipt of order for Battalion to advance from RED LINE.
They will be commanded by 2/Lieut R.C.W.MAY and 2/Lieut C.W.PHILIPS respectively and will act in accordance with special instructions already issued to these Officers.

EQUIPMENT 5.(a) 150 rounds S.A.A. and 4 No.23 Mills bombs per N.C.O. and man (except Rifle Bombers and L.Gunners).
(b) Rifle Bomb Sections...100 rounds S.A.A. and 4 No.23 Mills per N.C.O. and man.
(c) Lewis Gun Sections...50 rounds S.A.A. per N.C.O. and man, and 4 Magazines per man (except Nos 1 & 2).
(d) 10% picks and 40% shovels slung by a cord.
(e) 1 flare per man.

REPORTS 6. Reports to Battalion HQs hourly.

                          (sgd) R.A.JONES
                                2/Lieut & A/Adjutant
                                13th Bn. ESSEX REGT.

Copy No.1. 6th Infantry Brigade
        2. Commanding Officer
        3. 2nd in Command
        4. Adjutant
        5. O.C. "A" Coy.
        6. O.C. "B" Coy.
        7. O.C. "C" Coy.
        8. O.C. "D" Coy.
        9. T.O. & Q.M.
       10. Signalling Officer
       11. Medical Officer
       12. 1st Kings Regt.
       13. War Diary
       14. Do.

The CO will hold a conference re above at these HQ's at 11pm today.

SECRET   13th Bn. ESSEX REGT ORDER No.108   Copy No.....
Ref.Map.GLOSTER WOOD 1/20000   10/6/17
(Marked 1st and 2nd Bounds).

INTENTION   1. In the event of enemy falling back from FRESNES - ROUVROY LINE the 13th ESSEX will, on completion of operations in ORDER No.107, advance through the 1st KINGS and occupy above line from U.27.c.2.0. to U.21.c.6.4.
Advance will be carried out in conjunction with troops on each flank.

ADVANCE   2. On order to advance being received :-
(a) "A" & "B" Coys will advance in artillery formation. preceded by patrols, to line of VILLAGE TRENCH.
Right of "A" on light railway at junction with Sunken road C.1.b.0.2.   Left of "B" on junction of road and trench U.25.d.1.7.
Here "A" & "B" Coys will extend (providing their own supports) and continue advance without delay, scouts being thrown out 300 yds ahead of firing line.
(b) "C" & "D" Coys will advance in artillery formation 300 yds in rear of "A" & "B" Supports. They will keep close touch with troops on flanks by patrols and be responsible for protection of outer flanks of Battalion (viz: "C" Coy Right Flank, "D" Coy Left Flank).

DIRECTION   3. Direction will be maintained by Officers on each flank of Coys.
(a) Right of "A" Coy moving along Light Rly (C.2.a & b).
(b) Left of "B" Coy moving along road to junction road and RUPERT TRENCH and thence on a line drawn through U.21.c.6.4. (True bearing 185½°).
(c) Dividing line between Coys U.26.d.3.1. - U.27.a.6.2. - S.end of EAST COPSE.

OCCUPATION   4. On reaching FRESNES - ROUVROY LINE :-
OF   (a) "A" & "B" Coys will each at once form 4 platoon
OBJECTIVE   strong points as follows :-
"A" Coy.....U.27.c.2.0.(100 yds N.of Light Rly) to U.27.a.3.1. (inclusive).
"B" Coy.....U.27.a.6.3.(track) to U.21.c.6.4.(incl).
These strong points will be constructed capable of all round fire in accordance with the instructions issued to all platoon commanders.

OUTPOSTS   5. "C" & "D" Coys will advance through "A" & "B" Coys and under cover of one platoon each pushed forward to line of Light Railway (U.27.b.) will establish an outpost line as follows :-
"C" Coy....No.1.Piquet at U.27.d.0.3.
            No.2.Piquet at U.27.b.3.1.
            Detached post (½ platoon and 1 Officer) W.end of BOIS-EN-T. (This post will patrol to E.end of Wood and observe every 2 hours).
"D" Coy....No.3.Piquet at E.end of WEST COPSE.
            No.4.Piquet at U.21.d.½.2½.(Light Rly).
            Detached post (½ platoon and 1 Officer) E.end of EAST COPSE.
Covering parties will be withdrawn when piquets are entrenched.

REPORTS   6. Hourly reports to road and light railway junction C.1.b.6.2.
After FRESNES - ROUVROY LINE is occupied, to relay post at road and light railway junction C.3.b.1.7.

                         (sgd) F.A.JENNS 2/Lt & A/Adjt.
                             13th Bn. ESSEX REGT.

Copy No.1. 6th Infy.Bde.   No.2.Commanding Officer
     3. 2nd in Command   4.Adjutant
     5. O.C. "A" Coy   6.O.C. "B" Coy
     7. O.C. "C" Coy   8.O.C. "D" Coy
     9. T.O. & Q.M.   10.Signalling Officer
   11. Medical Officer   12.1st Kings Regt.
             13 & 14. War Diary.

SECRET   13th. Bn. ESSEX REGT. ORDER No. 109   Copy..13..

Ref.Map. 51BN.W. 1/20000   June 13th. 1917

RELIEF 1. The Battalion will be relieved by the 1st. D.C.L.I. in the Support Line (RED LINE) ARLEUX SECTOR tomorrow night 14th/15th June, and will proceed on relief to the Camp at G.4.d. vacated by the 12th. GLOSTER REGT.

GUIDES 2. One guide from each of "B", "C" & "D" Coys. will report to Battalion HQs at 9.30 p.m. 14/6/17 where they will meet "taking over" parties of corresponding coys of the 1st D.C.L.I. and guide them to their positions in the RED LINE.
"A" Coy will be relieved at dusk by "A" Coy of the 1st. D.C.L.I., who are already in WILLERVAL North. A guide will be sent by "A" Coy to this Coy of the D.C.L.I. at a place and time to be notified later, in order to guide them to their position.
"B", "C" & "D" Coys of the D.C.L.I. will be working in the forward area tomorrow at 11.10 p.m. and the corresponding Coys of the 13th ESSEX REGT will move off at 11.10 p.m. provided all positions, etc. have been previously handed over to the "taking over" party.
Battalion Headquarters will be relieved about 10.45 p.m.

ROUTE 3. Companies will move off independently commencing at 11.10 p.m. via LUMINOUS TRACK and TOMMY TRENCH. Intervals of 1 minute must be maintained between platoons and 5 minutes between Companies.

POSITIONS 4. Every care must be taken that all positions, etc., are handed over correctly.

TRENCH STORES 5. Lists of Trench Stores to be handed over, to reach this Office by 9 p.m. 14th inst.

DUGOUTS 6. All Dugouts, etc., to be handed over in a scrupulously clean condition, and all trenches clear of rubbish, etc. Certificate to be rendered to this effect by Noon on 15th inst.

KITS 7. Trench Kits, Mess Canteens, etc., will be stacked at Battalion Headquarters by 10.30 p.m. where they will be collected by the Transport. The Pioneer SERGt. and Pioneers will remain until same are loaded.

BILLETING 8. The Coy Q.M.Sgts under Capt.S.E.COLLIER M.C. will take over accommodation in the Camp at G.4.d. tomorrow, reporting to 2/Lieut F.TAYLOR at Rear Bde. HQs, ECURIE at 11 a.m.

(sgd) F.A.JENNS

2/Lieut & A/Adjutant

Issued at 9 p.m.   13th Bn. ESSEX REGT.

Copy No. 1   Commanding Officer.
" No. 2   Second in Command.
" No. 3   Adjutant.
" No. 4   O.C. "A" Coy.
" No. 5   O.C. "B" Coy.
" No. 6   O.C. "C" Coy.
" No. 7   O.C. "D" Coy.
" No. 8   Transport Officer.
" No. 9   Quarter Master.
" No. 10   Medical Officer.
" No. 11   Signalling Officer.
" No. 12   R.S.M.
" Nos. 13 & 14   War Diary.

ANNEX   13th. ESSEX REGT. ORDER NO. 110   Copy No. 13
                                                        June 26th, 1917

Ref. Maps   51B N.W. 1/20000
                 51C N.W. 1/20000

RELIEF   1. The Battalion will move to new billets today at
                    MONT ST. ELOY.

STARTING   2. Quartermaster's Stores.
POINT
                    Order of March
                        Headquarters
                        "A" Coy.
                        "B" Coy.
                        "C" Coy.
                        "D" Coy.

                    Headquarters to pass Starting Point at a time to be
                    notified later (probably 8 p.m.).

                    DRESS Full Marching Order. Steel helmets under
                    valise straps.

ROUTE   3. MADAGASCAR CROSS ROADS and CROSS COUNTRY TRACK.
                    Intervals of 5 minutes to be maintained between
                    Companies.

KITS,   4. Officers' Kits, Mess Boxes, Canteen, Orderly Room
GUNS etc.   Boxes, to be stacked at Q.M. Stores by 5 p.m. for loading.
                    Lewis Guns, Spare Parts, Ammunition, etc., to be
                    at same place, at same time.

BLANKETS   5. To be rolled tightly in bundles of 10 and stacked
                    at Q.M. Stores, ready for loading at 4 p.m.

KITCHENS   6. To move off independently.

MESS CART   7. To be at Battalion Headquarters at 7 p.m.

COMPLETION   8. To be notified personally by Company Commanders.
of RELIEF

CAMP   9. Lines to be left scrupulously clean and tidy and
                    certificates to this effect to be rendered to Orderly
                    Room by 7 p.m.

                                              (Sgd.) F.A.JENNS.

                                              2/Lieut. & A/Adjutant.
        Issued at 3 p.m.   13th. Bn. ESSEX REGT.

        No. 1 Copy   Commanding Officer.
            2   "   Second in Command.
            3   "   Adjutant.
            4   "   O.C. "A" Coy.
            5   "   O.C. "B" Coy.
            6   "   O.C. "C" Coy.
            7   "   O.C. "D" Coy.
            8   "   Transport Officer.
            9   "   Quartermaster.
           10   "   Signalling Officer.
           11   "   Medical Officer.
           12   "   R.S.M.
         13 & 14 "   War Diary.

SECRET   13th ESSEX REGT ORDER No.111   Copy No. 13

Ref.Map. Sheet 36B 1/40000   June 20th 1917

RELIEF   1.   The Battalion will relieve the 2/8th LANCS. FUSILIERS in the Reserve Area, GORRE, GIVENCHY SECTOR, today.
Starting Point............Old French Barracks.
Order of March........Headquarters.
                        "A" Coy.
                        "B" Coy.
                        "C" Coy.
                        "D" Coy.
Headquarters will pass the Starting Point at 5.35.pm. followed by Companies at 1 minute intervals.
Dress...........Full Marching Order with Steel Helmets in Valise Straps.

KITS, etc.   2.   Officers Kits, Mess Canteens, Orderly Room Boxes, Lewis Guns, Spare Parts, Ammunition, etc., will be stacked at Q.M.Stores ready for loading at 5.30.pm.

BLANKETS   3.   To be stacked at Q.M.Stores at 3.pm. rolled in bundles of ten ready for loading.

TRENCH STORES   4.   Lists of Trench Stores (if any) taken over to reach Battalion HQs by 9.am. 21st inst.

COMPLETION OF RELIEF   5.   Completion of relief to be notified to Battalion HQs by Company Commanders personally.

BILLETS   6.   To be left scrupulously clean and certificates to this effect to be rendered to Battalion Orderly Room not later than 5.pm.

MEALS   7.   Tea to be served at 4.30.pm. today.

                                 (sgd) F.A.JENNS
                                 2/Lieut & A/Adjutant
Issued at 12.30.pm.   13th Bn. ESSEX REGT.

                Copy No.   1.   Commanding Officer
                           2.   Second in Command
                           3.   Adjutant
                           4.   O.C. "A" Coy.
                           5.   O.C. "B" Coy.
                           6.   O.C. "C" Coy.
                           7.   O.C. "D" Coy.
                           8.   Transport Officer
                           9.   Quartermaster
                         10.   Signalling Officer
                         11.   Medical Officer
                         12.   R.S.M.
                         13.   War Diary
                         14.   War Diary.

2nd Division
6th Infantry Bde.
13th Essex Regt.
July. To 31st December
1917

6th Brigade
2nd Division.

13th BATTALION

THE ESSEX REGIMENT

J U L Y   1917.

Army Form C. 2118.

WAR DIARY
or
INTELLIGENCE SUMMARY.
(Erase heading not required.)

CONFIDENTIAL

WAR DIARY

of

13th (Service) Bn. ESSEX Regt

from

July 1st to July 31st 1917

WAR DIARY or INTELLIGENCE SUMMARY

Army Form C. 2118.

Place	Date	Hour	Summary of Events and Information	Remarks and references to Appendices
GIVENCHY SECTOR FESTUBERT	1st	—	Battalion holding front line system as follows:- Right front — D Coy Centre — B Coy Left front — C Coy Support in O.B.L. — A Coy General refusing to trenches carried out during day & night. Battalion working hard as about. Intermittent shelling on both sides.	
	2nd	9.30 pm	Battalion relieved by 11th Middlesex Regt and moved into Support area, WINDY CORNER, as follows:- B Coy to GIVENCHY KEEPS. C Coy to O.R.L. under orders of O.C. 14th OC 1st Kings Regt A & D Coys to billets at WINDY CORNER. Middlesex Regt. 1 Officer (2nd Lt E.L. CORPS and 45 Other Ranks attached to 5th Field Coy R.E. as Sapper Workers.	

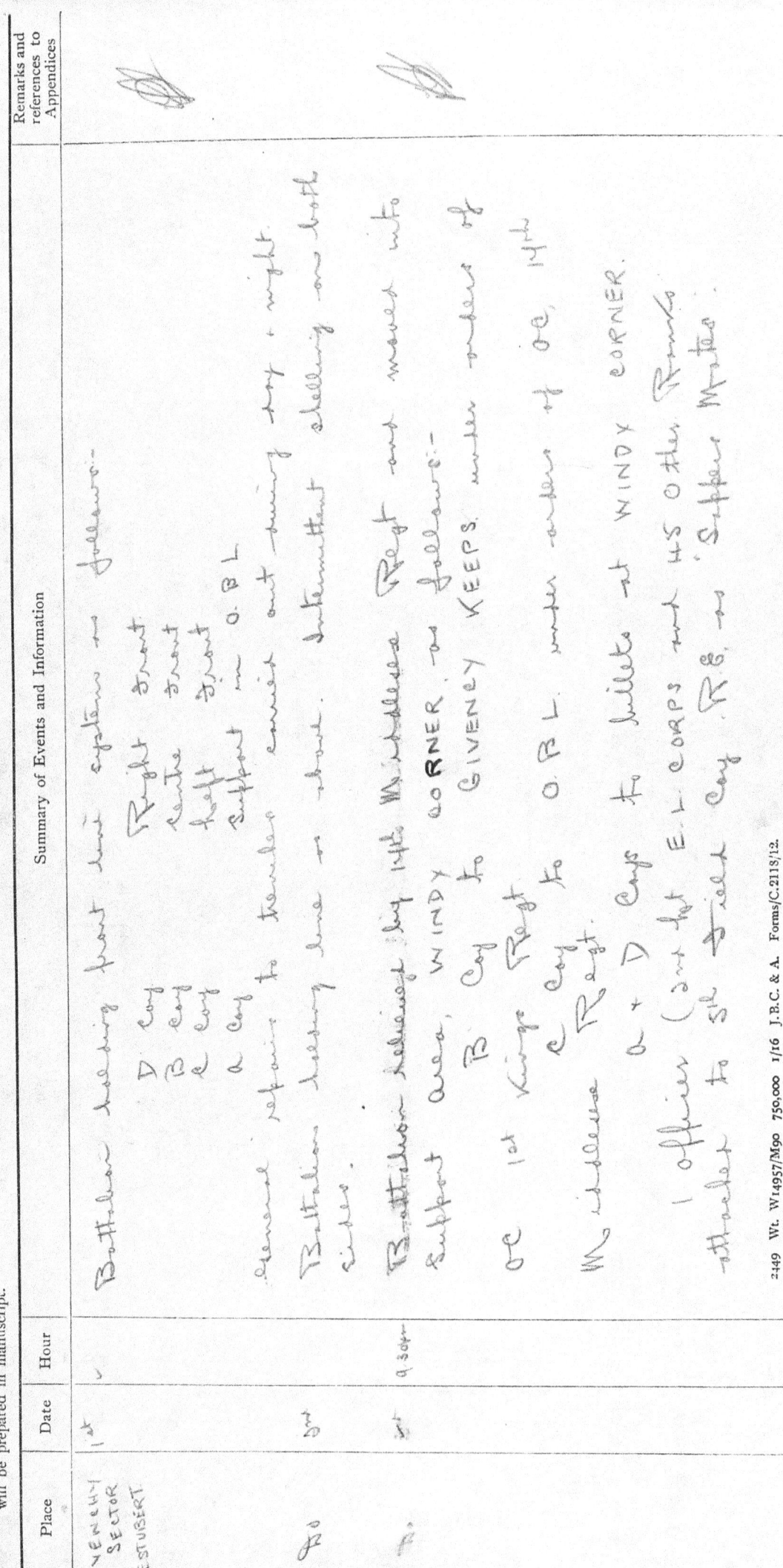

Army Form C. 2118.

WAR DIARY
or
INTELLIGENCE SUMMARY
(Erase heading not required.)

Instructions regarding War Diaries and Intelligence Summaries are contained in F. S. Regs., Part II. and the Staff Manual respectively. Title Pages will be prepared in manuscript.

Place	Date	Hour	Summary of Events and Information	Remarks and references to Appendices
Subject Area WINDY CORNER	3/4/14	—	Working parties supplies to Tunnelling Coy. R.E. & to Brigade. Training carried out by D Coy. Snipers under 2nd Lt F.J. SOUTHERN, and observers under 2nd Lieut A.C. TIMMS. Authority given for 2/Lt H.T. JESSOP to wear the badges of the rank of Captain, whilst commanding a Company. 2nd Lieut R. & H. MAY & 2nd Lieut H.L. BROOKE returned from leave to PARIS.	
Do	4th		Working parties supplies for Tunnelling Coys. R.E. and Brigade. 2/Lt G.G. SMYTH + 1 O.R. slightly gassed. Sniping training carried out by A Coy. Snipers under 2/Lt F.J. SOUTHERN Observers under 2/Lt A.C. TIMMS Bombers under Sergt ROLPHE	

Army Form C. 2118.

WAR DIARY
or
INTELLIGENCE SUMMARY.
(Erase heading not required.)

Instructions regarding War Diaries and Intelligence Summaries are contained in F. S. Regs., Part II. and the Staff Manual respectively. Title pages will be prepared in manuscript.

Place	Date	Hour	Summary of Events and Information	Remarks and references to Appendices
Support area	5/4/17		Working parties supplied for Tunnelling Coy, R.E. and Brigade. Training carried out by Coy. Snipers, Observers + Bombers under their instructors. 2nd Lieut E. A. PATTERSON and 3 O.R. rejoined from Corps School of Instruction at VIIth Corps School. Major A A MACFARLANE-GRIEVE, M.C. returned to 2nd Bn. H.L.I. Working parties supplied for Tunnelling Coy. R.E. and Brigade.	
WINDY CORNER	6/4/17		"B" Coy relieved "B" Coy in GIVENCHY KEEP under of O.C., 1st KINGS Regt. Training carried out by "D" Coy Snipers, Observers + bombers under their instructors. Major W H CARTER, D.S.O, M.C. took over the duties of 2nd in Command to the Battalion. No. 18040 Pte G.A. GREENO "C" Coy accidentally wounded by a revolver shot.	

A5834 Wt W4973/M687 750,000 8/16 D.D. & L. Ltd. Forms/C.2118/13.

WAR DIARY
INTELLIGENCE SUMMARY

Army Form C. 2118.

Place	Date	Hour	Summary of Events and Information	Remarks and references to Appendices
Support Line	6/4/19 cont		Runners sent repeated owing to their guns registering on certain portions of our front line system.	
WINDY CORNER		9.30 pm	B & D Coys went up the Communication Trench A.E.F. HARRIS D.S.O. moved up to the O.R.L in close support to the 14th Middlesex Regt. Lieut Col HARRIS resumed the Command of the LEFT Subsector. Capt. S.E COLLIER M.C. took over the duties of Acting Adjutant. 2nd Lieut F.A JENNS appointed Assistant Adjutant. 2nd Lieut R.T TREBILEO proceeded to 6th Trench Mortar Battery for attachment.	
	7/4/19	4 am	A Coys in O.R.L returned to billets. D Coy relieved C Coy & were relieved at O.C 14th Middlesex Regt. Training carried out by B Coy. Snipers, Observers & Bombers under their instructors	

WAR DIARY
or
INTELLIGENCE SUMMARY.

Army Form C. 2118.

Place	Date	Hour	Summary of Events and Information	Remarks and references to Appendices
Support Area WINDY CORNER	4/4/17		Working parties supplied for Tunnelling Coy. & Burgoyne No 180 qu 2/6/66 F A JAMES received a bar to his MILITARY MEDAL for gallantry. (Auty-in-Div R.O. No 3/16.)	
		9.30pm	B & C Coys resumed their positions in the O.B.L. in case of attack. Lieut. Col. A E F HARRIS, D.S.O. resumed command of the LEFT Subsector. Billets vacated by B & C Coys at WINDY CORNER taken over by 2 Coys of 1st SOUTH STAFFS Regt.	
	5/4/17	9.30pm	Battalion relieved 14th Welsh Regt in LEFT Subsector. Dispositions. Right Front A Coy Centre Front B Coy Left Front C Coy O.B.L. D Coy	
			Intermittent shelling but little else during night. Hs R.G. Box + 2nd Lt H.V.COOK proceeded for course at XIth Corps School.	

WAR DIARY or INTELLIGENCE SUMMARY

Place	Date	Hour	Summary of Events and Information	Remarks and references to Appendices
Left Subsector	8/4/14		Battalion holding front line. O.B.L. shelled with 5.9's during morning. QUINQUE RUE was also shelled. Our guns retaliated effectively. Repairs to trenches & wiring carried out.	
"	10/4/14		Battalion holding front line. Shetland Road work and constructions commenced. From a reference plan. Twenty infantrymen and wiring parties taken. Sent out.	
"	11/4/14		Intermittent shelling by both sides. Battalion holding line. Construction of defensive front in fact of SHETLAND Road continues. Wiring parties in front line. ♱ Lieut. T. D. STEELE proceeded on leave to England. Bomber's continual instruction under Sergt. ROLPHE. Intermittent shelling by Light S.A. a Coy relieved B Coy on Right front.	

Army Form C. 2118.

WAR DIARY
or
INTELLIGENCE SUMMARY.
(Erase heading not required.)

Instructions regarding War Diaries and Intelligence
Summaries are contained in F. S. Regs., Part II.
and the Staff Manual respectively. Title pages
will be prepared in manuscript.

Place	Date	Hour	Summary of Events and Information	Remarks and references to Appendices
LEFT Subsector	11/1/17		Battalion holding line Defences thinned at SHETLAND Front continued. Trenches improved generally. Wiring parties out in power patrols.	
			1 AM NEW groupe for duty. Capt A E BUNTING and Lieut A E BUNTING and Lieut BUNTING took over the Command of Coy from 2/Lieut W A HARVEY who however to the 2nd Divisional Draft Training School as an instructor for Bombers notified. Enemy went Sergt ROLPHE	
	12/1/17		Battalion holding line. 1 O.R. killed. Enemy were quiet. M.G's active at night. Consolidation work apparent to line commenced at SHETLAND Front continued to fourth front.	
	13/1/17		Battalion holding line. Situation slowly as before. 1 O.R. killed. Weather the day.	

WAR DIARY or INTELLIGENCE SUMMARY

Army Form C. 2118.

(Erase heading not required.)

Instructions regarding War Diaries and Intelligence Summaries are contained in F.S. Regs., Part II. and the Staff Manual respectively. Title pages will be prepared in manuscript.

Place	Date	Hour	Summary of Events and Information	Remarks and references to Appendices
Left our Billets	11/1/17	9.30 p.m.	Battalion relieved by 14th Middlesex Regt and two Coys wanted by 1st Kings Regt at GORRE.	
GORRE	12/1/17		Training continued. 150 men found for working parties. Line. 2/Lt H L BROOKE + 1 OR proceeded to 1st Army School of Instruction. 2/Lt W S MACLAREN proceeded for attachment to 14th Bde R.T.O. 2nd Lieut G.G. SMYTH returned from hospital. Capt J LYONS RAMC ceased to be attached to Battalion on Medical Officer from 13th Lieut J MARTIN took over the duties of Medical Officer from MOL.	
	13/1/17		Programme of Training carried out. Working parties supplied. 2/Lt (a/Capt) H.T. JESSOP proceeded on course of training and instruction in working and in supply of working parties at MALO.	

Army Form C. 2118.

WAR DIARY
or
INTELLIGENCE SUMMARY.
(Erase heading not required.)

Instructions regarding War Diaries and Intelligence Summaries are contained in F. S. Regs., Part II. and the Staff Manual respectively. Title pages will be prepared in manuscript.

Place	Date	Hour	Summary of Events and Information	Remarks and references to Appendices
GORRE	14/4/14		The following Officers joined the Battalion & report for duty — W. STUART BROWNE (actg & Capt) " H. R. E. KING (2o Lt) " F. C. RANSOM (2o Lt) on working party	
"	15/4/14		Major W. H. CARTER D.S.O. M.C. proceeded to U.K. on assumption of command of the 1/4th SOUTH STAFFS Regt, not relinquishing attachment of Second in Command. Capt. A. A. MACFARLANE - GRIEVE M.C. 2/Lt. 1/5 reported for duty and took over the duties of Second in Command. Training carried out. Working parties supplied at night.	
"	16/4/14	9.30pm	Battalion Sports carried out. Rifles inspected by Brigade Armourer Sergeant. Working parties supplied during day. Battalion relieved 14th Worcester Regt. in the LEFT Subsector. Inkertans	

WAR DIARY
or
INTELLIGENCE SUMMARY

Army Form C. 2118.

Place	Date	Hour	Summary of Events and Information	Remarks and references to Appendices
CORBIE Cnt	1/4/17		Dispositions:- Right front. Centre do Left do O.R.L. (Support) to Coy B do C do D do Wiring parties & wire also patrols active throughout night	
Left Sub Sector	2/4/17		Battalion holding line. Consolidation & repairs to trenches carried out. Intermittent shelling by both sides throughout day.	
		2.50am	Bangalore Torpedo successfully exploded under enemy wire north of OLD MANS CORNER by a party from 17th Middlesex Regt.	
Do	3/4/17		Battalion holding line. Consolidation & repairs to trenches continued. Enemy snipers & M.G's active also our Machine Guns. Enemy M.G's and Sniper Lewis gun detachments sent out to England.	

A5834 Wt. W4973/M687 750,000 8/16 D.D. & L. Ltd. Forms/C.2118/13.

WAR DIARY
or
INTELLIGENCE SUMMARY.

(Erase heading not required.)

Army Form C. 2118.

Place	Date	Hour	Summary of Events and Information	Remarks and references to Appendices
Left Shorncliffe	2/4/17		2/Lt. W.S. McLAREN rejoined from 11th Battery R & a 2/Lt. E.W. PHILLIPS + 3 O.R. proceeded for bombing course at XIth Corps School.	
	3/4/17		H.H. GLEN + 3 O.R. proceeded for Lewis Gun course at XI Corps School. 28 O.R. proceeded to Divisional Draft Training School for 21 days intensive training. Battalion having line. Every quiet day but intermittently shelled past line + RICHMOND TERRACE tuning day with TM's + 4.5's. Consolidation of trenches carried on. 2/Lt A.R. WELLS. MC rejoined from Course.	
	22/4/17		Battalion holding line continued intermittent shelling by both sides. Consolidation of line continued. 2/Lt A.R. WELLS. M.C. proceeded for course of instruction at	

WAR DIARY
or
INTELLIGENCE SUMMARY
(Erase heading not required.)

Army Form C. 2118.

Place	Date	Hour	Summary of Events and Information	Remarks and references to Appendices
Left Béthune	23/4/16 24/4/16		1st Army Signal School. Battalion relieved by 14th Middlesex Regt and took over the Support Area as follows:- "A" Coy GIVENCHY KEEPS under OC 1st Kings "C" " O.B.L. under OC 14th Middlesex Regt "B" " Coy to billets at WINDY CORNER	↙
Support Area	25/4/16		Training carried out + working parties supplied. Snipers, Observers + Bombers under their instructors + Rifle Bomb Sections (1 O.R.) under Lieut A E BUNTING carried out + fired others in conjunction with the 1st Trench Mortar Battery on the enemy's line North of OLD MAN'S CORNER for the purpose of assisting a minor which was being carried out by the 1st Kings Regt on our right. The party got within 40 yards of the enemy wire + at 2 a.m., viz 10.30 p.m. sent over 6 H.E. + 3 Rifle bombs, after which they	↙ ↙

Army Form C. 2118.

WAR DIARY
or
INTELLIGENCE SUMMARY.
(Erase heading not required.)

Instructions regarding War Diaries and Intelligence Summaries are contained in F.S. Regs., Part II. and the Staff Manual respectively. Title pages will be prepared in manuscript.

Place	Date	Hour	Summary of Events and Information	Remarks and references to Appendices
Winty Cover.	25/1/17		Successfully withdrew. When our Rifle bombs reaches the enemy front line & not very light was sent up in response to which a barrage was put down on our own front line. Casualties 1 O.R. Wounded.	
Do	26/1/17		Training carried out not working parties 2/Lieut. Supfire Observers + bombers under their instructors. Capt. J.G.H. KENNEFICK proceeds on leave to England. 2/Lt T.D STEELE proceeds for attachment to 147th Battery R.F.A. Lieut G. SIMPSON rejoins the Battalion. 2/Lieut V.E. BLOOMFIELD joins for duty.	
Do	27/1/17		Training carried out + working parties supplied. Snipers, Observers + bombers under their instructors. Enemy shelled vicinity of Battalion H.Q. with shells of large calibre intermittently during morning. R.S.M. M. COCKRAIN joins for duty.	

2353 Wt W2544/1454 700,000 5/15 D.D.&L. A.D.S.S./Forms/C. 2118.

WAR DIARY or INTELLIGENCE SUMMARY

Army Form C. 2118.

Place	Date	Hour	Summary of Events and Information	Remarks and references to Appendices
Winty Camer	28/4/17		Training carried out + working parties supplies. Specialists under their instructors. 2/Lt (a/Capt) H.T. JESSOP proceeded to R.F.C. 2/Lieut C.C. COLE proceeded to R.F.C. as an Observer. 2/Lt G. SIMPSON took over the Command of C Coy. 2/Lieut T. MARTIN R.A.M.C. relinquishes in duties of Medical officer. 2/Lieut L. FARMER R.A.M.C. took over the duties of Medical officer. (O.R. Wavrans) Battalion relieves 1st Wiltshire Regt in LEFT Subsector. Dispositions:—	
	29/4/17	9.30pm	A Coy Right front. B Coy Centre. C Coy Left. D Coy O.B.L. (Support) Right Front. Working parties + patrols also consolidation of line continued. M.G. fire from both sides during night.	

Army Form C. 2118.

WAR DIARY
or
INTELLIGENCE SUMMARY.
(Erase heading not required.)

Instructions regarding War Diaries and Intelligence Summaries are contained in F. S. Regs., Part II. and the Staff Manual respectively. Title pages will be prepared in manuscript.

Place	Date	Hour	Summary of Events and Information	Remarks and references to Appendices
Left Subsector	29/1/17		2/Lt A.R.WELLS + 2/Lt E.H.SHERMAN awarded the "MILITARY CROSS" (Supplement to London Gazette dated 26/1/17)	
To	30/1/17		Consolidation of line continued. Wiring parties + patrols active. Intermittent shelling by both sides.	
Do	31/1/17		Battalion holding line. Consolidation of line continues. Intermittent shelling by enemy to which our artillery replies effectively.	
			Strengths of Battalion —	
			Effective Strength 35 Officers. 886. O.R.
			Fighting 31 to 669 to
			Trench 14 to 548 to
			A.M.Annis Lieut Colonel
			Commanding 13th Essex Regiment.

3.2.17.

6th Brigade
2nd Division.

13th BATTALION

THE ESSEX REGIMENT

AUGUST 1917.

Army Form C. 2118.

WAR DIARY
or
INTELLIGENCE SUMMARY.
(Erase heading not required.)

Vol 21

G.22

CONFIDENTIAL

WAR DIARY

of

13th (S) Bn. The Essex Regt

from

August 1st – 31st 1917

Army Form C. 2118.

WAR DIARY
or
INTELLIGENCE SUMMARY.
(Erase heading not required.)

Instructions regarding War Diaries and Intelligence Summaries are contained in F. S. Regs., Part II. and the Staff Manual respectively. Title pages will be prepared in manuscript.

Place	Date	Hour	Summary of Events and Information	Remarks and references to Appendices
Left Subsector GIVENCHY SECTOR	1/8/17		Battalion holding front line system as follows:— "A" Coy. Right Front. B Do. Centre Do. C Do. Left Do. D Do. O.B.L. (Support). Lieut (a/Capt) F.R. KEEBLE M.C. admitted to Hospital & relinquished command of "B" Coy. Lieut A.W. NEW took over command of "B" Coy. The undermentioned Officers granted permission to wear the badge of the ranks set against their names. Lieut F.R. KEEBLE M.C. Captain. " A.E. BUNTING Do. 2/Lieut L.P. CHANDLER Lieut. " H.T. JESSOP Do. " J.D. STEELE Do. " A.R. WELLS M.C. Do. " F.J. SOUTHERN Do. " W.A. HARVEY Do.	Authy:— 2/Div. Q2589/823 dated 1/8/17.

WAR DIARY
or
INTELLIGENCE SUMMARY.
(Erase heading not required.)

Army Form C. 2118.

Place	Date	Hour	Summary of Events and Information	Remarks and references to Appendices
Left Subsector	2/8/17		Battalion holding line. Consolidation & repairs to trenches carried out. Intermittent shelling by both sides throughout day. 1. O.R. wounded	
GIVENCHY SECTOR.	3/8/17		Battalion holding line. General situation very quiet. 2/Lieut H.A. MUCKERN joined for duty & posted to 'A' Coy. 4 Others proceeded to Divisional Riflemen's School for course of instruction. Battalion relieved by 17th MIDDLESEX REGT and on relief moved into billets at GORRE. Vacated by 1st Bn. KING'S REGT.	
GORRE	4/8/17		Training carried out. 2/Lieut A.H.D. CARPENTER joined for duty & posted to "A" Coy. Lieut W.A. HARVEY returned from 2/Divisional Staff School and was replaced by 2/Lieut F.C. RANSOM. Lieut J.D. STEELE returned from 17th Battery R.F.A. 2/Lieut W. STUART-BROWNE proceeded to 19th Battery R.F.A. for instruction	
Do.	5/8/17		Firing carried out on the Range by 'A' & 'B' Coys. from 12.30 pm. to 9 pm; otherwise the day was observed as a holiday by the	

WAR DIARY
or
INTELLIGENCE SUMMARY.
(Erase heading not required.)

Army Form C. 2118.

Place	Date	Hour	Summary of Events and Information	Remarks and references to Appendices
GORRE	5/8/17 (contd)		Battalion. 1 officer and 50 O.Rs per Coy & 25 O.Rs of H.Qs attended a service in the Y.M.C.A. Hut, GORRE, in commemoration of the outbreak of war. Lieut W.A. HARVEY & 10 O.Rs proceeded on leave 2/Lieut H.H. GLEN & 3 O.Rs returned from XI Corps I.G. School & 2/Lieut C.W. PHILIPS & 3 O.Rs returned from XI Corps Bombing School	✓
Do.	6/8/17		Programmes of training carried out by 'C' & 'D' Coys. while 'A' & 'B' Coys observed the day as a holiday, as far as possible. Musketry test were carried out, according to 2I Division Competition Rules. Capt. J.G.H. KENNEFICK granted extension of leave to 10/8/17. Working parties supplied.	✓
Do.	7/8/17		Programmes of training carried out by Coys. & Working Parties supplied.	✓
Do.	8/8/17		Training continued. "D" & "C" Coys. used the Range between 12.30 p.m. to 3 p.m. and 4 p.m. to 8 p.m. respectively. Lewis Gun Section of all Coys. fired on the Range between 3 p.m. to 4 p.m.	✓

Place	Date	Hour	Summary of Events and Information	Remarks and references to Appendices
GORRE	8/8/17 (cont'd)		under 2/Lieut. H.H. GLEN. "D" & "C" Coys. NCO's and "A" & "B" Coys. NCOs handed under the R.S.M. for instruction at 10.15 am & 2 pm respectively.	
Do.	9/8/17		2/Lieut. C.S. JAMES joined for duty and posted to "D" Coy. Training carried out as per programmes submitted by Company Commanders. 19 O.R's. returned from 2/Divisional Draft School, on completion of their 21 days intensive training. Lieut. J.D. STEELE proceeded to Divisional Draft School for 2 days preliminary instruction in the Lewis gun before proceeding on a course at the First Army School. 6 O.R's. attached to Brigade as caretakers to tramways. 2/Lieut. R.C.H. MAY granted extension of leave to 15/8/17 on grounds of ill-health (H.Q. 2/Div. Q629/645, dated 8/8/17). 2 O.R's. proceeded to England as Candidates for Commissions.	

Army Form C. 2118.

WAR DIARY
or
INTELLIGENCE SUMMARY.
(Erase heading not required.)

Instructions regarding War Diaries and Intelligence Summaries are contained in F.S. Regs., Part II. and the Staff Manual respectively. Title pages will be prepared in manuscript.

Place	Date	Hour	Summary of Events and Information	Remarks and references to Appendices
GORRE & Left Subsector	9/8/17		2/Lieut H.L. BROOKE and 1 O.R. returned from Course at First Army School of Instruction. Battalion relieved 17th Bn. MIDDLESEX REGT in the LEFT SUBSECTOR GIVENCHY SECTOR. Disposition :— "D" Coy Right Front "B" " Centre Front "C" " Left Front "A" " Support (O.B.L.)	
LEFT SUBSECTOR GIVENCHY SECTOR.	10/8/17		Intermittent shelling by both sides during night & snipers active. Battalion holding line as above. Trenches improved and wiring parties active. Usual Patrols sent out. 2/Lieut W. STUART-BROWNE returned from 17th Batt. R.F. Bombers continued training under Sgt. ROLFE.	
Do.	11/8/17		Battalion holding line. Situation generally very quiet. SHETLAND POST and L.O.B.L. repaired and parapets thickened. Work only carried out by night, owing to enemy balloons being	

WAR DIARY
or
INTELLIGENCE SUMMARY.
(Erase heading not required.)

Army Form C. 2118.

Place	Date	Hour	Summary of Events and Information	Remarks and references to Appendices
LEFT SUBSECTOR GIVENCHY SECTOR	12/8/17		up and to excellent visibility during hours of daylight. Battalion holding line. Patrols sent out but no enemy working parties or patrol were seen or heard. Strengthening of defences continued. Lieut A.W. NEW and C.S.M. BLOWES proceeded on a course at First Army School. Lieut A.W. NEW relinquished command of "B" Coy and 2/Lieut H.A. MULKERN took over command. 2/Lieut J.G.H. KENNEFICK Lieut F.V. SOUTHERN returned from leave to England. 2 O.Rs. accidentally wounded.	
	13/8/17		Battalion holding line. Situation generally quiet. Usual patrols sent out and useful information obtained. One patrol reported that OLD MAN'S CORNER was occupied by the enemy. "A" Coy relieved "D" Coy in the Right front and "D" Coy took over "A" Coy's position in the O.B.L.	

Army Form C. 2118.

WAR DIARY
or
INTELLIGENCE SUMMARY.
(Erase heading not required.)

Instructions regarding War Diaries and Intelligence Summaries are contained in F. S. Regs., Part II. and the Staff Manual respectively. Title pages will be prepared in manuscript.

Place	Date	Hour	Summary of Events and Information	Remarks and references to Appendices
Left Dunsectoe	13/8/17		Lieut. Col. A.E.T. HARRIS D.S.O. took over the command of 6th Infantry Brigade during the absence of Brig. Gen. R. WALSH'S D.S.O. leave to England. Major A.A. MacFARLANE-GRIEVE M.C. took over command of the Battalion.	
	14/8/17		Battalion holding line. Own wiring parties active. Patrol sent out but no enemy were seen or encountered and no work was heard in progress in enemy's lines. Situation normal. Lieut. J.D. STEELE proceeded on course at First Army School from 2/8/17 rejoined Staff School on completion of his preliminary training.	
	15/8/17		6 O.R. detached for duty with 6th T.M. Battery. Battalion holding line. Lively bombardments on right throughout day & night but no unusual activity on Battalion front. Battalion was relieved by 17th Bn. MIDDLESEX REGT and on relief the Bn. (less "B" Coy) over billets vacated by MIDDLESEX REGT at WINDY	

2353 Wt. W.2544/1454 700,000 5/15 D. D. & L. A.D.S.S./Forms/C. 2118.

WAR DIARY or INTELLIGENCE SUMMARY

Army Form C. 2118.

Place	Date	Hour	Summary of Events and Information	Remarks and references to Appendices
WINDY CORNER	15/8/17		CORNER. "B" Coy. remained in support to 17th MIDDLESEX REGT. in the O.B.L., near its junction with BARNTON ROAD. "D" Coy occupied the GIVENCHY KEEPS. 2/Lieut A.H.D. CARPENTER proceeded to XI Corps Infantry School for a course of instruction. 2/Lieut H.R.E. KING & 2/Lieut R.B. TONKIN proceeded on a course at XI Corps Infantry School. 2/Lieut W. STUART-BROWNE proceeded on one month's leave to England.	
Do.	16/8/17		R.E. 130 O.R's found fou working parties at the BRASSERIE, PONT FIXE & at head of light Rly. near GIVENCHY KEEP in WOOD LANE. The latter party was engaged in carrying bags of bricks and sand. A party of 13 O.R's were found for 6th Div. Pottery but these were returned as not required. Snipers under Lieut F.J. SOUTHERN, training of observers under 2/Lieut A.C. TIMMS. Bombers under Sgt. ROLFE. 2/Lieut E.A. PATTERSON proceeded to 14th Supporting Pottery R.F.A. for instruction for period of 6 days.	

WAR DIARY
or
INTELLIGENCE SUMMARY.

(Erase heading not required.)

Army Form C. 2118.

Place	Date	Hour	Summary of Events and Information	Remarks and references to Appendices
WINDY CORNER	16/8/17		The following Officers joined for duty and were posted to Coys as shown:— 2/Lieut. H.L. BALL "B" Coy. (2/Lieut) Lieut. H.L. HUGHES "C" " 2/Lieut. N.K. BESSEX "A" " 2/Lieut. W.A. HERYET "D" "	
Do.	17/8/17		1 O.R. wounded, whilst attached to 170th Tunnelling Coy R.E. Capt. F.R. KEEBLE returned to Battalion from hospital. Lieut. L. FARMER, to England on leave of duties taken over by Capt. LEITH WILSON. Working parties supplied as on 15th except from 10th In. Battery. Snipers, Observers & Bombers under their respective 2/Lieut. G.G. SMYTH admitted to Hospital.	
Do.	18/8/17		Usual working parties supplied for 251st Tunnelling Coy R.E. and training carried out. Defences at Potton Headquarters strengthened and repaired and general repairs carried out. Lieut W.A. HARVEY returned from England. 2/Lieut H.L. BROOKE admitted to Hospital. "C" Coy relieved "D" Coy in the Keeps.	

Army Form C. 2118.

WAR DIARY
or
INTELLIGENCE SUMMARY.
(Erase heading not required.)

Place	Date	Hour	Summary of Events and Information	Remarks and references to Appendices
WINDY CORNER	19/8/17		Working parties supplied to Tunnelling Coys R.E. and Brigade. Snipers, Observers, & Bombers under their instructors. Lieut G. SIMPSON given permission to wear badges of rank of Captain.	
Do.	20/8/17		Working parties supplied to Tunnelling Coy R.E. and Brigade. 2/Lieut W.S. McLAREN proceeded on leave. 2/Lieut M.S. CLAYDON joined Battalion for duty & posted to "B" Coy. 1 O.R. wounded by buried bomb when lowering a firestep in the keeps.	
In & Left Subr	21/8/17		Working parties supplied up to 6 p.m. Battalion relieved 17th Bn. MIDDLESEX REGT in LEFT SUBSECTOR, GIVENCHY SECTOR and 1st KING'S REGT took over billets vacated at WINDY CORNER. Dispositions:— "D" Coy RIGHT FRONT.	

WAR DIARY
or
INTELLIGENCE SUMMARY.
(Erase heading not required.)

Army Form C. 2118.

Place	Date	Hour	Summary of Events and Information	Remarks and references to Appendices
LEFT SUBSECTOR GIVENCHY SECTOR	21/8/17 (contd)		"B" Coy CENTRE FRONT "C" Coy LEFT FRONT "A" Coy SUPPORT (O.B.L.) Normal machine gun fire & sniping during night.	
Do.	22/8/17		Battalion holding line as above. Wiring parties and patrols active. Patrol located enemy working party but no further activity discerned. 2/Lieut. E.A. PATTERSON returned from 176th Supporting Battery, R.F.A. Capt. F.R. KEEBLE resumed command of "B" Coy.	
Do.	23/8/17		Battalion holding line. Enemy shelled the Brewery with 4.2s and took areas intermittently. Otherwise situation normal. 2/Lieut M.H. GLEN attended a Flying Demonstration at AUCHEL.	
Do.	24/8/17		Battalion holding line. Normal sniping & machine gun fire during night. Occasional shelling to which own artillery replied effectively. Patrols sent out but no enemy movement	

Army Form C. 2118.

WAR DIARY
or
INTELLIGENCE SUMMARY.
(Erase heading not required.)

Place	Date	Hour	Summary of Events and Information	Remarks and references to Appendices
Left Subsector GIVENCHY SECTOR	24/8/17		was defected. "A" Coy relieved "D" Coy in the Right Front. 4 O.R's wounded.	
Do.	25/8/17		Battalion holding line. Enemy wiring party located by patrol and dispersed by machine gun fire. Enemy shelled Brewery with several 4.2's between noon & 2 p.m. Lieut.Col. O.B.J. HARRIS D.S.O. returned from 6th. Infantry Brigade and Major (A/Lt.Col.) MacFARLANE-GRIEVE M.C. resumed the duties of Second in Command to the Battalion. 2/Lieut V.E. BLOOMFIELD proceeded on a course of instruction at the Divisional Lewis School ESSARS. 2/Lieut. H.L. BROOKE returned to Battalion from Hospital.	
Do.	26/8/17		Battalion holding line. Enemy were unaffected by our patrols and found to be in sound condition on left Coys front. Further wiring by enemy heard to be in progress.	

2353 Wt. W2344/1454 700,000 5/15 D. D. & L. A.D.S.S./Forms/C. 2118.

Army Form C. 2118.

WAR DIARY
or
INTELLIGENCE SUMMARY.
(Erase heading not required.)

Instructions regarding War Diaries and Intelligence Summaries are contained in F.S. Regs., Part II. and the Staff Manual respectively. Title pages will be prepared in manuscript.

Place	Date	Hour	Summary of Events and Information	Remarks and references to Appendices
Left Dubluchon	26/8/17		2/Lieut G.G. SMYTH rejoined from Hospital. 2/Lieut A.C. TIMMS attached to 6th Inf. Bde. as Intelligence Officer.	
Do.	27/8/17		Battalion holding line. Several rifle grenades & light trench mortars exchanged. Normal machine gun & rifle fire. Battalion relieved by 17th Bn. MIDDLESEX REGT and on relief, took over billets vacated by MIDDLESEX REGT in GORRE. Hon Lieut N. LANG proceeded for 6 days Special leave to PARIS. 2/Lieut A. NETHERCOTT joined Battalion for duty and posted to 'C' Coy. Lieut J.D. ROBINSON classified "T.B" for 2 weeks from 15/5/17.	
GORRE	28/8/17		Fatigue parties of 1 N.C.O. & 12 men found for Town Major for Sanitary duties. 2/Lieut W.A. HERYET proceeded to 17th Battery R.F.A. for instruction. 2/Lieut V.E. BLOOMFIELD returned from Divisional Gas School. Lieut L. FARMER returned from leave & resumed duties of Medical	

WAR DIARY
or
INTELLIGENCE SUMMARY.

(Erase heading not required.)

Army Form C. 2118.

Place	Date	Hour	Summary of Events and Information	Remarks and references to Appendices
GORRE	28/8/17		Officers to the Battalion. 2/Lieut R.C.H. MAY ordered a Medical Board whilst on leave and struck off strength accordingly. Major A.A. MacFARLANE-GRIEVE M.C. proceeded on leave.	
Do.	29/8/17		Training carried out. L.G. Section Commanders and all Bombing Section Commanders paraded for instruction, under 2/Lieut G.G. SMYTH proceeded on leave to TOURNEHEM for the purpose of getting married. Lofgen J. LEITCH-WILSON ceased to be attached. 2/Lieut H.A. MULKERN admitted to Hospital.	
Do.	30/8/17		Training continued. Commanding Officer inspected Bomber Sections. Capt. S.E. COLLIER M.C. having completed period of instruction as Adjutant, resumed the duties of Transport Officer. Capt. A.E. BUNTING took over the duties of Adjutant. Lieut. J.D. STEELE returned from Irish Army Lewis Gun School.	

WAR DIARY
or
INTELLIGENCE SUMMARY.

Army Form C. 2118.

Place	Date	Hour	Summary of Events and Information	Remarks and references to Appendices
GORRE	30/8/17 (Contd)		Lieut W.A. HARVEY took over command of "A" Coy. 2 Officers & 60 ORs provided as carrying party to T.2 Trench Mortar Battery.	
B.O.	31/8/17		Training continued. A usual fatigue party found. Battalion fired on Range at LE QUESNOY. Officers attended lectures upon and Bombing Classes.	
			Strength of Battalion	
				Officers	ORs
			Effective Strength	43	848
			Fighting ,, ,,	29	631
			Trench ,, ,,	23	524
			A. Hown Lieut. Colonel	
			Comdg :- 13th Sussex Regt.	
	3.9.17.			

6th Brigade.

2nd Division.

13th BATTALION

THE ESSEX REGIMENT

SEPTEMBER 1917.

Army Form C. 2118.

WAR DIARY
or
INTELLIGENCE SUMMARY
(Erase heading not required.)

Vol 22

G.23

CONFIDENTIAL

WAR DIARY
of
13th (S) Bn. The Essex Regt.
from
September 1st – 30th 1917.

Army Form C. 2118.

WAR DIARY
or
INTELLIGENCE SUMMARY.
(Erase heading not required.)

Instructions regarding War Diaries and Intelligence Summaries are contained in F. S. Regs., Part II. and the Staff Manual respectively. Title pages will be prepared in manuscript.

Place	Date	Hour	Summary of Events and Information	Remarks and references to Appendices
GORRE	1/9/17		Training carried out. Battalion (including Headquarters) used the Range at LE QUESNOY between 11 a.m. and 4 p.m. HQs & "A" Coy. carried out a successful cross-country march, wearing box respirators, in the dark. Part of the men held a rope, as a means of keeping touch and direction, while the remainder held the bayonet scabbards of the men in front. 30 O.Rs under 2/Lieut H.L. BALL and 30 O.Rs under 2/Lieut M.S. CLAYDON carried trench mortar bombs for Z.2 Battery between the hours of 9 p.m. & midnight. 2/Lieut. W.S. McLAREN returned from leave to England.	
do. & Left subsection GIVENCHY SECTOR.	2/9/17		Day observed, as far as possible, as a holiday. Two Officers per Company and other ranks not on duty attended a Church Parade Service on Battalion Parade ground at 10 a.m. Battalion relieved 17th Battn. MIDDLESEX REGT in the Left Sub. Sector, GIVENCHY SECTOR. First relieving Coy. moved	

Army Form C. 2118.

WAR DIARY
or
INTELLIGENCE SUMMARY.
(Erase heading not required.)

Instructions regarding War Diaries and Intelligence Summaries are contained in F.S. Regs., Part II. and the Staff Manual respectively. Title pages will be prepared in manuscript.

Place	Date	Hour	Summary of Events and Information	Remarks and references to Appendices
GORRE and LEFT-SUBSECTOR	2/9/17		Starting Point at 8 p.m. and entire relief completed by 10.50 p.m. The Battalion was accompanied by No.3 Company, 1st Battalion, PORTUGUESE INFANTRY attached for 3 days general instruction. Lieut A. R. WELLS M.C. & servant returned from First Army Signalling School. 2Lieut A.H.D. CARPENTER returned from XI Corps Sniping School. 2Lieut W.S. McLAREN interviewed C.R.A., 2 Division with a view to transfer to R.F.A. Usual fatigue of one N.C.O. and 12 men supplied to Town Major, GORRE for Sanitary Duties.	
LEFT SUBSECTOR GIVENCHY SECTOR	3/9/17		Battalion holding line. Between 10 and 11 a.m. enemy dropped several H.E. just in rear of O.B.L. Otherwise situation very quiet. Usual patrols and wiring parties; and repairs to trenches carried out. Lieut M.L. FARMER, R.A.M.C. posted as Officer in Medical Charge of Battalion.	

Army Form C. 2118.

WAR DIARY
or
INTELLIGENCE SUMMARY.
(Erase heading not required.)

Instructions regarding War Diaries and Intelligence Summaries are contained in F.S. Regs., Part II. and the Staff Manual respectively. Title pages will be prepared in manuscript.

Place	Date	Hour	Summary of Events and Information	Remarks and references to Appendices
LEFT SUB-SECTOR GIVENCHY SECTOR	4-9-16		Battalion holding line. During the early hours of the morning, enemy shelled O.B.L and RUE DE CAILLOUX with shrapnel. At 10 a.m. several H.E. were fired in the vicinity of the Brewery. Several enemy aeroplanes crossed our lines during the morning.	
— do —	5-9-16		Battalion holding line. Five light high explosive shells fell between O.B.L and Brewery about midnight 4th/5th. Short bursts of M.G. fire during the night and normal rifle fire. Enemy fired 30 light shells, on RUE DE CAILLOUX, and 8 - 4.7" shells fell near the Brewery the majority of which did not explode. At 4.30 p.m. Our light trench mortars supported by Field Artillery bombarded tender spots in the enemy line. Enemy artillery retaliated. The following Officers and 1 Other Rank were wounded:— Lieut W.A. HARVEY 2/Lieut W.A. HERYET 2/Lieut A.H.D. CARPENTER.	

Army Form C. 2118.

WAR DIARY
or
INTELLIGENCE SUMMARY.
(Erase heading not required.)

Place	Date	Hour	Summary of Events and Information	Remarks and references to Appendices
LEFT. SUBSECTOR GIVENCHY SECTOR	3/9/17		Battalion holding line. Enemy fired about 20 - H.E's on BARNTON TEE. Short bursts of machine gun fire. Barnton Road was shelled between 9 a.m. and 10.30 a.m. with 4.4 m/m. The usual patrol was sent out by each Front Line Company but no enemy patrols were encountered, and no work was heard to be in progress in the enemy lines. Consolidation and repairs to our trenches which were damaged by the enemy artillery the previous day were carried out, and a large quantity of wire was placed in position. Capt. L. DYER was struck off the establishment of the Battalion.	
- do -	4/9/17		Battalion holding line. An enemy captive balloon was brought down at about 2.30 p.m. opposite BARNTON CENTRAL. Eight high explosive shells fell on RUE DE CAILLOUX between 12 m.n. and 1 a.m. The Battalion was relieved by the 22nd Bn ROYAL FUSILIERS, and on relief took over billets vacated by that Battalion in the TOBACCO FACTORY,	

Army Form C. 2118.

WAR DIARY
or
INTELLIGENCE SUMMARY.
(Erase heading not required.)

Place	Date	Hour	Summary of Events and Information	Remarks and references to Appendices
LEFT SUB-SECTOR & BETHUNE	7/9/17		BETHUNE. The Portuguese Company continued their instruction under the relieving Battalion. The Battalion moved by half platoon to GORRE thence by Companies to BETHUNE via South Bank of the LA BASSEE CANAL.	
BETHUNE	8/9/17		The day was spent in cleaning up, kit and other inspections. 2/Lieut J.D. ROBINSON returned to Battalion from 2nd Divisional Rest Depot. 2/Lieut H.A. MULKERN returned from Hospital. 2/Lieut H.L. BROOKE proceeded on leave to England.	
BETHUNE	9/9/17		The day was observed as a holiday as far as possible. Divine Services were held at 9.30 a.m. and 10 a.m. in the Unfinished Church, RUE D'AIRE. The undermentioned Officers were given permission to wear the badges of the rank of Captain:- Lieut A.W. NEW. Lieut J.D. STEELE. 2/Lieut R.G. BOX proceeded for six days attachment to the 14th Supporting Battery	

Army Form C. 2118.

WAR DIARY
or
INTELLIGENCE SUMMARY.
(Erase heading not required.)

Instructions regarding War Diaries and Intelligence Summaries are contained in F. S. Regs., Part II. and the Staff Manual respectively. Title pages will be prepared in manuscript.

Place	Date	Hour	Summary of Events and Information	Remarks and references to Appendices
BETHUNE	9.9.17	8.15	R.F.A. Major A.A. MACFARLANE-GRIEVE returned from leave to England.	
BETHUNE	10.9.17	8.15	"A" and "B" Coys carried out Range practice at the Divisional Range, LE QUESNOY from 8.a.m to 12 noon. From 2pm. to 3pm drills on Divisional Training Ground RUE DE VILLE. "C" and "D" Coys paraded for inspection at 8.30 a.m., and proceeded to the Divisional Training Ground for instruction by the Divisional Draft Training School instructors. From 2 p.m. do 3 p.m. Musketry Parade. 2/Lieut H.A.MULKERN took over command of "A" Coy.	
BETHUNE	11.9.17	8.15	Training carried out as per programme. A football match was played between this Battalion and the 1st Batt. Essex Regiment. Kick off 5.30 pm. Result drawn 1goal each. 2/Lieut G.G. SMYTH returned from leave to TOURNE' HEM. 2/Lieut R.C.H. MAY. Medical Board 19/1/17. FIT G.S. Received 14 days Cy.	

Army Form C. 2118.

WAR DIARY
or
INTELLIGENCE SUMMARY.
(Erase heading not required.)

Instructions regarding War Diaries and Intelligence Summaries are contained in F. S. Regs., Part II. and the Staff Manual respectively. Title pages will be prepared in manuscript.

Place	Date	Hour	Summary of Events and Information	Remarks and references to Appendices
BETHUNE	12.9.15		Training carried out during morning. Games during afternoon	
BETHUNE	13.9.15		"A" "B" Coys paraded at 8 a.m and marched to Bombing Ground, LE QUESNOY and carried out Bombing practice. Exercises were also carried out in formation of attack over broken trench ground, and bombing along trenches. "C" & "D" Coys paraded at 8.30 a.m for inspections. These two companies were handed over to the instructors at the Divisional Training School at 9 a.m. Bombing practices were carried out in the afternoon. 2/Lieut C.W. PHILIPS proceeded on leave to England.	
BETHUNE	14.9.15		Companies carried out training as in previous day. Games during the afternoon. The undermentioned proceeded for a course of instruction at the XI Corps Infantry School. 2/Lieut. H.L. HUGHES. 2/Lieut. M.S. CLAYDON.	

WAR DIARY
or
INTELLIGENCE SUMMARY.
(Erase heading not required.)

Army Form C. 2118.

Place	Date	Hour	Summary of Events and Information	Remarks and references to Appendices
BETHUNE	16.9.14		This day was observed as a holiday as far as possible the inferior shots of the Battalion were practised on the Range from 9.30 a.m. till 12 noon. One Officer per Company, and all ranks not on duty attended a church parade service in the unfinished church, RUE D'AIRE. The following were presented with medal ribbons by the Divisional-General:-	

Major A.A. MACFARLANE-GRIEVE M.C.
Capt S.E. COLLIER M.C.
Lieut A.R. WELLS M.C.
18169 Sgt H. PIERCY M.M.
28403 Sgt A. MANNING M.M.
17348 Sgt J.J. ASH D.C.M.

24161 Sgt G.J. WRIGHT M.M.
19914 Pte W.J. PEACOCK M.N.
14184 Pte J.F. WILKINSON M.M.
23940 Pte H.E. WOOD M.M.
13363 Sgt T. PEARTREE M.M.

Capt A.W. NEW returned from 1st Army School.
2 Lieut A.C. TIMMS admitted to Hospital whilst with 64th Infantry Brigade

Army Form C. 2118.

WAR DIARY
or
INTELLIGENCE SUMMARY.
(Erase heading not required.)

Place	Date	Hour	Summary of Events and Information	Remarks and references to Appendices
BETHUNE	15.9.17		"A" and "B" Companies. Route March under Major A.A. MACFARLANE-GRIEVE M.C. starting at 8.45 a.m. "C" and "D" Coys paraded at 8.30 a.m. for inspection and were handed over to the Officer commanding at the @ Divisional Training Ground at 9 a.m for instruction. Games at 2.30 p.m. Regular and Reserve Signallers paraded at 9 a.m. under the Signalling Officer for instruction in the theory and manipulation of the Power Buzzer. Stretcher Bearers paraded under the Medical Officer at 9 a.m. The undermentioned returned from Corps Infantry School 2/Lieut. H.R.E.KING 2/Lieut. R.B.TONKIN. 2/Lieut R.G.Box returned from 14th Battery R.F.A.	

Army Form C. 2118.

WAR DIARY
or
INTELLIGENCE SUMMARY.
(Erase heading not required.)

Instructions regarding War Diaries and Intelligence Summaries are contained in F.S. Regs., Part II. and the Staff Manual respectively. Title pages will be prepared in manuscript.

Place	Date	Hour	Summary of Events and Information	Remarks and references to Appendices
BETHUNE	14.9.17		"A" & "B" Coys carried out training as per programme. "C" & "D" Coys proceeded to Divisional training ground for instruction as on previous days.	
BETHUNE & WINDY CORNER	18 & 19		"A" & "B" Coys carried out Bombing practice in the morning, also Musketry over rough trench ground. "C" & "D" Coys. Training at Divisional training ground. Signallers paraded under the Signalling Officer. The Battalion relieved the 22nd Bn ROYAL FUSILIERS in the Support Area at WINDY CORNER. "A" Coy in Keeps. "B" Coy. O.B.L. "C" & "D" Coys WINDY CORNER. 2/Lieut H.V. COOK returned from leave to England. 2/Lieut W. STUART-BROWNE granted extension of leave.	
WINDY CORNER to	19.9.17 to		Working parties supplied for Brigade, 252nd Royal Engineers, 54th Field Coy. R.E, and assistance was rendered to Z2 Trench Mortar Battery in digging emplacements.	

Army Form C. 2118.

WAR DIARY
or
INTELLIGENCE SUMMARY.
(Erase heading not required.)

Instructions regarding War Diaries and Intelligence Summaries are contained in F. S. Regs., Part II. and the Staff Manual respectively. Title pages will be prepared in manuscript.

Place	Date	Hour	Summary of Events and Information	Remarks and references to Appendices
WINDY CORNER	19.9.17 to 23.9.17		2/Lieut F.H. AUSTIN rejoined from Hospital 20/9/17. 2/Lieut E.A. PATTERSON proceeded on leave 20/9/17. A/Capt A.W. NEW transferred from "D" Coy to "B" Coy 21-9-17. 1 Other Rank "wounded at duty" 21/9/17.	
WINDY CORNER & LEFT. SUBSECTOR GIVENCHY SECTOR	24.9.17	4.30	At 4.30 a.m. Enemy carried out a raid on LEFT. SUBSECTOR. A heavy barrage was put up on the SUPPORT AREA. Battalion stood-to till all was quiet. The raid was carried out under cover of a dense mist, and the enemy entered front line, from which he was promptly ejected. The Battalion relieved the 14th Bn MIDDLESEX REGT in the LEFT. SUBSECTOR, GIVENCHY SECTOR. The relief was completed by 9.30 p.m.	
LEFT. SUB-SECTOR GIVENCHY SECTOR	24/25.9.17		The night 24/25th passed quietly with no further action by the enemy. Front line Companies sent out the usual patrols and wiring parties. No enemy patrols or working parties were encountered. Heard on	

Army Form C. 2118.

WAR DIARY
or
INTELLIGENCE SUMMARY.

(Erase heading not required.)

Instructions regarding War Diaries and Intelligence Summaries are contained in F. S. Regs., Part II. and the Staff Manual respectively. Title pages will be prepared in manuscript.

Place	Date	Hour	Summary of Events and Information	Remarks and references to Appendices
LEFT SUB. SECTOR	25.9.17		Rem: During afternoon Enemy Trench Mortars and Machine Guns were active	
GIVENCHY SECTOR			Capt F.R.KEEBLE M.C. proceeded on leave to England. 2/Lieut H.H.QLEN was admitted to Hospital	
— do —	26.9.17		During the night of 25th/26th there was very little activity on either side. Artillery occasionally active during the day. C.W. PHILLIPS Returned from leave to England. The undermentioned Officers were given permission to wear the badges of the rank of Lieutenant. 2/Lieut H.L. HUGHES. 2/Lieut A. NETHERCOTT.	
— do —	24.9.17		At 5.30 a.m. our Indian Trench Mortar Batteries supported by the Artillery carried out an operation, and a party under Lieut F.J. SOUTHERN greatly assisted in making the operation an entire success.	

WAR DIARY
or
INTELLIGENCE SUMMARY.

(Erase heading not required.)

Army Form C. 2118.

Place	Date	Hour	Summary of Events and Information	Remarks and references to Appendices
LEFT SUBSECTOR GIVENCHY SECTOR	27/9/17	6 p.m	"A" Coy relieved "D" Coy in the RIGHT FRONT. "D" Coy returning to the O.B.L.	
—do—	28/9/17	6 p.m	Our Artillery carried out several organised shoots in selected spots in the enemy's lines assisted by our Trench Mortars. Retaliation was slight. One of our observation balloons was brought down by an enemy aeroplane. The occupants descended by means of parachutes. 2/Lieut G.G. SMYTH was admitted to hospital. 2/Lieut V.E. BLOOMFIELD proceeded for a course of instruction at the Corps Lewis Gun School. 2/Lieut F.A. JENNS proceeded on leave to England.	
—do—	29/9/17	6 p.m	Enemy Machine Guns active in the early hours of the day. Patrols and wiring parties were sent out, and met with no resistance in carrying out their duties.	

WAR DIARY
or
INTELLIGENCE SUMMARY.
(Erase heading not required.)

Army Form C. 2118.

Place	Date	Hour	Summary of Events and Information	Remarks and references to Appendices
LEFT SUBSECTOR GIVENCHY SECTOR	28/9/17	2.15	2/Lieut W.K. BESSEX proceeded for a course of instruction at the 1st Army School. 1 Other Rank Wounded.	
—do—	30/9/17	12.13	At about 12.30 a.m. enemy bombarded GIVENCHY KEEPS with Gas shell. The necessary precautions were taken in our Sector. All clear was received at 3. a.m. 1 Other Rank Killed.	

STRENGTH OF BATTALION.

Effective Strength. 41 Officers 845 Other Ranks
Fighting   do.   24   "   554   "   "
Trench   do.   23   "   442   "   "

[signature] Major
Commanding:- 13th Res. Essex Regt.

6th Brigade.

2nd Division.

13th BATTALION

THE ESSEX REGIMENT

OCTOBER 1917.

Army Form C. 2118.

WAR DIARY
or
INTELLIGENCE SUMMARY
(Erase heading not required.)

**CONFIDENTIAL
WAR DIARY
of
13TH (SERVICE) BATTN ESSEX REGIMENT
October 1st to 31st
1917**

WAR DIARY
or
INTELLIGENCE SUMMARY.

(Erase heading not required.)

Army Form C. 2118.

Place	Date	Hour	Summary of Events and Information	Remarks and references to Appendices
GORRE	1-10-19		Baths were allotted to the Battalion, and the day was spent in cleaning up, and inspections of kit etc. Lieut. Colonel A.E.F. HARRIS. D.S.O. took over command of the Infantry Brigade on 30-9-19, during the absence of Brig. Gen. R WALSH D.S.O. Major A.A. MacFARLANE-GRIEVE M.C. took over the command of the Battn. a/Major J. WALSH joined the Battalion for duty.	
GORRE	2-10-19		"A" and "B" Coys carried out practices on the Range at LE QUESNOY "C" and "D" Coys carried out tactical training. Stretcher Bearers received instruction from the Medical Officer. 3/Lieut Ranks rejoined the Battalion via 2 Divisional Draft School. " " " " " joined " " " " " 2/Lieut E.A. PATTERSON returned from leave to England 2/Lieut R.G. BOX proceed to 3 Div Draft School for attachment as an instructor. Major A.A MACFARLANE-GRIEVE M.C. proceeded to Senior Infantry School ALDERSHOT for a course of instruction, and is struck off the Battalion accordingly	

WAR DIARY or INTELLIGENCE SUMMARY

Army Form C. 2118.

(Erase heading not required.)

Instructions regarding War Diaries and Intelligence Summaries are contained in F.S. Regs., Part II. and the Staff Manual respectively. Title pages will be prepared in manuscript.

Place	Date	Hour	Summary of Events and Information	Remarks and references to Appendices
GORRE	2.10.14		Major J. WALSH took over command of the Battalion during the absence of Lieut. Colonel A.E.F. HARRIS D.S.O. Comdg: 64th Infantry Brigade. A Carrying Party of 1 Lance Cpl and eleven men was provided for the Z 2 Trench Mortar Battery.	
GORRE	3.10.14		Left Half Battalion fired on 30 yards Range from 8.30 a.m. to 10.30 a.m.	
			Right " " " " " " 10.30 a.m. to 12.30 p.m.	
			Left Half Battalion carried out a tactical scheme under Company arrangements from 10.30 a.m. to 12.30 p.m.	
			Right " " " " " " " " 8.30 a.m. to 10.30 a.m.	
			Regular and Reserve Signallers paraded under Signalling Officer for instruction.	
			Stretcher Bearers received instruction from the Medical Officer.	
			The Regimental Band played selections on the Chateau Parade Ground from 2 p.m. to 4 p.m.	
			2/Lieut W.S. McLAREN proceeded for attachment to R.F.C. for instructional purposes.	
GORRE	4.10.14		Left half Battalion fired on 30 yards Range from 8.30 a.m. to 10.30 a.m.	
			Right " " " " " " 10.30 a.m. to 12.30 p.m.	

Army Form C. 2118.

WAR DIARY
or
INTELLIGENCE SUMMARY.
(Erase heading not required.)

Instructions regarding War Diaries and Intelligence Summaries are contained in F. S. Regs., Part II. and the Staff Manual respectively. Title pages will be prepared in manuscript.

Place	Date	Hour	Summary of Events and Information	Remarks and references to Appendices
GORRE	4-10-17		Regt Half Battalion carried out a tactical scheme under Company arrangements from 10.30 a.m to 12.30 p.m.	
			Right " " " " " " " " 8.40 a.m to 10.30 a.m	
			Bombers and Rifle Bombers paraded under their instructors	
			31 Other Ranks rejoined the Battalion for duty	
			90 " " " joined	
			2nd Lieut R.G. Box Returned from 2nd Divisional Draft School	
			2nd Lieut A. C. TIMMS " " " " "	
			2nd Lieut HAMULKERN to Hospital.	
			Lieut J.D. ROBINSON proceeded on leave to England	
GORRE	5-10-17		The day was occupied in cleaning up billets and surroundings.	
			The Battalion was relieved in the Reserve Area by the 8th Batln. LOYAL NORTH LANCS and on relief moved to BETHUNE via GORRE DRAWBRIDGE and Road running parallel to and SOUTH of CANAL, and took over billets at ECOLE des JEUNES FILLES	
			Pvt. F.J. SOUTHERN admitted to Hospital.	
			5 Other Ranks rejoined the Battalion via 2nd Divisional Draft School.	
			2 Lieut E.L. CORPS and 34 Other Ranks returned from 5th Field Company, R.E.	

253 Wt W₃544/1454 700,000 5/15 D. D. & L. A.D.S.S./Forms/C. 2118.

Army Form C. 2118.

WAR DIARY
or
INTELLIGENCE SUMMARY.
(Erase heading not required.)

Instructions regarding War Diaries and Intelligence Summaries are contained in F.S. Regs., Part II. and the Staff Manual respectively. Title pages will be prepared in manuscript.

Place	Date	Hour	Summary of Events and Information	Remarks and references to Appendices
BETHUNE	6/10/1917		The Battalion was medically inspected. Companies were inspected in full marching order under Company arrangement. 18 Other Ranks returned to the Battalion from 401st Sumelding Coy. R.E. 2/Lieut. W.S. McLAREN returned from R.F.C.	
BETHUNE & LOZINGHEM	7/10/17		The Battalion moved into billets at LOZINGHEM starting from BETHUNE at 8.25 am. Starting point:- PAON DOR at corner of the Marche Aux Chevaux and Boulevard of Victor Hugo. Order of march:- HQs. "A" "B" "C" "D" Coys. Transport. Route:- CHOCQUES - LE REVEILLON - ALLOUAGNE. Relief was complete at 12.730p.m. Capt. F. R. KEEBLE returned from leave to England. 2/Lieut. Col. A.E.F. HARRIS D.S.O. relinquished command of 6th Infantry Brigade. Major J. WALSH relinquished command of the Battalion.	
LOZINGHEM	8/10/17		Training carried out under Company arrangements. Lieut. Col. A.E.F. HARRIS D.S.O. resumed command of the Battalion.	

WAR DIARY
or
INTELLIGENCE SUMMARY.

(Erase heading not required.)

Army Form C. 2118.

Instructions regarding War Diaries and Intelligence Summaries are contained in F. S. Regs., Part II. and the Staff Manual respectively. Title pages will be prepared in manuscript.

Place	Date	Hour	Summary of Events and Information	Remarks and references to Appendices
LOZINGHEM	8-10-17		Major J. WALSH resumed the duties of Second-in-command. Capt. F.R. KEEBLE resumed command of "B" Coy.	
LOZINGHEM	9-10-17		Training was carried out on the following subjects under Company arrangements: CLOSE ORDER DRILL, MUSKETRY, SPECIALIST TRAINING, EXTENDED ORDER DRILL, BAYONET FIGHTING, PHYSICAL TRAINING, and Company exercise for Officers and N.C.Os. 2/Lieut A.E. TIMMS proceeded on leave to England.	
LOZINGHEM	10-10-17		Training was carried out on the programme on subjects so as to qualify by Coy. by Coy. the Brigade Range at U.29.9.0 was alloted to "A" Coy from 9am to 11am, and to "B" Coy from 11am to 1pm. Stretcher bearers paraded for instruction under the Medical Officer. Scouts and Observers of "A" Coy paraded for instruction under Officer E.C. HALL. Signallers paraded under the Signalling Officer. He 1.2. and 4. platoons of "B" Coy used the morning stationed in the 2nd Echelon as practice musketry competition.	

WAR DIARY
or
INTELLIGENCE SUMMARY.

(Erase heading not required.)

Army Form C. 2118.

Place	Date	Hour	Summary of Events and Information	Remarks and references to Appendices
LOZINGHEM	11/10/19		Training was carried out in the following subjects under Company arrangements:- MUSKETRY, SPECIALIST TRAINING, CLOSE ORDER DRILL, RIFLE EXERCISES, PHYSICAL TRAINING, SALUTING, SKIRMISHING. During which Preparations were made for a shoot fired. Practice "A" of Divisional Lewis Competition was fired on the 30 yards Range. 4 Other Ranks rejoined the Battalion for duty. 13 Other Ranks joined the Battalion for duty.	
LOZINGHEM	12/10/19		Training was carried out similar to previous to above. Fatigues were allotted to the Battalion. Captain F. A. JENNS returned from leave to England. Lieut. Col. A.E.F. HARRIS D.S.O. took over command of 4th Infantry Brigade. Major J. WALSH took over command of the Battalion. 21 Other Ranks joined the Battalion for duty.	
LOZINGHEM	13/10/19		Training was carried out in the following subjects under Company arrangements:- TRENCH TO TRENCH ATTACK, CLOSE ORDER DRILL, ANTI-GAS DRILL, PHYSICAL DRILL, BAYONET FIGHTING.	

Army Form C. 2118.

WAR DIARY
or
INTELLIGENCE SUMMARY.
(Erase heading not required.)

Instructions regarding War Diaries and Intelligence Summaries are contained in F. S. Regs., Part II. and the Staff Manual respectively. Title pages will be prepared in manuscript.

Place	Date	Hour	Summary of Events and Information	Remarks and references to Appendices
LOZINGHEM	13.10.19		The Lumpline Section paraded for instruction. The undermentioned Officers proceeded for a special course of instruction at XVIII Corps School. Capt. G. SIMPSON Capt. F.R. KEEBLE M.C. 2/Lieut (acpt) H.T. JESSOP 2/Lieut (acpt) H.A. MULKERN. The undermentioned returned from XI Corps Infantry School. 2/Lieut. (Lieut) H.L. HUGHES 2/Lieut M.S. CLAYDON 2/Lieut V.E. BLOOMFIELD returned from XI Corps Lewis Gun School.	
LOZINGHEM	14.10.19		A practice parade was carried out on the Battalion Drill ground in drill Order at 10 a.m. followed by a Church Parade. Services were also held for other denominations. Captain. S.E. COLLIER and Captain A.E. BUNTING proceeded on leave to England. Capt. J.G.H. KENNEFICK took over the duties of Transport Officer during the absence of Capt. S.E. COLLIER 2/Lieut. F.A. JENNS took over the duties of Adjutant during the absence of Capt. A.E. BUNTING. The undermentioned Officers took over the command of Companies during the absence of the	

Army Form C. 2118.

WAR DIARY
or
INTELLIGENCE SUMMARY.
(Erase heading not required.)

Place	Date	Hour	Summary of Events and Information	Remarks and references to Appendices
LOZINGHEM	4-10-19		Company Commanders at XVIII Corps School. 2/Lieut R.B.TONKIN "A" Coy. 2/Lieut (Lieut) A. NETHERCOTT "C" Coy Lieut (Capt) A.W. NEW "B" Coy. Lieut (Capt) J.D. STEELE "D" Coy. 9 Other Ranks joined the Battalion for duty.	

LOZINGHEM	5-10-19		The 6th Infantry Brigade was inspected by the General Commanding First Army.
			 The Battalion formed up on the Battalion Drill Ground and marched to the Brigade
			 Training Ground at RAIMBERT.
			 The Battalion were represented by a Platoon from "B" Company in the Brigade Competition of
			 the 2nd Divisional Rifleman and Marksmen's Competition.
			 The undermentioned Officers returned from Hospital
			     Lieut. F.J. SOUTHERN.
			     2/Lieut. F.C. RANSOM.
			 2/Lieut (Lieut) took over command of "C" Coy vice 2/Lieut (Lieut) A. NETHERCOTT.	

LOZINGHEM	6-10-19		Training was carried out by "A" and "B" Coys.	

Army Form C. 2118.

WAR DIARY
or
INTELLIGENCE SUMMARY.
(Erase heading not required.)

Place	Date	Hour	Summary of Events and Information	Remarks and references to Appendices
LOZINGHEM	16-10-14		The Range at U.29.C. was allotted to "C" and "D" Coys, as follows:– "C" Coy 1pm to 3pm "D" Coy 3pm to 5pm The Battalion was represented by a Section from "B" Coy in the Brigade Lewis Gun Competition on the Range at U.29.C.	
LOZINGHEM	17-10-14		Training was carried out by the Battalion in the following subjects:– CLOSE ORDER DRILL, RIFLE EXERCISES, PHYSICAL TRAINING, BAYONET FIGHTING, MUSKETRY, TACTICAL INSTRUCTION, and lectures to Officers and N.C.O. Six Snipers paraded for instruction under Lieut F.J. SOUTHERN. Stretcher Bearers paraded for instruction under the Medical Officer. Signallers from Company Signal Stations paraded for instruction under the Signalling Officer. The undermentioned Company Commanders returned from XVIII Corps School 2/Lieut (Capt) H.A. MULKERN "A" Coy. Capt G. SIMPSON "C" Coy. Capt F.R. KEEBLE "B" Coy. Lt (Capt) H.T. JESSOP "D" Coy.	
LOZINGHEM	18-10-14		"A" and "B" Coys carried practices on the Range at C.15.C. as follows:–	

Army Form C. 2118.

WAR DIARY
or
INTELLIGENCE SUMMARY.
(Erase heading not required.)

Instructions regarding War Diaries and Intelligence Summaries are contained in F. S. Regs., Part II. and the Staff Manual respectively. Title pages will be prepared in manuscript.

Place	Date	Hour	Summary of Events and Information	Remarks and references to Appendices
LOZINGHEM	18-10-14		"A" Coy Second class figure target (normal sighting) from 9am to 11am.	
			Full length figure target (using battle sight) " 11am to 1pm	
			"B" Coy as above	
			"C" and "D" Coys carried out training on 30 yards Range and Drill ground in COMPANY DRILL, PHYSICAL TRAINING and BAYONET FIGHTING, and SALUTING, also a Company Tactical Exercise	
			Stretcher Bearers paraded for instruction under the Medical Officer	
			All other Specialists of "A" and "B" Coy paraded under their respective instructors	
			Specialists of "C" and "D" Coys paraded with their respective Companies.	
			Lieut. J.D. ROBINSON returned from leave to England.	
			Hon. Lieut. & Quartermaster N. LANG proceeded on one month's leave to England	
LOZINGHEM	19-10-14		Training was carried out in subjects chosen by Company Commanders.	
			Battalion Snipers carried out Practices on the 50 yards Range from 8am. to 11am.	
			Headquarters " " " " " 11am. to 1pm	
			"A" and "C" Coys 8.30-10.15am. "B" and "D" Coys 10.15am. to 12 noon	
			Companies carried out a tactical scheme.	

Army Form C. 2118.

WAR DIARY
or
INTELLIGENCE SUMMARY.
(Erase heading not required.)

Instructions regarding War Diaries and Intelligence
Summaries are contained in F. S. Regs., Part II.
and the Staff Manual respectively. Title pages
will be prepared in manuscript.

Place	Date	Hour	Summary of Events and Information	Remarks and references to Appendices
LOZINGHEM	19.10.17		Specialists paraded under their instructors	
LOZINGHEM	20.10.17		Training was carried out as per programme. Specialists paraded under their respective instructors. 2/Lieut. R.B. TONKIN proceeded on leave to England.	
LOZINGHEM	21.10.17		A Church Parade was held on the Battalion Drill Ground, commencing at 11.15 a.m. Services for other denominations were also held during the day. 2nd Lieut. A.C. TIMMS returned from leave to England. 2nd Lieut. F.H. AUSTIN was admitted to Hospital.	
LOZINGHEM	22.10.17		Training was carried out on the Tactical Ground and Drill Ground by all Companies. The Brigade Range at U.G.E. was allotted as follows:- "B" Coy 9 a.m. to 11 a.m. "C" Coy 11 a.m. to 1 p.m. practices were carried out at full length figure with battle sight, rapid. Other practices were desired by O.C. Coys. The 30 yards range was allotted to "A" Coy's Lewis Guns from 10.45 a.m. to 1 p.m., and to "B" Coy's	

2353 Wt. W2544/1454 700,000 5/15 D. D. & L.   A.D.S.S./Forms/C. 2118.

WAR DIARY
or
INTELLIGENCE SUMMARY.
(Erase heading not required.)

Army Form C. 2118.

Place	Date	Hour	Summary of Events and Information	Remarks and references to Appendices
LOZINGHEM	22.10.14		Lewis Guns 8 a.m. to 10.15 a.m.	
LOZINGHEM	23.10.14		A Practice Scheme was carried out by the Battalion. The 50 yards Range was allotted to the Battalion Snipers from 8 a.m. to 12.30 p.m. 2/Lieut. E.L. CORPS proceeded on leave to England. Lieut. Colonel A.E.F. HARRIS D.S.O. relinquished command of 6th Infantry Brigade on return of Brig. Gen. R. WALSH. D.S.O., and resumed command of the Battalion. Major J. WALSH resumed the duties of Second-in-Command of the Battalion. A Brigade tactical exercise was carried out, in which the Battalion took part. The Battalion was formed up in the Battalion Drill Ground, and moved off at 9 a.m.	
LOZINGHEM	24.10.14		The Baths at Raimbert were allotted to the Battalion as follows:- "A" Coy 10 a.m. to 11 a.m. "B" Coy 11 a.m. to 12 noon "C" Coy 8 a.m. to 9 a.m. "D" Coy 9 a.m. to 10 a.m. Tactical training was carried out by "A" Coy from 12 noon to 1 p.m., and by "B" Coy from 8 a.m. to 10 a.m.	

WAR DIARY
or
INTELLIGENCE SUMMARY.
(Erase heading not required.)

Army Form C. 2118.

Place	Date	Hour	Summary of Events and Information	Remarks and references to Appendices
LOZINGHEM	25-10-17		"A" Coy carried out training on the Drill Ground from 9 a.m. to 9 a.m. Specialists paraded under their respective instructors. "C" and "D" Coys and 30 men from Headquarters attended a demonstration on ground in C.15.c, showing the different phases in the daily training of a platoon. A football match was played versus ROYAL BERKS. Result ROYAL BERKS 1, ESSEX nil.	
LOZINGHEM	26-10-17		The Brigade Range was allotted as follows:- "A" Coy's Lewis Guns 9 a.m. to 10 a.m. "C" Coys Lewis Guns 11 a.m. to 12 noon "B" Coy's " 10 a.m. to 11 a.m. "D" Coys " 12 noon to 1 p.m. (Practices at full length figures with battle sights) The 50 yards Range was allotted as follows:- "A" Coy 11 a.m. to 12 noon "C" Coy 8.15 a.m. to 9.15 a.m. "B" Coy 12 noon to 1 p.m. "D" Coy 9.15 a.m. to 10.15 a.m. Training was carried out on the Drill Ground and Tactical Ground by all Companies. Specialists paraded under their respective instructors.	

Army Form C. 2118.

WAR DIARY
or
INTELLIGENCE SUMMARY.
(Erase heading not required.)

Instructions regarding War Diaries and Intelligence Summaries are contained in F. S. Regs., Part II. and the Staff Manual respectively. Title pages will be prepared in manuscript.

Place	Date	Hour	Summary of Events and Information	Remarks and references to Appendices
LOZINGHEM	24/10/17		Training was carried out as selected by Company Commanders. Specialists paraded under their respective instructors. Night operations were practised.	
LOZINGHEM	28/10/17		Church Parade was held on the Battalion Drill Ground, commencing at 11.15 a.m. A Roman Catholic Church Parade was held at the Parish Church. LOZINGHEM at 9 a.m. Divine Services for other denominations were also held during the day. The undermentioned Officers returned from leave to England. Capt. S. E. COLLIER M.C. Capt. A. E. BUNTING. Capt. A.E. BUNTING resumes the duties of Adjutant. 2/Lieut. F.A. JENNS resumes the duties of Assistant Adjutant. Capt. S.E. COLLIER M.C. resumes the duties of Transport Officer vice Capt J.G.H. KENNEFICK 2/Lieut E.A. PATTERSON was transferred from "B" Coy to "A" Coy.	

2353 Wt. W2514/1454 700,000 5/15 D. D. & L. A.D.S.S./Forms/C. 2118.

Army Form C. 2118.

WAR DIARY
or
INTELLIGENCE SUMMARY.
(Erase heading not required.)

Instructions regarding War Diaries and Intelligence Summaries are contained in F. S. Regs., Part II. and the Staff Manual respectively. Title pages will be prepared in manuscript.

Place	Date	Hour	Summary of Events and Information	Remarks and references to Appendices
LOZINGHEM	29.10.17		The Range at U.29.c.2.6 was allotted as follows:- "A" Coy 1 p.m. to 3 p.m. "B" Coy 3 p.m. to 5 p.m. "C" and "D" Coys carried out training in the following subjects:- CLOSE ORDER DRILL, PHYSICAL TRAINING, BAYONET FIGHTING and TACTICAL INSTRUCTION A Battalion Exercise was carried out for Officers and N.C.Os from 2 p.m. to 3.30 p.m. Specialists paraded under their respective instructors	
LOZINGHEM	30.10.17		A Brigade Tactical Exercise was carried out during the day in which the Battalion took part.	
LOZINGHEM	31.10.17		Training was carried out as per programme in the following subjects:- CLOSE ORDER DRILL PHYSICAL TRAINING and BAYONET FIGHTING BATTALION TACTICAL SCHEME BATTALION EXERCISE for Officers & N.C.Os.	

Army Form C. 2118.

WAR DIARY
or
INTELLIGENCE SUMMARY.

(Erase heading not required.)

Instructions regarding War Diaries and Intelligence Summaries are contained in F. S. Regs., Part II. and the Staff Manual respectively. Title pages will be prepared in manuscript.

Place	Date	Hour	Summary of Events and Information	Remarks and references to Appendices
LOZINGHEM	31-10-19		Specialists paraded under their respective instructors. A football match was played between 13th Essex and 3rd Canadian Reinforcement. Result:- a draw with no score.	
			Strength of Battalion	
			Effective Strength 39 Officers. 1042 Other ranks	
			Fighting Strength 39 " 1041 " "	
			Trench Strength 28 " 884 " "	
	1-11-19			

A. Adam Lieut. Colonel.
Comndng: 13 Battn The Essex Regiment

6th Brigade.

2nd Division.

13th BATTALION

THE ESSEX REGIMENT

November (handwritten)

~~DECEMBER~~ 1917.

For narrative of Operations up to night 4/5th see War Diary for November 1917.

CONFIDENTIAL

WAR DIARY
of
13th (S) Batn Essex Regiment

NOVEMBER 1st to 30th 1917

WAR DIARY or INTELLIGENCE SUMMARY

Army Form C. 2118.

Place	Date	Hour	Summary of Events and Information	Remarks and references to Appendices
LOZINGHEM	1-11-14		Training was carried out by the Battalion as follows:-	

"C" and "D" Coys were allotted the Range at U.29.c.2.6 and carried out practices at full length figure (200 yards) fixed bayonets and battle sight.

"A" and "B" Coys carried out practices in forming up, and rushing strong points, special attention being paid to meeting and dealing with the unexpected.

The Lewis Gunners and Snipers of "A" and "B" Coys carried out practices on the 30 yards Range.

"A" and "B" Coys were passed through the Brigade Gas Chamber.

A Battalion Parade was carried out at 5 p.m., and practised "Forming up for attack".

A Court of Enquiry assembled in the Recreation Room, to investigate the circumstances of the shortage of luminous sights.

| LOZINGHEM | 2-11-14 | | Training was carried out by the Battalion in the following subjects:- | |

Tactical Instruction
Physical Training
Bayonet Fighting
Drill

Army Form C. 2118.

WAR DIARY
or
INTELLIGENCE SUMMARY.
(Erase heading not required.)

Instructions regarding War Diaries and Intelligence Summaries are contained in F. S. Regs., Part II. and the Staff Manual respectively. Title pages will be prepared in manuscript.

Place	Date	Hour	Summary of Events and Information	Remarks and references to Appendices
LOZINGHEM	2-11-19		"C" and "D" Coys passed through the Brigade Gas School. "A" and "B" Coys and Battalion Snipers carried out practices on the 30 yards Range. The Lewis Guns of the Battalion were inspected by the D.A.D.O.S. The undermentioned Officers proceeded on leave to England. Capt. F.R. KEEBLE M.C. Lieut A.R. WELLS. Capt. A.W. NEW. took over command of "B" Coy during the absence of Capt. F.R. KEEBLE M.C. 2/Lieut R.B. TONKIN returned from leave to England.	↓
LOZINGHEM	3-11-19		A Battalion Scheme was carried out in continuation of night operations of 1/11/19. The Battalion Lewis Gunners carried out practices on the Range at U.29.C.2.6 at full length figure.	↓
LOZINGHEM	4-11-19		A Church parade was held on the Battalion Drill Ground at C.12.d.2.3 at 11.15 a.m. A Roman Catholic Church parade was held in the Church at 9 a.m. Services for other denominations were held during the day. 2/Lieut W.K. BESSEX returned from the Army School of Instruction.	↓

Army Form C. 2118.

WAR DIARY
or
INTELLIGENCE SUMMARY.
(Erase heading not required.)

Instructions regarding War Diaries and Intelligence Summaries are contained in F.S. Regs., Part II. and the Staff Manual respectively. Title pages will be prepared in manuscript.

Place	Date	Hour	Summary of Events and Information	Remarks and references to Appendices
LOZINGHEM	4-11-14		2/Lieut E.L. CORPS returned from leave to England.	
LOZINGHEM & STEENBECQUE	5-11-14		The Battalion marched to STEENBECQUE, via HAM-en-ARTOIS - BERGUETTE - ISBERGUES thence along the AIRE ROAD to junction of Road and track 400 yards N. of LA LACQUE RIVER, thence by track over Canal D'AIRE - PECQUEUR - PECQUEUR LOCK, thence via Cross Roads 800 yards N. of the third E in BOESEGHEM, starting at 8 a.m. and completing the journey at 1:30 p.m.	
STEENBECQUE & EECKE Area	6-11-14		The Battalion marched to EECKE AREA, via HAZEBROUCK - St SYLVESTRE CAPPEL starting at 8.20 a.m. and completing the journey at 12. noon. The camp at which the remainder of the day and the night was occupied by the Battalion was situated in Squares P4 and 5 on Sheet 24 BELGIUM & FRANCE. 2/Lieut V.E. BLOOMFIELD proceed on leave to England.	
EECKE Area & HOUTKERQUE	7-11-14		The Battalion marched to a Camp situated in Square D 24 on Sheet 24 BELGIUM & FRANCE near HOUTKERQUE starting at 4.30 a.m. and completing the journey at 11 a.m. Route:- STEENVOORDE - DROGLANDT	

2353 Wt. W2544/1454 700,000 5/15 D. D. & L. A.D.S.S./Forms/C. 2118.

Army Form C. 2118.

WAR DIARY
or
INTELLIGENCE SUMMARY.
(Erase heading not required.)

Instructions regarding War Diaries and Intelligence Summaries are contained in F. S. Regs., Part II. and the Staff Manual respectively. Title pages will be prepared in manuscript.

Place	Date	Hour	Summary of Events and Information	Remarks and references to Appendices
HOUTKERQUE Area	8-11-19		Training was carried out in Areas D.30.e., J.6.a and e. All specialists proceeded to the Training Ground and were instructed by their respective Officers or C.O.s. Stretcher Bearers received instruction from the Medical Officer at the Aid Post.	
HOUTKERQUE Area	9-11-19		Training was carried out by Companies in Areas D.30.e., J.6.a and e in the following subjects:- Physical Training & Bayonet fighting, Musketry, Anti-Gas Drill, Tactical Instruction. Specialists paraded under their respective instructors. Lieut H.R.E. KING proceeded on leave to England.	
HOUTKERQUE Area	10-11-19		Training for all Companies was carried out in the following subjects:- Musketry, Physical Training & Bayonet fighting	

Army Form C. 2118.

WAR DIARY
or
INTELLIGENCE SUMMARY.
(Erase heading not required.)

Instructions regarding War Diaries and Intelligence Summaries are contained in F. S. Regs., Part II. and the Staff Manual respectively. Title pages will be prepared in manuscript.

Place	Date	Hour	Summary of Events and Information	Remarks and references to Appendices
HOUTKERQUE Area	10-11-17		Practice of Advance to Objective followed by consolidation. Specialists paraded under their respective instructors.	
HOUTKERQUE Area	11-11-17		A Church Parade Service was held in the Y.M.C.A Marquee at 9.30 a.m. A Parade Service for Roman Catholics was held in Houtkerque Church at 9.15 a.m. A Parade Service for Nonconformists was held in the Barn at Battalion H.Qs at 10 a.m. Other Services were held throughout the day. Companies paraded as follows for instruction under the Brigade Gas Officer. "A" Coy 11 a.m "B" " 11.30 a.m "C" " 12 noon "D" " 12.30 p.m. A special drill was practised in adjusting the gas mask when wearing the steel helmet, not letting the latter drop on the ground. (2/Lieut) A/Capt H.A. MULKERN proceeded to First Army School of Instruction. 2/Lieut W.K. BESSEX took over command of "A" Company during the absence of (2/Lieut) A/Capt H.A. MULKERN.	

2353 Wt. W2344/1454 700,000 5/15 D. D. & L. A.D.S.S./Forms/C. 2118.

Army Form C. 2118.

WAR DIARY
or
INTELLIGENCE SUMMARY

(Erase heading not required.)

Instructions regarding War Diaries and Intelligence Summaries are contained in F. S. Regs., Part II. and the Staff Manual respectively. Title Pages will be prepared in manuscript.

Place	Date	Hour	Summary of Events and Information	Remarks and references to Appendices
HOUTKERQUE Area	12-11-17		Training was carried out by all Companies in ground situated at D.29.d. D.30.a D.30.b and D.30.d in the following subjects:— Musketry Physical Training Bayonet Fighting Platoon and Company Drill Intensive digging Specialists paraded under their respective Instructors as usual. Captain J. AYLMER attached to Battalion and took over command of "A" Company, vice 2/Lieut W.K. BESSEX.	
HOUTKERQUE Area	13-11-17		Companies moved to training Areas at 9.30 a.m. and practised "Advance and consolidation" between 11 a.m. and 12.30 p.m. Field Kitchens accompanied the Battalion. Half Battalion scheme "forming up in the dark for the attack" was carried out at 5.15 p.m. on ground immediately West of camp. Specialist training continued.	

Army Form C. 2118.

WAR DIARY
or
INTELLIGENCE SUMMARY
(Erase heading not required.)

Instructions regarding War Diaries and Intelligence Summaries are contained in F. S. Regs., Part II. and the Staff Manual respectively. Title Pages will be prepared in manuscript.

Place	Date	Hour	Summary of Events and Information	Remarks and references to Appendices
HOUTKERQUE area	13-11-17		One N.C.O. per Platoon paraded at Q.M. Stores at 9.55 a.m. for instruction in the Yerman Maxim. A similar party received instruction at 1.55 p.m. 2/Lieut F.H. AUSTIN returned from Hospital. 8 O.R. proceeded to 2) Division Depôt Battalion for instruction.	
HOUTKERQUE area	14-11-17		Fire direction attack and consolidation carried out by Companies on Training Ground between 7.30 a.m. and 11 a.m. Half Battalion scheme carried out at 5.15 p.m. as on 13th. Special 2/Lieut training continued. 2/Lieut R.B. TONKIN proceeded to 13th Corps Headquarters for attachment as Corps Pierriere Officer. "A" Coy carried out Company scheme at 11 a.m. and "B" Coy at 12 Noon. "C" and "D" Coys "Advance and to consolidation" between 11 a.m. and 12.30 p.m.	
HOUTKERQUE area	15-11-17		Officers practised at 5 p.m. "Laying out in the dark". Special training continued.	

Army Form C. 2118.

WAR DIARY
or
INTELLIGENCE SUMMARY.
(Erase heading not required.)

Place	Date	Hour	Summary of Events and Information	Remarks and references to Appendices
HOUTKERQUE Area.	16-11-17		Companies moved to Training Areas at 7.40 a.m. Tactical Training was carried out in Wood and on Tactical ground. Range allotted to "C" Coy. Battalion returned to Camp at 11 a.m. Instruction to Lewis gun Section, Observers, Signallers and Stretcher Bearers continued. Lieut. (a/Capt) A.W. NEW proceeded on leave to England. Lieut. H.L. HUGHES proceeded to 6th Infantry Brigade Headquarters for temporary attachment as Gas Officer.	
HOUTKERQUE Area	17-11-17		Battle on the HOUTKERQUE - WATOU ROAD used by Battalion between 8.30 a.m. and 3.30 p.m. "A" and "B" Coys. carried out training under Company arrangements previous to proceeding to Battle on vicinity of Camp. "C" Coy practised "forming up on the tape in the dark" at 6 p.m. and "D" Coy. at 5 p.m. Lewis gun Section paraded as usual but no other Specialists received instruction. 2/Lieut C.S. JAMES proceeded to II Corps Bombing School for	

(A7092). Wt. W12839/M1293. 75,000. 1/17. D.D. & L., Ltd. Forms/C.2118/24.

Army Form C. 2118.

WAR DIARY
or
INTELLIGENCE SUMMARY.
(Erase heading not required.)

Instructions regarding War Diaries and Intelligence Summaries are contained in F. S. Regs., Part II. and the Staff Manual respectively. Title pages will be prepared in manuscript.

Place	Date	Hour	Summary of Events and Information	Remarks and references to Appendices
HOUTKERQUE Area	18-11-17		Course of instruction. A Parade Service was held in the Y.M.C.A. Marquee at 11.30 a.m. at which 2 Officers and 95 other ranks were present. Battalion formed up on ground immediately East of Camp at 11.5 a.m. Captain T.R. KEEBLE M.C. and Lieut A.R. WELLS M.C. returned from leave to England. Lieut A.W. KAYE rejoined the Battalion and posted to "C" Coy. Captain J. AYLMER taken on strength of Battalion with effect from 14th and transferred to "D" Coy. Captain H.J. DUFF attached to Battalion from duty and takes over command of "A" Coy, vice Captain J. AYLMER. Captain T.R. KEEBLE M.C. resumes Command of "B" Coy.	
HOUTKERQUE Area	19-11-17		Battalion carried out training near Camp between 9 a.m. and 12.30 p.m. in the following:- Live instruction. Anti-gas drill. Musketry.	

(A7092). Wt. W12859/M1293. 75,000. 1/17. D. D. & L., Ltd. Forms/C.2118/14.

Army Form C. 2118.

WAR DIARY
or
INTELLIGENCE SUMMARY.
(Erase heading not required.)

Instructions regarding War Diaries and Intelligence Summaries are contained in F. S. Regs., Part II. and the Staff Manual respectively. Title pages will be prepared in manuscript.

Place	Date	Hour	Summary of Events and Information	Remarks and references to Appendices
	19-11-17		"A" and "B" Coys practiced "forming up for the attack" in the dark" at 5 A.m. Lewis Gun Section, Observers, Signallers and Stretcher Bearers paraded for special instruction at usual times. Hon. Mark N. LANG returned from leave to England.	
HOUTKERQUE Area	20-11-17		Companies carried out training, under Company arrangements between 8 a.m. and 12.30 p.m. on ground in vicinity of Camp. Specialist instruction continued. Captain J. AYLMER took over command of "D" Coy, vice Captain H.T. JESSOP, who assumed the duties of Second in Command to the Company.	
HOUTKERQUE Area	21-11-17		Companies carried out the following in Sub Area "A" at 9.30 a.m. (i) Rapid extension from close formation to artillery formation. (ii) Formation of advance guard. (iii) Outposts (posting of piquets and sentries). Range "A" at F.25.a. belonging to Corps Reinforcements Camp was allotted to "A" Coy from 2 p.m. to 4 p.m. Road State	

Army Form C. 2118.

WAR DIARY
or
INTELLIGENCE SUMMARY.
(Erase heading not required.)

Instructions regarding War Diaries and Intelligence Summaries are contained in F. S. Regs., Part II. and the Staff Manual respectively. Title pages will be prepared in manuscript.

Place	Date	Hour	Summary of Events and Information	Remarks and references to Appendices
	21-11-17		"A" Company use of the Range. Specialists training carried out at usual times. Major (A/Lt Col) A.E.F. HARRIS D.S.O. proceeded to England and struck off strength of Battalion. Major J. WALSH took over command. Lieut F.J. SOUTHERN proceeded on leave to England.	
HOUTKERQUE Area	22-11-17		Warning order received that Battalion would move to an unknown destination very shortly. Day spent in packing up. Officers' surplus kits despatched to England.	
HOUTKERQUE Area and PROVEN	23-11-17		Battalion in readiness to move. Pioklett ing Party under 2/Lieut A.C.TIMMS left Camp at 3 a.m. Battalion left Camp at 10.30 a.m. and marched via WATOU to PROVEN. Lieut M.L. FARMER proceeded on leave to England and duties of Medical Officer to Battalion were taken over by Lieut T. DRYSDALE R.A.M.C.	
PROVEN and ROCQUIGNY	24-11-17 25/11/17		Battalion reached PROVEN about 1 a.m. and entrained at PROVEN Station. Train left PROVEN about 3 a.m. and arrived at MIRAUMONT at 3 p.m. Battalion detrained and proceeded in motor lorries via BAPAUME to	

WAR DIARY
INTELLIGENCE SUMMARY

Army Form C. 2118.

Place	Date	Hour	Summary of Events and Information	Remarks and references to Appendices
	24-11-17		ROCQUIGNY, where the night was spent in Huts and under canvas. Battalion arrived at ROCQUIGNY at about 5.30 p.m.	See W.D. Sheet 11
ROCQUIGNY and DOIGNIES	25-11-17		Battalion left Camp at ROCQUIGNY at 9 a.m. and marched via BARASTRE, HAPLINCOURT, VELU and BEAUMETZ to DOIGNIES, which was reached at about 12.30 p.m. Battalion in bivouacs in field immediately South of DOIGNIES. Enemy artillery shelled BAPAUME – CAMBRAI Road at intervals during afternoon and several shells exploded over Battalion Camp and Brigade transport lines. Our batteries lively during afternoon. The Battalion moved up to reserve trenches East of MEUVRES + relieves the 14th Bn. IRISH Rifles	See Appx SCENE 3 10.30
DOIGNIES and Trenches	26-11-17 27-11-17 28-11-17 29-11-17 30-11-17		Battalion engaged in wiring + consolidating generally. Enemy attacked our positions in great strength of which we had been informed to War Diaries. See 31st M.W.	

Willis
Commdg 13th Essex Regt

6th Infantry Brigade.  CONFIDENTIAL.

Herewith a short narrative of the recent operations from November 30th, 1917 to night 4/5th December 1917.

1. On night of 29/30th November 1917., 13th ESSEX REGIMENT relieved 2nd S.STAFFS REGIMENT in the line astride the CANAD DU NORD, and took over their dispositions and orders.

2. On completion of relief, the Battalion was disposed as follows:-

   (a) "B" RIGHT FRONT COMPANY (Capt. F.R.KEEBLE commanding)

   3 Platoons in and under LOCK 5.
   1 Platoon in Reserve in TRAMWAY ROAD, E.21.c.9.6.

   (b) "D" LEFT FRONT COMPANY (Capt. H.T.JESSOP commanding)

   3 Platoons occupying STREET TRENCH from E.20.b.95.55 to SUNKEN ROAD at E.20.d.6.8.
   1 Platoon Company reserve E.20.d.7.6.

   (c) "A" RIGHT SUPPORT COMPANY (CAPT HJ DUFF COM DG)

   3 Platoons in TRENCH E.26.d.9.8 to E.27.b.5.3.
   1 Platoon in CANAL TRENCH E.27.c.3.8.
   NIGHT POST (including 1 Officer) at junction of ROAD and TRENCH E.21.b.6.3.
   NIGHT POST SUNKEN ROAD E.27.b.5.3.

   (d) "C" LEFT SUPPORT COMPANY (Lieut. A.NETHERCOTT commanding)

   2 Platoons in TRENCH E.20.d.5.6.
   2 Platoons in TRENCH E.20.d.4.6.

   (e) BATTALION HEADQUARTERS K.3.a.3.7.

3. Enemy activity through night was normal.

   (a) RIGHT FRONT COMPANY improved their defensive position by digging small trenches for Lewis Gun and Rifle Sections at NORTH and EAST edges of LOCK No. 5, and reconnoitring underground passages.
   An Officer patrol (Capt. F.R.KEEBLE) reconnoitred open ground E.21 Westward with a view to its occupation on noght 30th/1st.

   (b) LEFT FRONT COMPANY reconnoitred wire all along their Company front, (2/Lieut. E.L.CORPS) and the platoons were employed in deepening trench in shallow places and clearing fire steps where blown in.

   (c) RIGHT SUPPORT COMPANY. An Officer party (Capt. H.J.DUFF) in reconnoitring open area in E.27.b, c and d, with a view to occupying this area on night 30th/1st Dec. 1olu.

   (d) LEFT SUPPORT COMPANY. Consolidating trenches in their area.

   N.B. No enemy patrols were seen or heard by "D" "B" or "A" Coys.
   Night was fairly quiet.
   Hostile shelling and M.G. fire - intermittent.

4. EAST OF CANAL -   Right Front Company.
                    Right Support Company.

At about 6.30 a.m., enemy began to put down a light barrage on LOCK No. 5 -- BRIDGE E.20.b -- in CANAL Southwards from BRIDGE -- CANAL TRENCH, and open ground Eastwards in E.21.d.

This fire was very ordinary, and not in any way intensive.

At about 7.30 a.m., it became intensive.

(It so happened that I was on my rounds and was in this Sector at this period).

At about 9.30 a.m., the enemy launched his first attack. He was seen on the Road in E.15.c and d in great numbers, also debouching from a gap in the wire at about E.21.a.9.8., also from Sunken Road in E.21.b and along CABLE TRENCH in E.21.b.

(At this period I was in SUNKEN ROAD E.20.c.0.5).

"B" Coy. in LOCK No. 5 beat off this attack using nearly the whole of their ammunition and bombs in doing so.

3 Sections of Reserve Platoon, also 1 Vickers Gun lined SUNKEN ROAD at E.20.c.0.5 facing Northeast.

1 Section at Bridge E.21.c.0.5, facing NORTH and NORTH WEST.

Bombing Blocks in CANAL TRENCH at E.21.c.1.6 and in CABLE TRENCH E.21.c.2.6.

These dispositions were made by myself on the spot as there was no Officer with this platoon.

(d) This reserve successfully beat off the attack that was coming from the North East and used up nearly the whole of the ammunition in doing so.

(e) It is impossible to state with accuracy the strength of the enemy who had launched the attack or what losses he sustained, but I estimate from what I saw in the open at about 500 to 700 men.

Heavy losses were inflicted on them, and they either went back in great disorder or went to go ground.

During the lull which followed the dugout in SUNKEN ROAD was searched and about 300 rounds of S.A.A were found there and were loaded in the Lewis Gun magazines.

At 9.50 a.m., in the SUNKEN ROAD, I intercepted a message from O.C."B" Coy informing me that "he had successfully beaten off the attack in LOCK No. 5, but was short of S.A.A."

Action taken -

Message in writing was sent off to O.C."A" Coy. repeated Battalion Headquarters and Brigade.

I.   "I am at SUNKEN ROAD, E.21.c.0.5.

II. "I have received following message from O.C."B" Coy - Begins "ADJT CHINGFORD - HAVE BEATEN OFF ATTACK - SEND MORE S.A.A. Ends.

III. "I have ordered O.C."A" Coy to send up S.A.A. to No. 5. LOCK AAA I have also ordered O.C. "C" Coy to send S.A.A. to LOCK No. 5 AAA"

- 3 -

IV. "I have ordered O.C. "A" Coy to send up ONE PLATOON to E.21.c.0.5, to reinforce O.C. "B" Coy."

V. "I have ordered "C" Coy to send an Officer to O.C. "B" Coy to ascertain if "B" Coy requires any further assistance, and to be prepared to send up TWO platoons if required."

VI. "Situation now fairly quiet."
Repeat to Battalion Headquarters and BROMPTON.

(Sgd) J.WALSH   Major.
29.11.17.
10.10 a.m.   BY RUNNER.

N.B. I had to draw on reserve platoon in SUNKEN ROAD for runners, and it is to their credit that my orders reached Os.C "A" "B" and "C" Companies, and immediate action was taken.

I then made out a report of the fight, and sent it off to O.C. "A" Coy, repeated Battalion Headquarters.

(I dare not leave this platoon, as they had no Officer and very little S.A.A., and I was afraid they would retire)

10.20 a.m. I could see my RIGHT FRONT COMPANY still in their original position in STREET TRENCH, West of CANAL.

10.25 a.m. I saw BRITISH TROOPS retiring Southwards from the SUNKEN ROAD about E.20.central, and then sent off following messages:-

O.C. "A" Coy.
Battn. H.Qs.

I. When attack was made, enemy were reported seen moving EAST along ROAD from about E.15.c.3.3 to about E.15.c.9.3 AAA Also along ROAD moving SOUTH about E.21.b.5.8 AAA This is all at present, NOT CONFIRMED. I am sending it for what it is worth AAA

II. I am trying to clear up situation and will send all information in via "A" Coy Hd Qrs.

III Situation 10.20 a.m. HOSTILE BARRAGE along SUNKEN ROAD E.21.c.1.8 AAA heavy BARRAGE in LOCK No. 5. Enemy M.Guns active from E.21 a and c.

J.WALSH   Major.
10.25 a.m.
30.11.17   BY RUNNER

In the meantime, I had sent for another platoon of "A" Coy and S.A.A.

10.30 a.m. BARRAGE was intense (Gas shell and heavies). At about 10.30 a.m., enemy again attacked from NORTH EAST, and just as ammunition was giving out 2/Lieut. E.C.HALL arrived with one platoon of "A" Coy and several boxes of S.A.A.
This platoon prolonged the line to the RIGHT about E.21.c.2.5 mostly in the open and

checked the enemy advance across open ground about E.21.central. The Lewis Gun of the platoon and the rifles did very effective work, but the attack was so determined that the S.A.A. began to give out.

We lost fairly heavily during this attack from hostile Machine Gun and barrage fire which fell directly on this garrison.

At about 11 a.m., I called 2/Lieut. E.C.HALL, "A" Coy, Sergt. L.FISHER (No. 8 Platoon, "B" Coy) and Sergt. T.PEARTREE ("A" Coy) together and issued orders that "if enemy again attacked, they were to fight to the last with bayonet only if necessary", to maintain themselves until "B" Coy retired or S.A.A. arrived, and I would go back to "A" Coy's H.Qs and control from there.

I would like to place on record the magnificent demeanour of this Officer and two N.C.Os when I gave them this order. They were under the most trying conditions, absolutely determined to fight to the last. (I am submitting their names for honours).

At about 11.15 a.m., I went to "A" Coy's H.Qs in CANAL TRENCH. I passed details of Bn. H.Qs under Corpl. C.LUCAS (Police Corporal) going up with S.A.A.

About 11.30 a.m., I arrived at "A" Coy's H.Qs and sent up another platoon to support "B" Coy. They left taking up all the S.A.A. they could carry.

About 11.30 a.m., an Orderly from Advanced Brigade arrived with a message for me to report to Advanced Brigade at once.

I left, handing over the command of the troops EAST of CANAL to O.C. "A" Coy (Capt. H.J.DUFF) having explained the situation and given orders that all ground was to be held to the last.

About half an hour later "B" Coy (about 40 rifles) had to retire, and passed through the SUNKEN ROAD by BRIDGE, taking with them the remainder of the garrison of SUNKEN ROAD, about 6 rifles, the remainder having all been killed or wounded (2/Lieut. E.C.HALL wounded and missing).

This party had no S.A.A. or Bombs, and were being followed by numbers of the enemy.

LOCK No. 5 and SUNKEN ROAD were occupied immediately by the enemy.

Capt. H.J.DUFF "A" Coy, rallied these men at about E.27.a.3.9.

Capt. F.R.KEEBLE "B" Coy, together with some of "A" Coy and a platoon of 2nd. S.STAFFS REGT under 2/Lieut. C.T.HINDE, having received S.A.A. and Bombs organised a counter attack and drove the enemy back to the SUNKEN ROAD.

This they could not hold as the enemy were too strong, also through lack of bombs and S.A.A. which they had expended.

Capt. F.R.KEEBLE "B" Coy formed a BOMBING BLOCK in CANAL TRENCH about 10 yards South of SUNKEN ROAD -- E.21.c.10.45, and manned the parapet of CANAL TRENCH facing EAST and WEST.

S.A.A. and bombs were beginning to arrive in plenty and the enemy was prevented from advancing further and was cleared off the open ground EAST and WEST of CANAL TRENCH, and retired to the SUNKEN ROAD.

Capt. F.R.KEEBLE, later, again organised a bombing attack combined with an attack over the open to clear the SUNKEN ROAD.

This attack failed, as the enemy were very strong and had brought up 4 Machine Guns also using Rifle Grenades freely on the BLOCK in CANAL TRENCH.

By this time CANAL TRENCH from BOMBING BLOCK Southwards to cross trenches at E.27.c.3.9 was garrisoned by one of "A" Coy's Platoons and 3 Platoons of a Company of 2nd. S.

STAFFS REGT.

Trench running EAST and WEST, E.27.c, a, and d was occupied by two platoons of "A" Coy and and one platoon of a Company of the 2nd S.STAFFS REGT under Capt. BAXTER in addition occupied this trench..

The conduct of Capt. F.R.KEEBLE "B" Coy., Capt. H.J.DUFF "A" Coy and 2/Lieut. C.T.HINDE, 2nd. S. STAFFS REGT was beyond praise

The determined shewn by these gallant Officers not to yield one inch to the enemy had, I am sure, a great stimulating effect on their men.

The enemy made repeated attempts to sally from SUNKEN ROAD and also to approach CANAL TRENCH from the North East, but were always beaten back by rifle and Machine Gun fire.

It is difficult to estimate the casualties inflicted on the enemy, but all reports agree that he suffered very heavily.

Capt. F.R.KEEBLE estimates that his men, before retiring from Lock No. 5 had put out of action at least 400 or 500 of the enemy, and this he states is a moderate estimate.

During the night that followed, three unsuccessful attempts were made to retake the SUNKEN ROAD. Two by Capt. F.R.KEEBLE and 2/Lieut. C.T.HINDE, and later a third which was carefully organised by Capt. H.J.DUFF and Capt. F.R.KEEBLE..

After thrid attack failed, I relieved the elements of "B" Coy and "A" Coy and 2/Lieut. C.T.HINDE'S platoon, and put fresh troops in the Northern Ends of CANAL TRENCH.

These were our dispositions as handed over to the 22nd Battn. ROYAL FUSILIERS on relief.

From the time I left "A" Coy's Hd Qrs at about 11.15 a.m., Capt H.J.DUFF commanded all troops in my SECTOR, EAST of CANAL.

I have submitted the names of Capt. H.J.DUFF., Capt. F.R.KEEBLE., 2/Lieut. E.C.HALL and 2/Lieut. C.T.HINDE, 2nd S.STAFFS REGT, for honours.

WEST OF CANAL.

(1) At 11.45 a.m., on 30/11/17, when I returned to Battn. Hd Qrs, I found the situation with regard to "D" and "B" Companies very obscure.
I at once sent out orderlies to get in touch with the Companies.
I had no news of LEFT FRONT COMPANY ("D" Coy) except when I had last seen them from my position in SUNKEN ROAD about E.20.d.9.5 when they were still in their normal position, but enemy had gone past them at about E.20.central.

(2) I sent written orders to O.C."D" Coy to the effect that if he had been driven out of his position, he was to at once counter attack and establish on a line running WEST from BRIDGE at E.20.d.8.5.
This message did not reach him as the enemy had come in from the WEST and from across the CANAL and completely cut him off, and as I ascertained later, he was still in his original position.

(3) I had a message from O.C. "C" Coy stating that his Hd Qrs was at TRENCH JUNCTION, E.20.d.3.3, and that his strength was 3 Officers and about 25 Rifles.

I sent my Intelligence Officer (Lieut. H.L. HUGHES), also runners with orders to the Company Commander to at once counter attack and re-establish himself in his former position.

This message he received and acknowledged, and together with troops of 2nd. S.STAFFS REGT and 1st KINGS REGT he counter attacked and retook trenches as far as E.20.d.3.6 and E.20.d.4.6, but was held up by the enemy and lack of bombs.

(4) I received a further report from this Officer stating that he had, before receipt of my order to retake his old position, already taken part in two counter attacks with his Company.

I sent him instructions to place himself under the orders of O.C. 1st. KINGS REGT.

(5) I sent off my acting 2nd in Command (Capt. J. AYLMER) to get in touch with 1st. KINGS REGT and ascertain the situation on WEST of CANAL, and to ask O.C. 1st. KINGS REGT to take the remnants of "C" Coy under his command.

Capt. J.AYLMER also had orders to acquaint O.C. 1st KINGS REGT of the situation EAST of CANAL, and inform him that I intended to act vigourously and retake the SUNKEN ROAD on the EAST of CANAL if it were possible.

(6) My runners who were sent out to "D" Coy returned with the information that the enemy were between this and "D" Coy.

This was confirmed by Capt. J.AYLMER when he returned from H.Qs 1st. KINGS REGT and from H.Qs of "C" Coy.

(7) Lieut. Col. ALBAN D.S.O., comdng: 2nd. S.STAFFS REGT had in the meantime arrived at my Headquarters and I ascertained from him that he was O.C. Forward Area.

From that time onwards I consulted him in all things concerning the WEST of CANAL and concentrated my efforts on holding on to my position EAST of the CANAL and retaking, if possible the SUNKEN ROAD and BRIDGE at E.20.d.8.5.

(8) I was in constant touch with Os. C. 1st KINGS., 17th MIDDLESEX and 2nd. S.STAFFS REGTS from about 12 noon 30/11/17 onwards.

(9) By this time Major. EDWARDS, 17th MIDDLESEX REGT was engaging the enemy who had penetrated our line immediately WEST of CANAL in E.20.d.

(10) On Instructions from Brigade, O.C. LEFT SUB SECTION had all troops on WEST of CANAL under his command, and I had all troops EAST of and including the CANAL.

(11) About 4 p.m., the strength of "C" Coy was two Officers and 15 Other Ranks.

(12) (a) What happened to "C" Coy in earliest stages of fight is rather obscure, the two platoons at E.20.d.3.6 were attacked from the North West and West, and as far as I can ascertain fought to the last with troops of 1st. KINGS REGT.

(b) The other two platoons under O.C.Company were suddenly engaged from SUNKEN ROAD about E.20.d.3.9 also from WEST, and by a strong party of the enemy who had crossed CANAL by BRIDGE at E.20.d.8.5.

They suffered very heavily owing to having to lie in the open, and for a few minutes checked the enemy but had to fall back owing to lack of S.A.A. lack of men, and to avoid being cut off from enemy advancing from the WEST.

(c) At about 10.10 a.m., O.C. "C" Coy had received my message which I had sent from SUNKEN ROAD EAST, and sent 2/Lieut. H.V.COOK at once to LOCK No. 5.

This Officer reached Capt. F.R.KEEBLE as he was retiring from LOCK No. 5.

He sent 1 Corporal and 10 men with 5 Boxes S.A.A. to LOCK No. 5., but these men did not reach there., and were not seen again.

(13) "D" Coy.

At about 8 p.m., Sergt. L.S.LEGG "D" Coy, and one man arrived at Battalion Headquarters and informed me that they had escaped, and gave me the following information:-

(a) "D" Coy. were surrounded.

(b) They had not been attacked from the NORTH or NORTH WEST.

(c) The platoon at E.20.d.6.9 and a STOKES MORTAR had been firing at the enemy in SUNKEN ROAD at E.20.central, and also at enemy advancing over the open at about E.20.b.central.
That they must have killed hundreds of the enemy by their enfilade rifle and Lewis Gun fire.

(d) The platoon in TRENCH E.20.d.6.7 had held trench facing both ways i.e., S.W. and N.E., those S.W. inflicting heavy loss on the enemy who had crossed the BRIDGE. Those facing N.E. on enemy as he was pursuing "B" Coy from LOCK No. 5.

(e) That enemy brought 3 Machine Guns to E.20.d.8.5 EAST of CANAL, and enfiladed them. One of the guns and teams were knocked out, the other two cleared off.

(f) That Company was short of S.A.A.

(g) That Capt. H.T.JESSOP, O.C. "D" Coy was wounded.

(h) That they had their dugout full of enemy as prisoners. These prisoners, he stated, were captured in TRENCH in E.20.d.6.8.

(i) That at about 4 p.m. a council of war - Lieut. J.D.ROBINSON (2nd in Command of Company), 2/Lieut E.L.CORPS, the Company Sergeant Major and Platoon Sergeants, was held, and it was decided to fight to the last - no surrender - and two volunteers were to attempt to break through with information to me..

I have no corroborative evidence of the above except of the man who accompanied Sergt. LEGG.

14. Brigade and all Units were at once informed, and most violent efforts were made by all Units to reach "D" Coy.
They all failed.

15. During night, position EAST of CANAL was organised so that all ground over which enemy would have to

- 8 -

advance was swept by oblique and cross rifle, Lewis Gun and Machine Gun fire.

This organisation greatly assisted in driving the enemy back next morning when he attempted to drive out BLOCK in CANAL TRENCH and advance from SUNKEN ROAD.

16. These were our dispositions when we handed over to the 22nd. ROYAL FUSILIERS on relief on night 1st/2nd. December 1917.

17. Battalion then withdrew to K.3.a, and having received the details who had been left out re-organised, became Support Battalion to 22nd ROYAL FUSILIERS.

18. On handing over to 22nd ROYAL FUSILIERS, there were 70.000 rounds S.A.A. in Company Reserve at E.27.c.4.8.

19. Until the 4th/5th, we were called on on three occasions to reinforce the 22nd ROYAL FUSILIERS. The first two our services were not required. The third time also, but I regret to say that my "B" Coy in passing through hostile barrage lost 1 Officer wounded, 5 Other Ranks killed and 14 Other Ranks wounded.

20. I regret to report that the following were the casualties sustained by this Battalion from 30th, November to night 4th/5th December 1917.

Lieut. (A/Capt) J.D.STEELE	Wounded
2/Lieut. W.S.McLAREN	"
" H.L.BALL	"
" CLAYDON M.S.	"
Capt. H.T.JESSOP	Wounded & Missing
2/Lieut. R.G.BOX	" "
" C.W.PHILIPS	" "
" E.C.WALL	" "
Lieut. J.D.ROBINSON	Missing.
2/Lieut. E.L.CORPS	"
16 Other Ranks	Killed.
78 " "	Wounded.
9 " "	Wounded & Missing.
269 " "	Missing.

21. At about 9.15 p.m. 4th/5th December 1917, I received orders from G.O.C. 5th Infantry Brigade to evacuate my position, passing a certain line by 1 a.m. 5/12/17.

This evacuation was successfully carried out without casualties, and Battalion arrived at LEBUCQUIERE, at 4.20 a.m. 5/12/17.

22. Notes on lesson learnt during the operations are appended.

Major.
Comdng: 13th Bn. Essex Regiment

7/12/17.

NOTES ON RECENT OPERATIONS

I beg to forward the following with reference to the operations described above.

1. **SUPPLY of S.A.A.**

    I humbly suggest that if troops in the future are to successfully hold up an enemy attack which is ~~delivered~~ determined and prolonged, that much larger dumps of S.A.A. be made all over the area to be defended, so that if troops are compelled to fall back by superior numbers, they fall back on to supplies with which they can fight.

    These dumps I suggest should be put everywhere in an area where supporting troops have to pass on the way up to reinforce, and in convenient places to obviate delay in picking it up.

    I am firmly convinced that if such had been the case in the present instance, LOCK No. 5., SUNKEN ROAD at E.21.c.0.5 and BRIDGE adjoining would not have fallen.

    The expenditure of S.A.A. by Riflemen and Lewis Gunners was beyond belief. As supplies arrived, it was at once "eaten up", and everybody was constantly crying for S.A.A..

    As long as S.A.A. was available, the enemy could not advance accordingly across the open EAST of CANAL.

2. **LEWIS GUNS.**

    The Lewis Guns more than justified their issue. The matter of magazines is a deep problem. They became empty so quickly in beating off a prolonged attack that it is impossible to refill them in time to keep pace with the expenditure.

3. **MUSKETRY.**

    The time spent during the last 6 months at Musketry Training brought home to me the necessity of concentration on this branch of training.

    All ranks used their rifles with great ability, and I feel sure that they could not have used their rifles so effectively had they been called upon to do this task 6 months ago.

4. **SIGNALLING.**

    (1) Speech over phone is indispensible for fighting.

    (2) The Brigade Forward Station was of greatest use in keeping flank communications.
    If the same number of lines were laid as would be laid to Battalions, there should be at least one line working all the time to Brigade H.Qs.

    (3) The Brigade Forward Station provides an excellent cable store for Battalions.

    (4) The number of Signallers when 33% have been left behind is none too many.

    (5) One instrument is not sufficient on a 4 x 3 Buzzer Unit.
    A second instrument connected to a spare jack was found very useful.

    (6) The communications held out EAST of CANAL

— 2 —

through the whole of the 5 days, and we were never out off for more than 1 hour.

(7) An Advanced Battle Headquarters was established in CANAL TRENCH at K.27.a.3.6, and this line was invaluable in keeping Battn. H.Qs in immediate touch with the situation EAST of CANAL.

5. RUNNERS and RELAY POST.

I humbly suggest that consideration should be given by the Higher Command to the Runners and Relay Posts.

They get more and more important and complicated in every successive action, and I feel sure that the Battalion Signalling Officer cannot deal with his own job and runners in addition.

The Intelligence Officer cannot be spared for this work.

I suggest that an Officer should be placed in command of Runners and Relay Posts to run the whole scheme.

6. BOMBS and GRENADES.

Having gone all out for musketry, it was found by one Company Commander (Lieut. A. NETTERCOTT) that the men could do with a little more training in bombing, but personally I think that all ranks were efficient in the use of this weapon.

Bombs and rifle grenades were the only weapons with which enemy could be driven out of the trenches that he had gained.

7. MEDICAL ARRANGEMENTS.

No remarks.

8. 'S.O.S' SIGNAL.

My O.C. "B" Coy states that in the course of the morning 30/11/17, he put up at least eleven 'S.O.S' lights, and the response of the Artillery was weak.

9. ARTILLERY DEFENSIVE BARRAGE.

In connection with above, I quite agree and was on the spot, the Barrage appeared to come down behind the GERMAN FRONT LINE in an EAST and WEST line between E.15.c and d and E.21.a and b, and everywhere South up to here, enemy was free of BARRAGE.

I do not wish in any way to belittle our gunners as they were splendid, and later got on to these targets and effected enormous losses on the enemy in E.21.a and b, but I certainly think the defensive barrage in the initial stages of the attack was too far back.

J. Walsh, Major.

7/12/17. Comdng: 13th Bn. Essex Regiment.

13th (S) Bn Essex Regiment

Ref 6th Bde GS 916/36.

Organised as follows:-

Battalion Headquarters.

Four Companies.

'A' Coy	Coy H.Q's 26 OR	Four platoons	113 Rifles	Four L.G Sections
'B' Coy	do 22 OR	Two do	68 do	Two do
'C' Coy	do 20 OR	Two do	38 do	Two do
'D' Coy	do 17 OR	One do	23 do	One Ayrie L.G Sections
	85 OR		242 Rifles	including 1st Rein 1.2 only

A.E Bentley Capt
Adjt for Major
Commdg: 13th Essex Regt

SECRET

To O/C HQ Coy

Have at present following my present dispositions:—

1. CENTRES

 (a) D Coy 3rd R.F.
   O.B.L. K.14.A.2.1. to K.14.C.1.7
   STRENGTH 65 RIFLES 4 LEWIS GUNS
   and Coy HQ ORs

 (b) D Coy 13th ESSEX Rgt.
   O.B.L. K.14.C.1.7 to K.14.C.10.25
   STRENGTH 14 RIFLES 12 LEWIS GUN
   and Coy HQ ORs

 (c) A Coy 13th ESSEX Rgt.
   O.B.L. K.14.C.10.25 to K.19.B.9.1
   STRENGTH 130 RIFLES 4 LEWIS GUNS
   and Coy HQ ORs

 (d) BN HQ K.13.D.8.3

2. ATTACHED TO WINGS
   'B' Coy 13th ESSEX Rgt K.7.4.2. to K.8.d.
   'C'   "   "   "   K.8.4.7.6 to K.8.A.5.3

10.20 AM
9.12.1   [signature]
                                 Comdg 13th Essex Rgt.

BY RUNNER + PIGEON POST

"A" Form
MESSAGES AND SIGNALS.

Army Form C. 2121 (in pads of 100).

TO: BROMPTON

Sender's Number: W 10
Day of Month: 12/12
In reply to Number: 1.69
AAA

Rough SKETCH shewing dispositions asked for aaa NO I CHINGFORD has sent you dispositions of all troops at present with FRONT BATTALION aa my SKETCH all troops at present with me aaa

B. Coy CHINGFORD — 3 off — 79 O.R. (includes two LEWIS GUNS)

'C' Coy CHINGFORD — 2 off — 44 O.R. (includes two LEWIS GUNS)

"A" Form
MESSAGES AND SIGNALS.

Army Form C. 2121 (in pads of 100).

No. of Message..................

Prefix....Code....m. Office of Origin and Service Instructions.	Words	Charge	This message is on a/c of	Recd. at........m.
	Sent At........m.		....................Service.	Date.................. From ....
	To.................... By....................		(Signature of "Franking Officer.")	By................

TO {			
		?	

Sender's Number.	Day of Month.	In reply to Number.	**A A A**
	D. Coy	CALADONIAN.	3 officers — 82 O R inclu
			FOUR LEWIS GUNS

From: CHINGFORD
Place:
Time: 8 pm

Signature: Walshhayes (?)

The above may be forwarded as now corrected.

Wt. W492/M1647 100,000 pads. 4/17

ROUGH SKETCH shewing disposition of Troops under Comd. of M.C. LEFT SUPPORT BN. at 7. pm. 12/13·12·17

(SQUARES R. 13.. 14.. 19 and 20)

ANTI·TANK GUN and CREW

SPARE ACCOMMODATION DUGOUTS AVAILABLE FOR 100 MEN

B Coy ESSEX RGT 3 Offrs & 79

D Coy KINGS 3 Offrs & 82.

C Coy ESSEX 2 Offrs & 44

⬤   BN. HD. QRS — ESSEX.
✕   S·O·S· OBSERVATION POSTS
◉   BN HD. QRS — KINGS

J. Walshmeyer
Comdg 13 ESSEX Rgt

SECRET   13th ESSEX REGT. ORDER No. 144   Order No. .....

Ref.Map DEMICOURT 1/10000   December 20th, 1917.

1. The Battalion will relieve 22nd Royal Fusiliers in the Support Area of the Right Sector of the 2nd Divn. Front on the night of 20th/21st December 1917.

2. ORDER OF MARCH   "B" "A" "C" "D" Coys. Headquarters.

3. DISPOSITIONS
   "B" Coy. 13th ESSEX will relieve "D" Coy. 22/R.F.
   "A" "   "   "   "   "   "C" "   "
   "C" "   "   "   "   "   "A" "   "
   "D" "   "   "   "   "   "B" "   "

4. Officers' Trench Bundles, Lewis Guns and Magazines, Trench Equipment, Dixies and Company Mess Boxes, will be stacked at Q.M.Stores by 1.30 p.m.
   Kits not required for the Trenches to be at same place at same time.

5. BLANKETS All blankets to be tightly and neatly rolled in bundles of ten and stacked at Q.M.Stores by 1.30 p.m.

6. Companies will leave Camp at the following times.
    "B" Company   ...   ...   2.40 p.m.
    "A"   "   ...   ...   2.45 p.m.
    "C"   "   ...   ...   2.55 p.m.
    "D"   "   ...   ...   3 p.m.
    Headquarters   ...   ...   3.5 p.m.
   An interval of 50 yards will be maintained between Platoons.

7. ROUTE AND GUIDES Companies will march to Spoil Heap J.35.d.2.4. by the same route as taken today.

8. The Battalion will rest for one hour at above and tea will be served.
   Companies will leave Spoil Heap at 5 monutes interval in the same order of march to rendezvous(by same route as reconnoitred today) to railway and canal crossing K.26 Central when they will meet guides at 6 p.m. as arranged.

9. DRESS. Fighting Order with packs slung.
   Great Coats will be worn and water bottles will be filled before leaving Camp.

9. RATIONS Rations for consumption on 21st. will be issued to men previous to leaving Camp.

10. TRANSPORT ARRANGEMENTS
   (a) Two Company Cookers, Lewis Gun Limbers will be at SPOIL HEAP J.35.d.2.4. at 3.45 p.m.
   Tea will be ready for the Battalion at 4 p.m.
   Companies will unload Lewis Guns, and magazines, Trench Equipment, Signalling Equipment and issue same.
   On completion of same, limbers and cookers will return to Transport Lines.
   (b) Limbers carrying cooking utensils for Companies, Officers' Mess Boxes, and Trench Kits, Water Tins, and all other equipment will be conveyed under arrangements made by Transport Officer to K.14.d.90.65 and should arrive at 8.30 p.m.
   Companies and Headquarters will, on arrival, send parties to collect Stores from this Dump.

11. RATION DUMP K.14.d.90.65 (in bed of Canal), until further orders.
12. B.H.Qrs. K.15.d.9.9.
13. Trench STORES Lists of Trench Stores taken over and sketch map shewing dispositions to be forwarded to Battalion Headquarters by 6 a.m., 21st instant.
14. RELIEF COMPLETE Relief Complete will be notified to B.H.Q. by the word "HARRIS" by phone and confirmed by Runner.
15. ACKNOWLEDGE

                (Sgd.) A. E. BUNTING Captain,
                Adjutant, 13th ESSEX REGT.

DEFENCE SCHEME

Copy No. 6

SUPPORT BATTN

1. The Battalion plus 1 Company of SLAG HEAP BATTN, is disposed as follows:—
   (a) Two Companies in WATSON TRENCH
       (Coy. HD.QRS. K.10.c.9.7).
   (b) One Company in TANK TRENCH
       K.15.c.35.75 to about K.15.c.60.40.
       (Coy. HD.QRS. K.15.c.60.70)
   (c) One Company in dugouts – K.15.c.40.78 and balance in dugouts K.15.c.02.12
       (Coy. HD.QRS. K.15.c.30.40)
   (d) One Company, SLAG HEAP BATTN., in TANK SUPPORT in dugouts K.15.c.02.12 and K.21.a.25.95
       (Coy. HD.QRS. K.21.a.80.40)
   (e) Battn. HD.QRS. K.15.d.90.90.

2. Two Companies, vide Para.1 (a) are placed under the direct orders of O.C. FRONT LINE BATTN:
   (a) Their function is to support Companies of FRONT LINE BATTN: by quickest and best route.
       There are three routes available:—
       (i) Via EAST END of WATSON TRENCH — HINDENBURGH SUPPORT COMMUNICATION TRENCH — to MAIN LINE.
       (ii) Over the top via HAVRINCOURT ROAD to CROSS ROADS – K.9.b.50.20 to HUGHES SWITCH K.10.a.0.5.
       (iii) Over the top from WATSON TRENCH to HUGHES SWITCH through gap in enemy wire.
            (Gap through wire will be located).
   (b) To counter attack at once over top if enemy succeed in gaining a footing in HUGHES SWITCH in MAIN LINE.

3. In event of hostile attack, it is certain that all lines will be broken.
   Senior Officer in WATSON TRENCH will organise relay runners at his Company HD.QRS. and send out continually to Coy. HD.QRS. in HUGHES SWITCH so as to be in constant touch with the situation.
   All information to be passed back to BATTN: HD.QRS. by 'phone if open, and runners.

4. The three Companies mentioned in Para.1 (b), (c) and (d) are under the orders of O.C. SUPPORT BATTN:
   (a) In the event of hostile attack, the code word "GEORGE" will be sent over 'phone and by runner to Company HD.QRS. of three Companies mentioned above.
   (b) On receipt of this, Companies will "stand to" and an officer from each Company, will at once report to BATTN: HD.QRS. for orders.
   (c) "A" Coy. BING will move at once, under the

Second-in-Command of Company and take up position in GEORGE STREET, between K.15.d.80.40 and HAVRINCOURT ROAD K.15.d.40.20.

This Company will then be held ready to reinforce garrison of WATSON TRENCH or HUGHES SWITCH, via GEORGE STREET and HINDENBURGH SUPPORT, or over the top in HALF-PLATOONS, EAST of HAVRINCOURT ROAD, through squares K.15.d and b. - K.9.d and K.10.a.

(d) Should this move take place, "D" Coy. BING, will immediately occupy the place vacated by "A" Coy. BING in GEORGE STREET.

(e) Should "D" Coy. BING be sent forward, the Company of SLAG HEAP BATTN: attached, will at once occupy the place of "D" Coy. BING.

5. For information of Companies of SUPPORT BATTN: the POLICY is to hold on to all POSTS to the last and MAIN LINE is to be held at all costs, COUNTER ATTACKS being immediately launched from WATSON TRENCH, should enemy gain a footing in MAIN LINE.

6. ADVANCED BATTN: HD: QRS. would probably be established in WATSON TRENCH, at present DOUBLE COY. HD: QRS. K.10.c.9.7.

7. All officers (except O.C. "D" Coy) have reconnoitred routes.
O.C. "D" Coy. will carry out reconnaissance of all routes forthwith.

8. To be handed over on relief.

9. ACKNOWLEDGE.

G S Bunting
Captain
Adjutant: 13th Essex Regt.

Copy No. 1   O.C. "A" Coy.
        2   O.C. "B" "
        3   O.C. "C" "
        4   O.C. "D" "
        5   O.C. 2nd. S. STAFFS
        6   6th INFANTRY BRIGADE.

ADDENDUM TO DEFENCE SCHEME

SUPPORT BATTN.

Reference PARA 2.

1. If the Companies of the FRONT LINE BATTN. in HUGHES SWITCH are attacked and require re-inforcements, they will fire a RED VERY PISTOL LIGHT from HUGHES SWITCH low along the ground in the direction of WATSON TRENCH.

2. This signal will mean that the O.C. Company who fired the RED LIGHT requires re-inforcing.

3. Senior officer in WATSON TRENCH will at once reinforce, using his initiative as to the number of PLATOONS or COMPANIES that he sends forward.

4. An Observation Post will be established in WATSON TRENCH, where lights fired from HUGHES SWITCH can be observed.

NOTE   Above does not cancel other precautions laid down in the DEFENCE SCHEME, but is supplementary.

A. S. Bunting
Captain
Adjutant 13th Essex Regt.

6th Brigade.

2nd Division.

13th BATTALION

THE ESSEX REGIMENT

DECEMBER.
~~NOVEMBER~~ 1917.

Attached:

Report on Operations 30th November-5th December

Army Form C. 2118.

WAR DIARY
or
INTELLIGENCE SUMMARY.
(Erase heading not required.)

G.96

Confidential

War Diary

13th (S) Bn Essex Regt

from Nov 1st – 31st 1917

Army Form C. 2118.

WAR DIARY
or
INTELLIGENCE SUMMARY.
(Erase heading not required.)

Instructions regarding War Diaries and Intelligence Summaries are contained in F. S. Regs., Part II. and the Staff Manual respectively. Title pages will be prepared in manuscript.

Place	Date	Hour	Summary of Events and Information	Remarks and references to Appendices
MOEUVRES Sector	1/9/17		Battalion relieved by the 2nd Bn ROYAL FUSILIERS and marched to K3a (west of GRAINCOURT) arriving after dark. enemy shelling heavy shelling but suffering at intervals. Casualties 1 OR killed 3 OR wounded	Moeuvres 2/9/17 all most refugees who in the area from month of a line drawn through HERMIES and GRANDCOURT and SOUTH of MOEUVRES
K3a	2/9/17		Battalion in Support. A 2nd ROYAL FUSILIERS Intermittent shelling on both sides. Major A.G. HAYWARD MC rejoined and assumed command of the Battalion	
	3/9/17		Battalion in Support to the 22nd ROYAL FUSILIERS Intermittent shelling on both sides + M.G: attn Casualties 1 OR killed 1 OR wounded. Capt A W NEW rejoined from leave. Lieut T. LAW (derogatory surname) + 2/Lt T CHRISTY (same surname) joined for duty + posted to A BELL ECLISE + C Coys	

Army Form C., 2118.

WAR DIARY
or
INTELLIGENCE SUMMARY.
(Erase heading not required.)

Instructions regarding War Diaries and Intelligence Summaries are contained in F.S. Regs., Part II. and the Staff Manual respectively. Title pages will be prepared in manuscript.

Place	Date	Hour	Summary of Events and Information	Remarks and references to Appendices
K3a	4/1/17		Heavy Shelling by enemy at intervals. Our artillery retaliate effectively. Casualties: 4 O.R. Killed, 10 O.R Wounded + 1 O.R. Wounded + Missing	
		9 a.m	Battalion withdrew from the forward area in conjunction with other Battalions of the 2nd Division and went into billets at LE BUCQUIERE. Relieved by the 11th the ROYAL FUSILIERS. The Battalion suffered no casualties during the movement.	
LE BUCQUIERE	5/1/17		Battalion at rest. 2/Lt W S MAC LAREN evacuated to England. Wounded	
	6/1/17	2.30 p.m	Battalion inspected by the Commanding Officer. Capt F R KEEBLE M.C. + 2/Lt W K BESSEX returned to Hospital. Capt A W NEW took over the Command of B Coy.	
	7/1/17		Training. Any arrangements. 2/Lt C S JAMES rejoined from IV Corps Bombing School	
	8/1/17	5 h	Battalion relieved 2nd O×s + Bucks Light Infantry in the Divisional Support	

WAR DIARY or INTELLIGENCE SUMMARY

Army Form C. 2118.

Place	Date	Hour	Summary of Events and Information	Remarks and references to Appendices
Suffolk area	9/12/17		Suffolk area in K13 West of DEMICOURT. Bn HQrs at K13 + 14. Capt G. SIMPSON + 2/Lt F.C. RANSOM proceeded on leave to England. 2/Lt A. HENDERSON- LIVESAY (base Learning) joined for duty + procured on a course of Instruction at the Divisional Base Battalion. 2/Lt W.K. BESSEX + 2/Lt M.S. CLAYDON returned from Hotchin Intermittent shelling on both sides.	DEMICOURT sheet
	10/12/17		B Coy relieved C Coy in trenches K1a35 to K1a09 NE of DEMICOURT – platoons of B Coy took over dugouts near Bn HQrs at K14c. These remaining 3 platoons also being relieved by a platoon of the 1st KINGS also moved into K14c. A Coy relieved C Coy + handed Conference of 1st KINGS Regt in KELLETT + WALSH trenches from K2b67 to K2a35 and in BULLEN trench from K2a15 to K2 & 3 1 SW of GRANCOURT C Coy after relief moved into way into OBL at K14d West of DEMICOURT	

Army Form C. 2118.

WAR DIARY
or
INTELLIGENCE SUMMARY.
(Erase heading not required.)

Instructions regarding War Diaries and Intelligence Summaries are contained in F. S. Regs., Part II. and the Staff Manual respectively. Title pages will be prepared in manuscript.

Place	Date	Hour	Summary of Events and Information	Remarks and references to Appendices
Support area	14/12/17		Intermittent shelling on both sides. Patrolling carried out	
do	12/12/17		2/Lt H V COOK wounded to Hospital	
do	13/12/17		Intermittent shelling on both sides. Enemy MG's active Capt J AYLMER proceed on leave to England Major J WALSH granted permission to wear the hostages of the rank of Lieut Colonel	
do	14/12/17 6pm		Battalion relieved by the 2nd Bn HIGHLAND L.I. and moved into billets at LE BUCQUIERE vacated by the 17th ROYAL FUSILIERS.	
LE BUCQUIERE	15/12/17		Capt H J DUFF proceeded on leave to England 2/Lt W K BESSEX took over the command of "A" Coy.	
do	16/12/17		Training owing to Company arrangements	

WAR DIARY
INTELLIGENCE SUMMARY

Army Form C. 2118.

Place	Date	Hour	Summary of Events and Information	Remarks and references to Appendices
LE BUCQUIERE	14/4/17		Training under Company arrangement	
do	18/4/17		Men re-fitted –	
do	19/4/17		Capt H A MULKERN rejoined from 1st Army School + assumed Command of A Coy during the absence of Capt H. J DUFF on leave.	

Army Form C. 2118.

WAR DIARY
or
INTELLIGENCE SUMMARY.
(Erase heading not required.)

Instructions regarding War Diaries and Intelligence Summaries are contained in F. S. Regs., Part II. and the Staff Manual respectively. Title pages will be prepared in manuscript.

Place	Date	Hour	Summary of Events and Information	Remarks and references to Appendices
LE BUCQUIERE	20/1/18	2.40pm	Battalion proceeded to the Support Area of the Right Sector of the 3rd Divisional Front and relieved the 20th ROYAL FUSILIERS. Enemy shelled the CANAL en route. Casualties:- 1 Pnt F J SOUTHERN Wounded.	MOEUVRES sheet
SUPPORT AREA.	21/1/18		4 OR Killed. 3 OR Wounded. Intermittent shelling on both sides. Enemy M.G. active. 1 OR Killed	
Do	22/1/18		Heavy shelling down on our right. Intermittent shelling on both sides. 1 OR Wounded.	
Do	23/1/18		Heavy shelling by enemy at intervals. Our artillery replies effectively. Battalion relieved 1 OR Wounded 1st KINGS Regt in the FRONT line	
Do	24/1/18		Disposition:- C Coy RIGHT front B Do CENTRE Do A Do LEFT Do D Do SUPPORT	
Front line	24/1/18		Intermittent Shelling by enemy. 1 OR (No 24951 Pte R FAIRCLOTH, B Coy) Missing. Capt G SIMPSON + 2/Lt F C RANSON rejoined from leave	

(A7092). Wt. W12859/M1293 75,000. 1/17. D. D. & L., Ltd. Forms/C.2118/14.

WAR DIARY
or
INTELLIGENCE SUMMARY.
(Erase heading not required.)

Army Form C. 2118.

Place	Date	Hour	Summary of Events and Information	Remarks and references to Appendices
Front Lines	24/1/17		The following were awarded the MILITARY MEDAL by the Corps Commander under authority delegated by the King.	
			N° 12965 A/CSM L. FISHER A/18444 Sergt L.S. HEGO 19330 a/Cpl J FARMER 18848 L/Cpl F. WOOLDRIDGE 10145 Pte H E MARKHAM H3308 Pte G WEBSTER (attached 6th T.M.B) 14303 Pte E L HILL 40163 a/Cpl G CHARLES (attached 6th T.M.B) N° 31580 Pte A DUCKETT.	
Do	25/1/17		Intermittent shelling on both sides. Enemy M.G. active. 2 O.R. Killed. 4 O.R. Wounded.	
			N° 14798 Sergt A MOORE proceeded to England on a Commission for Commission.	
			Enemy systematically bombarded our trenches during the day. Our artillery retaliated vigorously. 3 O.R. Killed 8 O.R. Wounded.	
Do	26/1/17		N° 1856 CSM CWD BOWRING to England for Commission for Commission.	

WAR DIARY
or
INTELLIGENCE SUMMARY.

Army Form C. 2118.

Place	Date	Hour	Summary of Events and Information	Remarks and references to Appendices
Front Line	26/10/17		2/Lt W.K. BESSEX proceeded on leave to ENGLAND. Battalion relieved by the 17th MIDDLESEX Regt & moved into billets at HERMIES. Relief complete at 11am.	
HERMIES	27/10/17	2pm	Battalion (less 'C' Coy) engaged in unloading MAXWELL Ave & digging Communication trench between O.B.L - PORTAJON Ave. No 14384 Pte T. FLYNN to England on Course for Commission.	
Do	28/10/17	3pm	Battalion (less D Coy) engaged in work on the 27th Lieut. A NETHERCOTT proceeded to Third Army School for a Course of Instruction.	
Do	29/10/17	4.45pm	Capt. T.G.H. KENNEFICK tried by G.C.M. at 5th Inf Bde Headquarters at BARASTRE for "When on Active Service drunkenness." Battalion proceeded to relieve the 1st KING'S Regt in the Support area, of the Right Bn of the Divisional front.	

Army Form C. 2118.

WAR DIARY
or
INTELLIGENCE SUMMARY.
(Erase heading not required.)

Instructions regarding War Diaries and Intelligence Summaries are contained in F. S. Regs., Part II. and the Staff Manual respectively. Title pages will be prepared in manuscript.

Place	Date	Hour	Summary of Events and Information	Remarks and references to Appendices
Support area	30/1/17		Dispositions 'B' + 'C' Coys WATSON TRENCH. A + D Coys TANK SUPPORT. Capt T AYLMER rejoined from sick leave. Intermittent Shelling. Enemy M.G. active. 1 O.R. Wounded. 2/Lt H.L HUGHES + 2/Lt M.S. CLAYDON proceeded on leave to England.	
do	31/1/17		2/Lt C.S JAMES rejoined from leave. 2/Lt C WARK + 2/Lt J. GAMPS (1/8th ESSEX Cyclists) joined the Battalion for duty.	
do	—		'A' + 'D' Coys relieved 'B' + 'C' Coys in WATSON TRENCH. hut No 164 Extracts from hut of affectionate Commanders in chief, The British Armies in the field. Letter dated 22/12/17 approved by the trades Marshal. Commanding in chief. 13th Bn Essex Regt. "Infant" (2/Major) J WALSH R trans to 1st Bn Essex Regt Casualty Bn + to be trans to Casualty Bn + to be trans to 7 So R Bank Regt (England) 22/11/17. Major (T/Lt Col) J G Thorne acting OC since Casualty 13th Ess. Regt.	

(A7092). Wt. W12839/M1293. 75,000. 1/17. D. D. & L., Ltd. Forms/C.2118/14.

SHORT NARRATIVE OF THE RECENT OPERATIONS
FROM NOVEMBER 30th, 1917 TO NIGHT OF
4th/5th DECEMBER 1917.

1. On night of 29/30th November 1917, 13th ESSEX REGIMENT relieved 2nd S.STAFFS REGIMENT in the line astride the CANAL DU NORD, and took over their dispositions and orders.

2. On completion of relief, the Battalion was disposed as follows:

   (a) "B" RIGHT FRONT COMPANY (Capt. F.R.KEEBLE commanding)

   3 Platoons in and under LOCK 5.
   I Platoon in Reserve in TRAMWAY ROAD, E.21.c.0.5.

   (b) "D" LEFT FRONT COMPANY. (Capt. H.T.JESSOP commanding)

   3 Platoons occupying STREET TRENCH from E.20.b.95.55 to SUNKEN ROAD at E.20.d.6.2.
   I Platoon Company Reserve E.20.d.7.6.

   (c) "A" RIGHT SUPPORT COMPANY (Capt. H.J.DUFF Commanding)

   3 Platoons in TRENCH E.26.D.9.8. to E.27.b.5.3.
   I Platoon in CANAL TRENCH E.27.c.3.8.
   NIGHT POST (including I Officer) at junction of ROAD and TRENCH E.21.b.6.3.
   NIGHT POST SUNKEN ROAD E.27.b.5.3.

   (d). "C" LEFT SUPPORT COMPANY (Lieut A.NETHERCOTT commanding)

   2 Platoons in TRENCH E.20.d.5.6.
   2 Platoons in TRENCH E.20.d.4.6.

   (e) BATTALION HEADQUARTERS E.3.a.3.7.

3. Enemy activity through night was normal.

   (a) RIGHT FRONT COMPANY improved their defensive position by digging small trenches for Lewis Gun and Rifle sections at NORTH and EAST edges of LOCK No. 5; and reconnoitring underground passages.
   An Officer patrol (Capt. F.R.KEEBLE) reconnoitred open ground E.21 Westward with a view to its occupation on night 30th/1st.

   (b) LEFT FRONT COMPANY reconnoitred wire all along their Company Front; (2nd Lieut.E.L.CORPS) and the platoons were employed in deepening trench in shallow places and clearing fire steps where blown in.

   (c) RIGHT SUPPORT COMPANY. An Officer party (Capt. H.J.DUFF) in reconnoitring open area in E.27.b, c , and d, with a view to occupying this area on night 30th/1st Dec.1917.

   (d) LEFT SUPPORT COMPANY. Cosolidating trenches in their area.

   N.B. No enemy patrols were seen or heard by "D" "B" or "A" Coys.
   Night was fairly quiet.

Hostile shelling and M.G. fire - intermittent.

4. EAST OF CANAL -   Right front Company.
   Right Support Company

At about 6.30 am; enemy began to put down a light barrage on LOCK No. 5 BRIDGE E.20.b. in CANAL Southwards from BRIDGE CANAL TRENCH, and open ground Eastwards in E.21.d.

This fire was very ordinary and not in any way intensive.

At about 7.30 a.m, it became intensive.

At about 9.30 a.m, the enemy launched his first attack. He was seen on the road in E.15.c and d in great numbers; also debouching from a gap in the wire at about E.26.a.9.6., also from Sunken Road in E.21.b and along CABLE TRENCH in E.21.b.

"B" Coy in LOCK 5 beat off this attack using nearly the whole of their ammunition and bombs in doing so.

3 Sections of Reserve Platoon, also 1 Vickers Gun lined SUNKEN ROAD at E.20.c.0.5 facing North East.

1 Section at Bridge E.21.c.0.5. facing NORTH and North West.

Bombing blocks in CANAL TRENCH at E.21.c.1.6 and in CABLE TRENCH E.21.c.2.6.

(d)   This reserve successfully beat off the attack that was coming from the North East and used up nearly the whole of the ammunition in doing so.

(e)   It is impossible to state with accuracy the strength of the enemy who had launched the attack or what losses he sustained, but it is estimated at about 500 to 700 men were seen in the open.

Heavy losses were inflicted on them, and they either went back in great disorder or went ot ground.

During the lull which followed, the dug-out in SUNKEN ROAD was searched and about 300 rounds of S.A.A. were found there and were loaded in the Lewis Gun magazines.

At 9.50 a.m. in the SUNKEN ROAD, a message was intercepted from O.C. "B" Coy informing the C.O. that "he had successfully beaten off the attack in LOCK N0;5. but short of S.A.A.

10.25 a.m.   BRITISH TROOPS were seen retiring Southwards from the SUNKEN ROAD at about E.20 Central.

10.20 a.m.   The RIGHT FRONT COMPANY could still be seen in their original position in STREET TRENCH, WEST of CANAL.

10.30 a.m.   Barrage was intense.(Gas shells and heavies). At about 10.30 a.m., enemy again attacked from NORTH EAST; and just as ammunition was giving out 2nd.Lieut. E.C.HALL arrived with one platoon of "A" Coy and several boxes of S.A.A.

This platoon prolonged the line to the Right about E.21.c.2.5. mostly in the open and and checked the enemy advance across the open ground about E.21 Central. The Lewis Gun of the platoon and the rifles did very effective work, but the attack was so determined that the S.A.A., began to give out.

We lost fairly heavily during this attack from hostile Machine gun and barrage fire which fell directly on this garrison.

About half an hour later "B" Coy (about 40 rifles) had to retire, and passed through the SUNKEN ROAD by BRIDGE, taking with them the remainder of the garrison of SUNKEN ROAD; about 6 rifles; the remainder having all been killed or wounded (2nd Lieut. E.C.HALL wounded and Missing).

This party had no S.A.A., or bombs and were being followed by numbers of the enemy.

LOCK No. 5 and SUNKEN ROAD were occupied immediately by the enemy.

Capt. H.H.DUFF "A" Coy., rallied these men at about E.27.a.3.9.

Capt. F.R.KEEBLE "B" Coy, together with some of "A" Coy and a platoon of the 2nd. SOUTH STAFFS Regt under 2nd. Lieut. C.T.HINDE, having received S.A.A., and bombs organized a counter attack and drove the enemy back to the SUNKEN ROAD.

This they could not hold as the enemy were too strong, also through lack of bombs and S.A.A., which they had expended.

Capt. F.R.KEEBLE; "B" Coy; formed a BOMBING BLOCK in CANAL TRENCH about 10 yards South of SUNKEN ROAD E.21.c.10.45, and manned the parapet of CANAL TRENCH facing EAST and WEST.

S.A.A., and bombs were beginning to arrive in plenty and the enemy was prevented from advancing further and was cleared off the open ground EAST and WEST of CANAL TRENCH, and retired to the SUNKEN ROAD.

Capt. F.R.KEEBLE, later; again organized a bombing attack combined with an attack over the open to clear the SUNKEN ROAD.

This attack failed as the enemy were very strong and had brought up 4 Machine Guns also using Rifle Grenades freely on the block in CANAL TRENCH.

By this time CANAL TRENCH from BOMBING BLOCK Southwards to cross trenches at E.27.c.3.9. was garrisoned by one of "A" Coys' Platoons and 3 Platoons of a Company of 2nd.SOUTH STAFFS REGT.

Trench running EAST and WEST E.27.c,a, and d; was occupied by two platoons of "A" Coy and one platoon of a Company of 2nd. S.STAFFS REGT under Capt. BAXTER in addition occupied this trench.

The conduct of Capt. F.R.KEEBLE "B" Coy., Capt. H.J.DUFF "A" Coy., and 2nd. Lieut. C.T.HINDE (2nd. S.STAFFS REGT) was beyond praise.

The determination shewn by these gallant Officers not to yield one inch to the enemy, had a great stimulating effect on their men.

The enemy made repeated attempts to sally from SUNKEN ROAD and also to approach CANAL TRENCH from the North East, but were always beaten back by rifle and Machine gun fire.

It is difficult to estimate the casualties inflicted on the enemy, but all reports agree that he suffered very heavily.

Capt. F.R.KEEBLE estimates that his men, before retiring from LOCK No. 5 had put out of action at least 400 or 500 of the enemy, but this, he states; is a very moderate estimate.

During the night that followed, three unsuccessful attempts were made to retake the SUNKEN ROAD.,two by Capt.F.R.KEEBLE and 2nd. Lieut. C.T.HINDE; and later a third which was carefully organized by Capt. H.J.DUFF and Capt. F.R.KEEBLE.

After the third attack failed,the elements of "B" Coy and "A" Coy and 2nd.Lieut HINDE'S platoon were relieved and fresh troops put in the Northern Ends of CANAL TRENCH.

These were our dispositions as handed over to the 22nd Battn,ROYAL FUSILIERS on relief.

WEST OF CANAL.

P.T.O/

WEST OF CANAL.

(1).　At 11.45 a.m., on 30/11/17, the situation with regard to "D" and "B" Coys' was very obscure.

Orderlies were at once sent out to get in touch with these Companies.

No news had been received from the LEFT FRONT COMPANY, ("D" Coy) since they had been seen by the C.O., from his position in the SUNKEN ROAD about E.20.d.9.5., when they were still in their normal position but the enemy had gone past them at about E.20.Central.

(2).　Written orders were sent to O.C., "D" Coy to the effect that if he had been driven out of his position, he was to at once counter attack and establish on a line running WEST from BRIDGE at E.20.d.8.5.

These orders did not reach him as the enemy had come in from the WEST and from across the canal and completely cut him off; and, as was ascertained later, he was still in his original position.

(3).　A message was received from O.C., "C" Coy stating that his Headquarters was at TRENCH JUNCTION, E.20;d.2.3. and that his strength was 3 Officers and about 25 rifles.

The Intelligence Officer (Lieut. H.L. HUGHES) and runners with orders to the Company Commander to at once counter attack and re-establish himself in his former position.

This message he received and acknowledged, and together with troops of 2nd. S. STAFFS Regt and 1st KINGS REGT, he counter attacked and retook trenches as far as E.20.d.3.6 and E.20.d.4.6, but was held up by the enemy and lack of bombs.

(4).　A further report was received from this Officer stating that he had, before receipt of his order to retake his old position, already taken part in two counter attacks with his Company.

Instructions were sent to him to place himself under the orders of O.C. 1st. KINGS REGT.

(5)　The acting 2nd in Command (Capt. J. AYLMER) to get was sent to get in touch with 1st. KINGS REGT and ascertain the situation on WEST OF CANAL, and to ask O.C. 1st KINGS REGT to take the remnants of "C" Coy under his command.

Capt. J. AYLMER also had orders to acquaint O.C. 1st KINGS REGT of the situation EAST OF CANAL, and inform him that the C.O. intended to act vigoursly and retake the SUNKEN ROAD on the EAST of CANAL if it were possible.

(6)　Runners who were sent out to "D" Coy returned with the information that the enemy were between his and "D" Coy.

This was confirmed by Capt. J. AYLMER when he returned from H.Qs 1st. KINGS REGT and from H.Qs of "C" Coy.

(7)　Lieut. Col. ALBAN D.S.O., comdng: 2nd. S. STAFFS REGT had in the meantime arrived at my Headquaters and the O.C. ascertained from him that he was O.C. Forward Area.

From that time onwards the O.C. consulted him in all things concerning the WEST of CANAL and concentrated his efforts on holding on to his position EAST of the CANAL and retaking, if possible the SUNKEN ROAD and BRIDGE at E.20.d.8.5.

(8)　The C.O. was in constant touch with Os. C. 1st KINGS., 17th MIDDLESEX and 2nd. S. STAFFS REGT From about 12 noon 30/11/17 onwards.

(9)　By this time Major EDWARDS, 17th MIDDLESEX REGT. was engageing the enemy who had penetrated our line immediately WEST of CANAL in E.20.d.

- 5 -

(10)   On instructions received from Brigade, O.C. LEFT SUB SECTION had all troops on WEST of CANAL under his command, and the C.O. had all troops EAST of and including THE CANAL.

(11)   About 4 p.m., the strength of "C" Coy was two Officers and 15 Other Ranks.

(12) (a)   What happened to "C" Coy in earliest stages of fight is rather obscure, the two platoons at E.20.d.3.6. were attacked from the North West and West, and as far as the C.O. can ascertain fought to the last with troops of 1st KING REGT.

(b)   The other two platoons under O.C. Company were suddenly engaged from SUNKEN ROAD about E.20.d.3.9 also from West, and by a strong party of the enemy who had crossed CANAL by BRIDGE at E.20.d.8.5.
They suffered very heavily owing to having to lie in the open, and for a few minutes checked the enemy but had to fall back owing to lack of S.A.A. lack of men, and to avoid being cut off from enemy advancing from the West.

(c)   At about 10.10 a.m., O.C. "C" Coy had received the C.Os message which he had sent from SUNKEN ROAD EAST, and sent 2Lieut. H.V.COOK at once to LOCK No. 5.
This Officer reached Capt. F.R.KEEBLE as he was retiring from LOCK No. 5.
He sent 1 Corporal and 11 men with 5 Boxes S.A.A. to LOCK No. 5., but these men did not reach there., and were not seen again.

(13) "D" Coy.

At about 8 p.m. Sergt. L.S. LEGG "D" Coy; and one man arrived at Battalion Headquaters and informed the C.O. that they had escaped, and gave him the following information:-

(a)   "D" Coy. were surrounded.

(b)   They had not been attacked from the North or NORTH WEST.

(c)   The platoon at E.20.d.6.9. and a STOKES MORTAR had been firing at the enemy in SUNKEN ROAD at E.20. central, and also at enemy advancing over the open at about E.20.b.central.
That they must have killed hundreds of the enemy by their enfilade rifle and Lewis Gun Fire.

(d)   The platoon in TRENCH E.20.d.6.7. had held trench facing both ways i;e;, S.W. and N.E., those S.W. inflicting heavy loss on the enemy who had crossed the BRIDGE. Those facing N.E. on enemy as he was pursuing "B" Coy from LOCK No.5.

(e)   That enemy had brought 3 Machine Guns to E.20.d.8.5 EAST of CANAL, and enfiladed them. One of them guns and teams were knocked out, and the other two cleared off.

(f)   That Company was short of S.A.A.

(g)   That Capt. H.J.JESSOP, O.C. "D" Coy was wounded.

(h)   That they had a dugout full of enemy as prisoners. These prisoners, he stated, were captured in TRENCH in E.20.d.6.8.

- 2 -

(i) That at about 4 p.m. a council of war, Lieut. J.D. ROBINSON (2nd in Command of Company), 2/Lieut. E.L. CORPS, the Company Sergt. Major and Platoon Sergeants was held, and it was decided to fight to the last - no surrender - and two volunteers were to attempt to break through with information to the C.O.

(14) Brigade and all Units were at once informed, and most violent efforts were made by all Units to reach "D" Coy. They all failed.

(15) During night, position EAST of CANAL was organised so that all ground over which the enemy would have to advance was swept by oblique and cross fire, rifle, Lewis Gun; and Machine Gun.

This organisation greatly assisted in driving the enemy back next morning when he attempted to drive out BLOCK in CANAL TRENCH and advance from SUNKEN ROAD.

(16) These were our dispositions when we handed over to the 22nd ROYAL FUSILIERS on relief on night 1st/2nd December 1917.

(17) Battalion then withdrew to K.3.a. and having received the details who had been left out re-organised and became Support Battalion to the 22nd ROYAL FUSILIERS.

(18) On handing over to 22nd ROYAL FUSILIERS, there were 70,000 Rounds S.A.A. in Company Reserve at E.27.c.4.8.

(19) Until the 4th/5th, the Battalion was called upon on three occasions by the 22nd ROYAL FUSILIERS; The first two its services were not required. The third also and "B" Coy in passing through hostile barrage lost 1 Officer wounded, 5 other Ranks killed, and 14 Other Ranks wounded.

(20) The following were the casualties sustained by this Battalion from 30th November to night 4th/5th December 1917.

Lieut. (A/Capt.) J.D. STEELE   Wounded.
2/Lieut. W.S. McLAREN   "
    "   H.L. BALL   "

Capt. H.T. JESSOP   Wounded and Missing.
2/Lieut. R.G. BOX   "   "   "
    "   C.W. PHILLIPS   "   "   "
    "   E.C. HALL   "   "   "

Lieut. J.D. ROBINSON   Missing.
2/Lieut. E.L. CORPS   "

16 Other Ranks   Killed.

78   "   "   Wounded.
 9   "   "   Wounded and Missing.

269 "   "   Missing/

(21) At about 9.15 p.m. 4th/5th December 1917 orders were received from G.O.C. 5th Infantry Brigade to evacuate our positions, passing a certain line by 1 a.m. 5/12/17.

This evacuation was successfully carried out without casualties, and the Battalion arrived at LEBUCQUIERE at 4.20 a.m. 5/12/17.

Lieut. Colonel.
Commanding. 13th. Bn. The Essex Regt.

6th Brigade.

2nd Division.

Battalion disbanded 10.2.18.

1/13th BATTALION

THE ESSEX REGIMENT

JANUARY 1918.

Army Form C. 2118.

WAR DIARY
or
INTELLIGENCE SUMMARY.
(Erase heading not required.)

Vol 26

CONFIDENTIAL
WAR DIARY
of
13TH (S) BN. ESSEX REGT
JANUARY 1918.

Instructions regarding War Diaries and Intelligence Summaries are contained in F. S. Regs., Part II. and the Staff Manual respectively. Title pages will be prepared in manuscript.

Place	Date	Hour	Summary of Events and Information	Remarks and references to Appendices

WAR DIARY
or
INTELLIGENCE SUMMARY.
(Erase heading not required.)

Army Form C. 2118.

Place	Date	Hour	Summary of Events and Information	Remarks and references to Appendices
	1/1/18		Front line. Winning parties & patrols active. Intermittent shelling on both sides.	
	2/1/18		Front line. Capt H.J. DUFF returned from leave & assumed command of "A" Coy.	
	3/1/18		Battalion relieved by 1st KINGS Regt and moved into billets at HERMIES. Intermittent shelling by enemy throughout the day.	
	4/1/18		Battalion relieved by 2nd LINCOLNS and marched to billets at ROCQUIGNY. Lieut M.L. FARMER, R.A.M.C. returned from hospital. Lieut C. WARK proceeded to LE TOUQUET for leave from Course. Capt H.A. MULKERN proceeded on leave to England.	

Army Form C. 2118.

WAR DIARY
or
INTELLIGENCE SUMMARY.
(Erase heading not required.)

Instructions regarding War Diaries and Intelligence Summaries are contained in F. S. Regs., Part II. and the Staff Manual respectively. Title pages will be prepared in manuscript.

Place	Date	Hour	Summary of Events and Information	Remarks and references to Appendices
ROCQUIGNY	5-1-18		Companies were placed at the disposal of Company Commanders. Feed up dying and pulling were carried out by the Battalion. 2/Lieut. E.A. PATTERSON proceeded on leave to England on 5/1/18 to awaunt dated 6-1-18 to 30-1-18. 2/Lieut V.E. BLOOMFIELD proceeded to 3rd Army Musketry Camp for general course of instruction. (Authy:- 2nd Div Q 4129/85 dated 30/12/19. Capt (A/Major) A.G. HAYWARD M.C. returned from Gas Course, ALBERT on 5/1/18.	
ROCQUIGNY	6-1-18		A Parade Service was held in the Recreation Hut at 12 noon, and was attended by all hands not on duty. Capt J. AYLMER was in charge of this parade. A Roman Catholic Parade Service was held in a Bessin Hut near the H. Qo. of the 1st KING'S REGT, at 10 a.m. the following divine Services were held during the day. 8.30 a.m. 10.30 a.m. 12.30 p.m. 6.45 p.m. } Holy Communion in the Recreation Hut At 6 p.m. a United Service was held for National Day of Intercession for the Nation.	

Army Form C. 2118.

WAR DIARY
or
INTELLIGENCE SUMMARY.
(Erase heading not required.)

Instructions regarding War Diaries and Intelligence Summaries are contained in F. S. Regs., Part II. and the Staff Manual respectively. Title pages will be prepared in manuscript.

Place	Date	Hour	Summary of Events and Information	Remarks and references to Appendices
ROEQUIGNY	6-1-18		2/Lieut J.G. AMPS is transferred from "C" Coy and posted to "D" Coy. 2/Lieut F.C. RANSOM returned to "A" Coy for duty.	
ROEQUIGNY	7-1-18		Companies carried out Platoon Training under Platoon Commanders from 9am to 1p.m. in the following subjects:- Saluting, with and without arms to Recr Section and Platoon Drill to " " Elementary Extended Order Drill by Sections and Platoons to " " Platoon Specialist Training to " " Gas Drill, including a short lecture on gas noticed by enemy. March discipline was practised while marching to and from training ground. Companies detailed 2 men per platoon for instruction in Bombing under Sergt ROLFE from 9am to 1p.m. Duration of course - 4 days. All signallers paraded under the Signalling Sergeant for instruction from 9 a.m. to 1p.m. Companies detailed 2 men per platoon to undergo a course of Observing, Scouting and Sniping under 2/Lieut H.L.BROOKE. Duration of course - 10 days. Stretcher Bearers paraded under the Medical Officer at the Regtl Aid Post at 9am.	

Army Form C. 2118.

WAR DIARY
or
INTELLIGENCE SUMMARY.
(Erase heading not required.)

Place	Date	Hour	Summary of Events and Information	Remarks and references to Appendices
ROEQUIGNY	7-1-18		The undermentioned Officers joined the Battalion, were taken on the strength and attached to the Companies shown against their names. 2/Lieut. H. FAIRBANK "B" Coy. 2/Lieut. A. R. GREEN "B" " 2/Lieut. T. W. GINDER "C" " 2/Lieut. F. W. DENHAM "C" " Lieut. A. R. WELLS M.C. was admitted to hospital. Baths in Recreation Hut were allotted to Companies as under:- "A" Coy. 9 a.m. to 9.45 a.m. "B" " 9.45 a.m. to 10.30 a.m. "C" " 10.30 a.m. to 10.50 a.m. "D" " 10.50 a.m. to 11.20 a.m. "H. Qs" 11.20 a.m. to 12 noon.	
ROEQUIGNY	8-1-18		Training was carried out in vicinity of Lillers, and under Company Commanders. Specialist training with their Companies. The undermentioned Officers attended a Conference at ROEQUIGNY Commanding Officer. 2/Lieut. H. L. BROOKE proceeded on leave. Warrant dated 9-1-18 to 23-1-18	

Army Form C. 2118.

WAR DIARY
or
INTELLIGENCE SUMMARY.
(Erase heading not required.)

Instructions regarding War Diaries and Intelligence Summaries are contained in F. S. Regs., Part II. and the Staff Manual respectively. Title pages will be prepared in manuscript.

Place	Date	Hour	Summary of Events and Information	Remarks and references to Appendices
ROEQUIGNY	8-1-18		Lieut (A/Capt) A.W. NEW proceeded on 14 days leave to PARIS. 2/Lieut F.H. AUSTIN took over command of "B" Coy during absence of Lieut (A/Capt) A.W. NEW. 2/Lieut C.S. JAMES took over the duties of Intelligence Officer during the absence of 2/Lieut H.L. BROOKE.	
ROEQUIGNY	9-1-19		Companies carried out Platoon Training under Platoon Commanders in training area from 9 a.m. to 1 p.m. in the following subjects:- 1 hour — Section and Platoon Drill ½ " — Saluting with and without arms ½ " — Elementary Extended Order Drill, by Sections and Platoons ½ " — Platoon Specialists Training ½ " — Gas drill, including short lecture. Specialists were trained under their respective Instructors on or on 4-1-18. A lecture by the Brigade Gas Officer was given to the Officers and N.C.O's of the Battalion at 5 p.m. Lieut. FIELD, Assistant Inspector of Armourers inspected the Lewis Guns and rifles of the Battalion at 3 p.m. Lieut (T/Lieut. Col.) J. WALSH D.S.O. proceeded on leave to England. Warrant dated 10-1-18 to 28-1-18 Capt (A/Major) A.G. HAYWARD M.C. took over command of the Battalion during the absence of Lieut (T) Lieut Col. J. WALSH D.S.O. on leave	

Army Form C. 2118.

WAR DIARY
or
INTELLIGENCE SUMMARY.
(Erase heading not required.)

Instructions regarding War Diaries and Intelligence Summaries are contained in F. S. Regs., Part II. and the Staff Manual respectively. Title pages will be prepared in manuscript.

Place	Date	Hour	Summary of Events and Information	Remarks and references to Appendices
ROE QUIGNY	10-1-18	9am to 1pm	Revetting of Hutments against Hostile Aircraft was carried out. Signallers, Observers, Scouts, Snipers and Bombers paraded under their respective instructors. 9 Other Ranks rejoined the Battalion. 2/Lieut C.W. PHILIPS previously reported "missing" now reported "Prisoner of war" in Germany	
ROE QUIGNY	11-1-18	9am to 1pm	Platoon Training was carried out by Companies under Platoon Commanders in vicinity of Camp in the following subjects:- Physical Training and Bayonet Fighting. Section and Platoon Drill. Saluting, with and without arms. Elementary Extended Order Drill by Sections and Platoons. Gas Drill, including short lecture. Lewis Gun Instruction. One N.C.O. and four men from each Company received instruction in wiring under an expert from the Royal Engineers. Specialists paraded under their respective instructors. The undermentioned Officers previously "missing" now reported Prisoners of war in Germany. Capt H.T. JESSOP. Lieut J.D. ROBINSON. 2/Lieut E.L. CORPS. 2/Lieut R.J. TREBILCO.	
ROE QUIGNY	12-1-18		Revetting of Hutments against Hostile Aircraft was continued. Specialist Training was carried out as on previous days.	

Army Form C. 2118.

WAR DIARY
or
INTELLIGENCE SUMMARY.
(Erase heading not required.)

Instructions regarding War Diaries and Intelligence Summaries are contained in F. S. Regs., Part II. and the Staff Manual respectively. Title pages will be prepared in manuscript.

Place	Date	Hour	Summary of Events and Information	Remarks and references to Appendices
ROEQUIGNY	12-1-18		2/Lieut. H.R.E. KING proceeded to 2nd Divisional Depot Battalion for attachment. 2/Lieut. A.C. TIMMS proceeded from 6th Infantry Brigade on 8/1/18 to V Corps Headquarters. 2/Lieut. W.K. BESSEX returned from leave to England on 12-1-18.	
ROEQUIGNY	13-1-18		A Parade Service was held in the Cinema Hut at 11.30 a.m. and was attended by all ranks not on duty. A Roman Catholic Parade Service was held in the Cinema Hut at 10 a.m. The meetting of Rudments was continued in the afternoon. Services for other denominations were held during the day. 2/Lieut. C.G. PURKISS joined the Battalion for duty. One other rank died. Lieut. (A/Capt) A.W. NEW returned from leave to PARIS, and resumed the command of "B" Coy. Capt. J. AYLMER took over the duties of Second-in-Command. 2/Lieut. W.K. BESSEX took over the command of "D" Coy.	
ROEQUIGNY	14-1-18	9a-1p	Platoon Training under Platoon Commanders was carried out in the following subjects:- March Discipline. Saluting. Section and Platoon Drill. Elementary Extended Order Drill. Gas Drill. Instruction in Lewis Guns. "A" Coy carried out firing practice on the Range at V.B.a. from 9a.m. to 1p.m. Specialists paraded under their respective Instructors. Another N.C.O. and four men from each Company received instruction in wiring under the expert from the Royal Engineers.	

Army Form C. 2118.

WAR DIARY
or
INTELLIGENCE SUMMARY.
(Erase heading not required.)

Instructions regarding War Diaries and Intelligence Summaries are contained in F.S. Regs., Part II. and the Staff Manual respectively. Title pages will be prepared in manuscript.

Place	Date	Hour	Summary of Events and Information	Remarks and references to Appendices
ROEQUIGNY	14-1-18	5 p.m.	A lecture by the Commanding Officer was given to all Officers and N.C.Os. on principles of defence of a position usually allotted to a Battalion on a certain front. The band of the ROYAL ARTILLERY played in the Cinema Hut at 2.30 p.m. and 5.30 p.m. 15 all ranks from each Company and Battalion Headquarters attended each performance.	
			145 Other Ranks joined 2nd Division Depot Battalion and were taken on the strength of the Battalion.	
			26 Other Ranks joined the Battalion.	
ROEQUIGNY	15-1-18	9 a.m.	Battalion Ceremonial Parade.	
		9.45 a.m to 4 p.m.	Companies carried out Platoon Commanders in Training Area No 3. in the following subjects:-	
			March Discipline	
			Musketry, including rapid manipulation of bolt, rapid loading and rapid adjustment of sights.	
			Lewis Gun Instruction.	
			Specialists as on previous days.	
			Wiring under the expert from the Royal Engineers.	
			Capt. A.E. BUNTING proceeded on leave to England. Warrant dated 14-1-18 to 31-1-18.	
			Capt. S.E. COLLIER. M.C. " " " " "	
			2/Lieut. F.A. JENNS took over the duties of Adjutant during the absence of Capt. A.E. BUNTING.	

Army Form C. 2118.

WAR DIARY
or
INTELLIGENCE SUMMARY.
(Erase heading not required.)

Place	Date	Hour	Summary of Events and Information	Remarks and references to Appendices

ROEQUIGNY.	16.1.18	9am 6pm	Companies carried out Platoon Training under Platoon Commanders in Training Area 9ox in the following subjects:-
			
			 Squad Discipline
			 Musketry
			 Saluting
			 Section & Platoon Drill
			 Elementary Extended Order Drill
			 Gas Drill
			 Lewis Gun Instruction
			
			 Specialists carried out training under their respective instructors. Company Commanders carried out a tactical exercise during the afternoon for their Officers and N.C.Os. Special instruction was carried out in wiring as on previous days. 44 Other Ranks joined Divisional Depot Battalion on 12.1.18, and are taken on the strength of the Battalion.
			 2/Lieut C.M. KEMP joined the Battalion for duty.
			 The undermentioned joined the Battalion for duty:-
			     Lieut T. LAW.
			     2/Lieut T. CHRISTY
			     2/Lieut A.J. HENDERSON - LIVESAY.
			
			 Lieut. H.L. HUGHES returned from leave to England on 16.1.18.	

Army Form C. 2118.

WAR DIARY
or
INTELLIGENCE SUMMARY.
(Erase heading not required.)

Instructions regarding War Diaries and Intelligence Summaries are contained in F. S. Regs., Part II. and the Staff Manual respectively. Title pages will be prepared in manuscript.

Place	Date	Hour	Summary of Events and Information	Remarks and references to Appendices
ROEQUIGNY	17-1-18	9.30am to 4.30pm	Companies were placed at the disposal of Company Commanders to be practised in subject in which they were backward. The Range at U.6.a was allotted to "C" Coy. Specialists trained under their perspective instructors. A demonstration of the Flammenwerfer was carried out at the Bombing Pits in O.33.a at 2.30 p.m. 156 Other Ranks joined the Battalion from Divisional Depot Battalion.	
ROEQUIGNY	18-1-18	9am to 1pm	Companies carried out Platoon training under Platoon Commanders to include the following subject:- Snare advanced musketry Wire Combat & Fire Discipline. Special instruction in wiring was given to 1 N.C.O. and 4 men from each Company by the expert from the Royal Engineers from 3pm to 5pm and from 6pm to 8pm. 1 Other Rank died of wounds in No. 3. General Hospital	
ROEQUIGNY	19-1-19	9am to 9.30am 10am to 10.30	Battalion Drill. Battalion (less "B" Coy) Route March. All specialists paraded with their Companies. "B" Coy was allotted to U.6.a. and the Battalion Observers The Range at U.6.a	

Army Form C. 2118.

WAR DIARY
or
INTELLIGENCE SUMMARY.
(Erase heading not required.)

Instructions regarding War Diaries and Intelligence Summaries are contained in F. S. Regs., Part II. and the Staff Manual respectively. Title pages will be prepared in manuscript.

Place	Date	Hour	Summary of Events and Information	Remarks and references to Appendices
ROCQUIGNY	20-1-18		A Parade Service was held in the Cinema hut at 10 a.m. Services for other denominations were held during the day.	
ROCQUIGNY	21-1-18	9am to 4pm	Companies carried out Platoon training in training Area & to special attention being paid to Moral Discipline, Rapid loading, Fire discipline & fire Control. 2/Lieut (A/Capt) H.A.MULKERN 2/Lieut E.A. PATTERSON } returned from leave to England 2/Lieut M.S. CLAYDON 2/Lieut (A/Capt) H.A. MULKERN took over command of "D" Coy vice 2/Lieut W.K.BESSEY	
ROCQUIGNY	22-1-18		A Battalion Scheme was carried out on the field firing Range	
ROCQUIGNY	23-1-18	9am to 4pm	Companies carried out Platoon training under Platoon Commanders, practising Counter Attacks and any subject Company Commanders considered the men backward in. All Box Respirators of the Battalion were inspected by the Brigade Gas Officer. 2/Lieut M.S. CLAYDON and 25 other Ranks proceeded for attachment to the 2nd Australian Tunnelling Coy	

Army Form C. 2118.

WAR DIARY
or
INTELLIGENCE SUMMARY.

(Erase heading not required.)

Instructions regarding War Diaries and Intelligence Summaries are contained in F. S. Regs., Part II. and the Staff Manual respectively. Title pages will be prepared in manuscript.

Place	Date	Hour	Summary of Events and Information	Remarks and references to Appendices
ROEQUIGNY & METZ	24-1-18		The Battalion moved from ROEQUIGNY into billets at METZ by light railway. 2nd Lieut. H.L. BROOKE returned from leave to England. 2nd Lieut. C.M. KEMP proceeded on leave to England.	
METZ	25-1-18		Lieut. T. LAW proceeded to 2nd/4th SOUTH LANCASHIRE REGT. with a view to transfer. HdQrs of the Battalion carried out work on the METZ DEFENCES under the supervision of Capt. GREENWOOD, 54th Field Coy R.E. 2/Lieut. E.A. PATTERSON proceeded for attachment 64th T.M. Battery. 2/Lieut. H.L. BROOKE resumed the duties of Intelligence Officer.	
METZ	26-1-18	9 a.m.	Anti Gas Drill and Foot-Rubbing were carried out under the supervision of the Company Commanders, the remainder of the time being occupied in improving the Battalion billets.	
METZ	27-1-18		The Brigade Gas Officer inspected the Box Respirators of the Battalion in the morning. 35 Other Ranks joined the Battalion from 2nd Division Depôt Battalion. 2/Lieut. V.E. BLOOMFIELD returned from 3rd Army Musketry Camp.	
METZ – RIGHT SUB SECTOR LEFT BRIGADE SECTOR	28-1-18		The Battalion relieved the 14th Battn. Royal Fusiliers in the RIGHT SUB SECTOR, LEFT BRIGADE SECTOR, (LA VACQUERIE)	

Army Form C. 2118.

WAR DIARY
or
INTELLIGENCE SUMMARY.
(Erase heading not required.)

Instructions regarding War Diaries and Intelligence Summaries are contained in F. S. Regs., Part II. and the Staff Manual respectively. Title pages will be prepared in manuscript.

Place	Date	Hour	Summary of Events and Information	Remarks and references to Appendices
RIGHT SUB-SECTOR	29-1-18		With the exception of occasional shelling by both sides the days were quiet. Considerable aerial activity. 2/Lieut. A.J. HENDERSON-LIVESAY proceeded on 24-1-18 for attachment to 5th Field Coy. R.E. Lieut. (T/Lieut. Col.) J. WALSH D.S.O. returned from leave to England, and resumed command of the Battalion on 30-1-18. Working parties found for work on FARM AVENUE & NELSON Support and Mining parties out on strengthening our wire. Patrols active.	
	9 30-1-18			
	31/1/18		Enemy intermittently shelled VILLERS PLUICH. Work on FARM AVENUE carried out by A + D Coys. (50 men) 4 officers + 45 men engaged on work in NELSON SUPPORT. Battalion relieved by 1st South STAFFS Regt and moved into trenches in the SUPPORT AREA, VILLERS PLUICH.	

Effective strength
	Officers	O.R.
	40	826
Ration strength
	26	662
Trench strength
	22	526

J Walsh
Commanding 13th Batt Essex Regt.

SECRET   13th Bn: The Essex Regt. Relief Order No. 5   Copy No. 14

Ref Map LA VACQUERIE
Special Sheet   FEB. 2nd. 1918

1. The BATTALION will relieve the 2nd. S.STAFFS REGT. in the RIGHT BATTALION SECTOR tomorrow night, the 3rd/4th.

2. "A" Coy will relieve "C" Coy 2nd. S.STAFFS in POSTS 15-22 R. FRONT
   "D" "   "   "B" "   "   "   " 23-30 L. FRONT
   "C" "   "   "A" "   "   "   " 1-6   R. SUPPORT
   "B" "   "   "D" "   "   "   " 7-14 L. SUPPORT.

3. RENDEZVOUS for GUIDES (one per post) will be at the head of the RAVINE at R. 14.2. 15.65 and COMPANIES with their POSTS already detailed and in the correct Sequence will arrive at the RENDEZVOUS at the following times:-
   "D" Coy (23-30) ... ... at 6 p.m.
   "A" " (15-22) ... ... at 6.15 p.m.
   "B" " (7-14) ... ... at 6.25 p.m.
   "C" " (1-6)   ... ... at 6.35 p.m.

4. DETAILS of "D" and "A" Coys. not required for POSTS or COMPANY HD.QRS. will follow in rear of their Coys. to BATTALION HD.QRS. in RAVINE.

5. Lists of all maps, defence schemes, trench stores, etc. taken over will be sent in to BATTALION HD. QRS. by 6 a.m. on the 4th instant.

6. LISTS of TRENCH STORES, etc. in this (SUPPORT) AREA to be handed over to ~~the ~~~~~~~~~~ REGT.※ will be sent in to these HD. QRS. by 12 Noon tomorrow.   ※ 17th MIDDSX REGT.

7. RELIEF COMPLETE will be notified by the Code Word "MONS".

8. ACKNOWLEDGE.

                    (Sgd) J. AYLMER Captain
                        A/Adjt: 13th Essex Regt.

        Copy No. 1 ... Commanding Officer
             2 ... Second-in-Command
             3 ... Adjutant
             4 ... O.C. 2nd. S.STAFFS REGT.
             5 ... O.C. "A" Coy
             6 ... O.C. "B" "
             7 ... O.C. "C" "
             8 ... O.C. "D" "
             9 ... Transport Officer
            10 ... Quartermaster
            11 ... R.S.M.
            12 and 13. War Diary.
            14 ... 6th Inf. Bde. H.Q.

2ND DIVISION
6TH INFY BDE

1-13TH BATTALION
THE ESSEX REGIMENT
JAN 1918
(DISBANDED 10TH FEB)

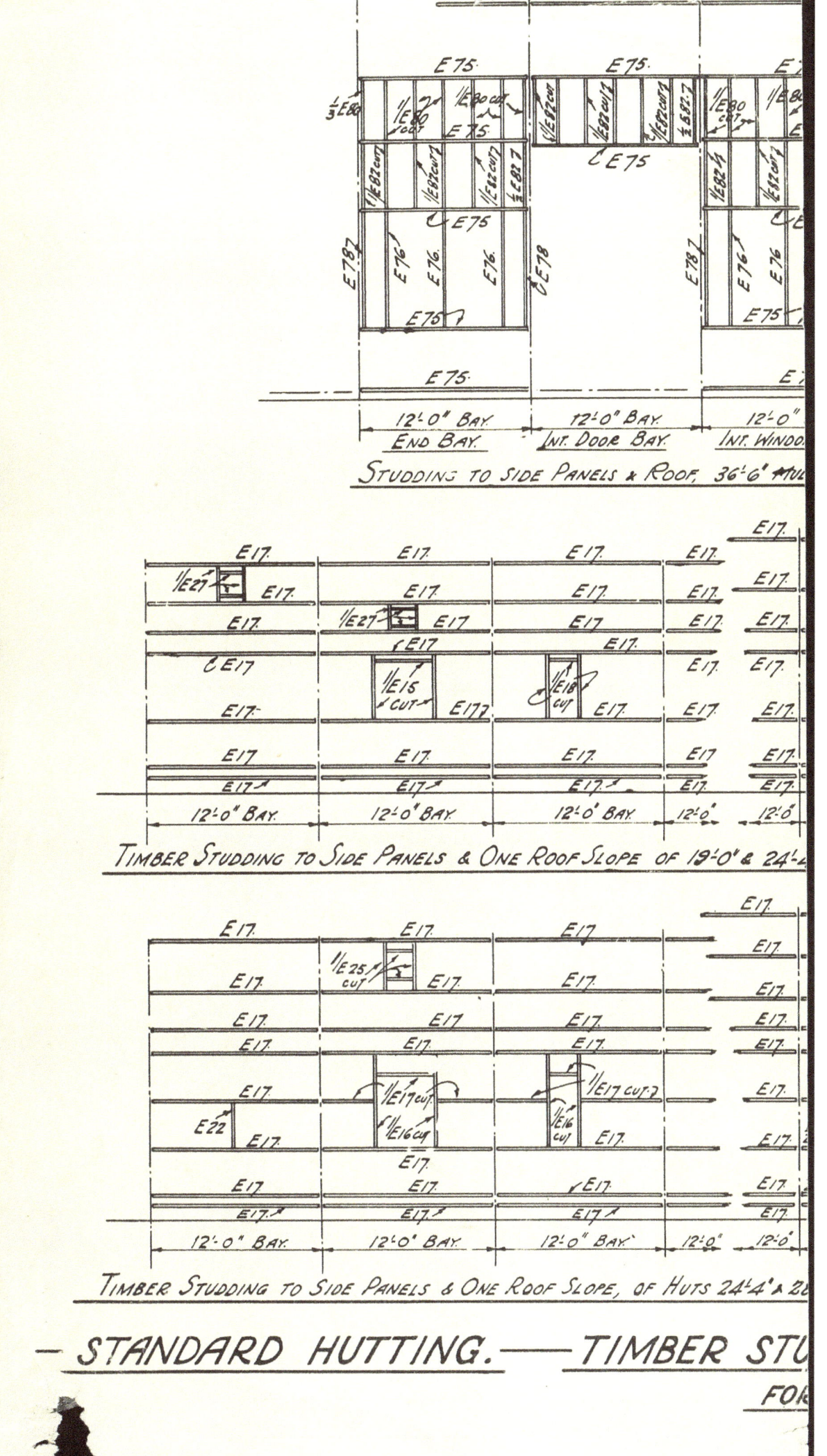

www.ingramcontent.com/pod-product-compliance
Lightning Source LLC
Chambersburg PA
CBHW082357010526
44113CB00039B/2330